ACTS

THEATER: THEORY/TEXT/PERFORMANCE

Series Editors: David Krasner and Rebecca Schneider

Founding Editor: Enoch Brater

Recent Titles:

Looking Into the Abyss: Essays on Scenography by Arnold Aronson

Avant-Garde Performance and the Limits of Criticism: Approaching the Living Theatre, Happenings/Fluxus, and the Black Arts Movement by Mike Sell

Not the Other Avant-Garde: The Transnational Foundations of Avant-Garde Performance edited by James M. Harding and John Rouse

The Purpose of Playing: Modern Acting Theories in Perspective by Robert Gordon

Staging Philosophy: Intersections of Theater, Performance, and Philosophy edited by David Krasner and David Z. Saltz

Critical Theory and Performance: Revised and Enlarged Edition edited by Janelle G. Reinelt and Joseph R. Roach

Reflections on Beckett: A Centenary Celebration edited by Anna McMullan and S. E. Wilmer

Performing Conquest: Five Centuries of Theater, History, and Identity in Tlaxcala, Mexico by Patricia A. Ybarra

The President Electric: Ronald Reagan and the Politics of Performance by Timothy Raphael

Cutting Performances: Collage Events, Feminist Artists, and the American Avant-Garde by James M. Harding

Illusive Utopia: Theater, Film, and Everyday Performance in North Korea by Suk-Young Kim

Embodying Black Experience: Stillness, Critical Memory, and the Black Body by Harvey Young

No Safe Spaces: Re-casting Race, Ethnicity, and Nationality in American Theater by Angela C. Pao

Artaud and His Doubles by Kimberly Jannarone

The Problem of the Color[blind]: Racial Transgression and the Politics of Black Performance by Brandi Wilkins Catanese

The Sarah Siddons Audio Files: Romanticism and the Lost Voice by Judith Pascoe

Paul Robeson and the Cold War Performance Complex: Race, Madness, Activism by Tony Perucci

Passionate Amateurs: Theatre, Communism, and Love by Nicholas Ridout

Dark Matter: Invisibility in Drama, Theater, and Performance by Andrew Sofer

Simming: Participatory Performance and the Making of Meaning by Scott Magelssen

Acts: Theater, Philosophy, and the Performing Self by Tzachi Zamir

Acts

THEATER, PHILOSOPHY, AND THE PERFORMING SELF

Tzachi Zamir

The University of Michigan Press
Ann Arbor

Published in the United States of America by
The University of Michigan Press
Manufactured in the United States of America
♾ Printed on acid-free paper

2017 2016 2015 2014 4 3 2 1

A CIP catalog record for this book is available from the British Library.

ISBN 978-0-472-07213-2 (cloth : alk. paper)
ISBN 978-0-472-05213-4 (paper : alk. paper)
ISBN 978-0-472-12029-1 (e-book)

To the memory of Avi Schiller

Acknowledgments

Over the seven years of work on this book, I acquired many debts. Some of these are to my colleagues in academia; others are to acting teachers, fellow performers, and directors with whom I trained and performed; still others relate to institutions which have proved surprisingly hospitable to unorthodox requests (I sympathize with The Hebrew University executive who had— nervously—approved my request to employ a research grant as tuition payment for an acting-class on buffoonery). Should these friends read this book, they would see the extent to which their comments, leads, suggestions, and institutional support have shaped my arguments—an effect over another's thinking that constitutes the real way in which appreciation for facilitating one's intellectual growth is expressed. But since repetition and explicitness in such matters is a pleasure, I wish to express my gratitude directly as well.

Criticisms, corrections, suggestions, supportive comments and encouraging feedback were generously given me by Tamar Aylat-Yaguri, Inbal Barel, Reut Barzilai, Shuli Barzilai, Isaac Benabu, Lawrence Besserman, Emily Budick, Sanford Budick, Matthew Cohen, David Fishelov, Elizabeth Freund, Ahuva Goldstand, Sigal Gooldin, David Heyd, Yael Inbar, Kerry McElroy, Galia Ofek, Talia Trainin, David Wallace, Kendall Walton, and John Vincent. I wish to thank all of them for their rich input to this book. The (at the time anonymous) referees of this book—Patrick Anderson, James Hamilton, and David Saltz—have been ideal readers, substantially upgrading the essay in many ways. The book owes much to their fine insights and meaningful suggestions.

Several acting teachers and directors have opened up valuable gateways for me into the acting process. The ones that had a particularly lasting impact on my thinking are Shirili Deshe, Tzvika Fishzon, Javier Katz, and Noam Meiri from the Lecoq School of Physical Theatre at Tel-Aviv. Directors Itzik Seidoff, Yevgeni Kushnir, and Rose Machichi enabled me to turn from acting exercises to performances. My understanding of work on role, rehearsal, and audience-performer interaction was profoundly guided by their intelligent and sensitive mediation of this process to me.

The following journals have kindly permitted me to rework and develop parts of the book they had previously published: *Critical Inquiry*, *The Journal of Aesthetics and Art Criticism*, *New Literary History*, *The Journal of Medical Humanities*, *The Philosophical Quarterly*, *Theatre Journal*, and *Theatre Topics*. I wish to thank them for granting me this permission, and for the comments their editors and anonymous readers have supplied. While the material in this book deviates—often significantly—from these incipient versions, the integration of these separate inquiries into a cohesive argument benefitted from the generous feedback received at the time.

Finally, I would like to thank the Israel Science Foundation for a research grant that enabled me to pursue this project.

Contents

INTRODUCTION

To reflect on acting is to rethink identity. It is to examine the playful withdrawal from established connections between self and embodied agency. Exploring this process in its manifestation as a performing art, involves an attempt to pinpoint the uniqueness of this imaginative metamorphosis, and the ways in which it affects an audience. Understanding the more evasive manifestations of acting outside art requires a probing into the rich experiential gateways that are established by role-playing and its consequences for others. This book will investigate both: it opens by asking very specific questions regarding stage acting, its definition, and the varieties of its experience; it ends with studies of anorexia and masochism, in which non-actors orchestrate wholesale stylized dramatizations of self-other relations.

I first became curious about acting after agreeing to be cast for a film made by a philosophy high school student of mine. I found the acting experience gripping and fulfilling in ways I could not fully understand. Consequently, I enrolled into a short-term acting program, which then led to joining an amateur company. My professional interest as a philosopher in what I was experiencing began to surface, and I started looking for useful literature. Very little was on offer: short essays by Diderot and Kleist, an ambiguous dialogue by Plato, a diatribe by Rousseau; these constituted virtually all that the philosophical tradition had to say about acting. Few contemporary Anglo-American aestheticians contributed inquiries in which acting was not independently examined, but was subsumed under broader questions relating to performance. Strangely, while music, literature and painting were (and are) extensively discussed by philosophers, acting—an art form that television mediates to most people on a daily basis—was neglected.

As I began performing, my questions no longer appeared to me musings over a hobby, but progressively took the shape of genuine philosophical curiosity: Why was I looking for more of the acting experience? How could a repeated rehearsal of a known sequence be invigorating? How to characterize the different insights I gained into the fictional character I was embodying when contrasted with insights yielded by merely reading the play attentively? Why do I need an audience? How to understand the willing embodied subordination to someone else's words, or the willing subordination to being directed? What was the 'energy' that performers were tirelessly looking for?

Gradually, my experiences as performer began to modify my teaching. As a philosopher of literature teaching in an English department, I was aware of a change of focus in my Shakespeare courses: previously I had attempted to bring my students into dialogue with the abstract insights the plays contain and their interpenetration with literary subtleties; instead, I was now devising exercises in which students were urged to examine how verbalizing Shakespeare's words affected their inner state, or the different feeling of the words when delivered standing up or while walking, or the inner potency of some words when memorized—alerting them to the contribution of such effects to the meaning of the lines. Such aesthetic values—I hoped to show them—could only surface when one no longer merely thought of the text as read language, but when the relationship of words, body, and voice acquired proximity and vitality. It was clear to me that I was beginning to look at acting as a unique access key into states: a studied attention to the texture of words. Does an incarnated migration into an imagined experience constitute knowledge? Is a gifted actor merely able to *do* something which a good close reader cannot accomplish, or does the actor practice a mode of attention, a form of wisdom, which at once enables a demanding imaginative expansion, and is, simultaneously, informed by such experience, thereby enabling the actor to *understand* something that a reading seldom or never reveals?

I began to look outside philosophy for orientation. Books by actors or contributions within theater studies provided partial illumination of such puzzles. Yet penetrating and rich as they were, such books were never intended to replace a philosophical investigation, with its characteristic attempt to patiently unearth the abstract underpinnings of complex clusters of intuitions, emotions, evaluations, and thoughts. It was then that I decided to undertake this study. It was obvious to me that the questions I was asking emerged out of actual acting experiences, and that, accordingly, armchair philosophy should be avoided as far as possible. But it was no less clear that I could never hope to attain a professional actor's ability or experience. I consulted a colleague regarding my hesitations. Her advice was that until a professional actor who also happens to be a trained philosopher offered such a study, there was room for mine. She also cautioned that, since my own acting experiences are only the hesitant gropings of a beginner, I should regard them as crucial stages of my own background research, but avoid basing anything directly upon them. "Do this," she said, "and actors would thereby recognize the vocabulary you use without sensing that they are being instructed by an amateur, and philosophers may justify your choice to engage with a practice prior to offering a philosophy of it."

I followed this advice. During the period in which this book was written, I joined, practiced, and performed with two other acting companies. I also underwent a more intense actor-training program at the Lecoq-inspired school of physical theatre in Tel-Aviv. Workshops in mime, mask-work, *commedia dell'arte*, buffoonery, and clown-work formed part of this training, progressively undermining my previously more psychologically-attuned understanding of the acting process. None of this work is mentioned or used as evidence in this book. It did, however, shape and guide the questions that seemed to me important to ask. It also enabled me to receive input from directors, teachers, and actors. The result is a philosophical study that aims to employ a vocabulary that professional actors would recognize, and which attempts to be responsive to the philosophical questions that the acting experience actually brings up.

As work on the book progressed, it expanded into forms of role-playing beyond the stage. It became clearer that acting mobilizes aspects of the living experience as such, and that these manipulations of the self are operative not only in the theater. A comprehensive philosophical inquiry needed to include such manifestations of acting. But in order to avoid the world-as-stage platitude, it was necessary to trace the relationship between such role-playing and acting as a performing art. Again, it seemed to me that the most fruitful way of engaging with such questions would be to work from the first-person perspective of a performer. The chapters devoted to such "life acting" in the contexts of pornography, masochism, or anorexia aim to both understand them as performances, and to achieve this by approximating the inner experience of the players. Methods adopted in order to achieve such faithful approximation varied: sometimes it made sense to work closely with testimonials; in the case of masochism, the most rewarding method to access the subjective nuances of the role-players called for a close reading of a semiautobiographical novel. I could obviously not treat first-person articulations as indisputable evidence. But even qualified reliance upon them showed how activities often perceived as potentially cold (masochism), objectifying (pornography), or lethal (anorexia), can also be experienced as empowering, intimate, and self-validating. To regard such episodes of self-theatricalization as acting, explains the warmth and self-assertion that, paradoxically, surfaces in practices that are usually dismissed as pathological, perverse, or abusive.

This book brings together and thinks together the results of these inquiries. Its four sections attempt to reveal different pathways that connect acting as a performing art with kinds of acting that are conducted outside the theater. The first part ("Life on Stage"), proposes a definition of acting couched in a process I call "existential amplification." Topics discussed in this section include the nature of theatrical inspiration, the actor's "energy" the difference between acting and pretending, the special role of repetition as part of live acting, the audience's function and its attraction to acting, and the unique significance of the actor's voice. The second section ("Staging Fictions"), undertakes to distinguish among various ways of "living more" through art. Readers and authors of literature repeatedly imagine themselves in the state of fictional characters. I propose ways in which these processes can be set apart from the specifically embodied nature of the actor's animation of a fiction. A contribution to the theory of drama is then attempted by arguing that texts written for the stage frequently mobilize themes that relate to their own projected enacted animation. The process of animation is then taken up in relation to adult puppetry—arguably the purest manifestation of the animation act.

The inquiries forming the third part of the book ("Between Life and Stage") focalize points of breakdown in the distinction between performance and identity. Ethical concerns relating to the acting process surface in episodes involving a role-identity collapse. Examples will be surveyed and a proposed explanation will be advanced; a foundation for an ethics of acting will thereby emerge. I then turn to pornography, a form of performance that offers the clearest example of a transition from represented role-playing into presented identity. Seeing through the performer's perspective (rather than via the moral prism through which it tends to be discussed) enables perceiving how the very properties that enable pornography to sometimes be liberating, empowering, or even intimate (as some performers enthusiastically maintain), are also responsible for its debilitating violence. A counterintuitive outcropping of this discussion is that the porn/art distinction does not correlate neatly with a moral opposition between exploitative and nonexploitative role-playing: some sexual acting in mainstream venues is more exploitative than some pornography.

The final section of the book ("Life as Stage") discusses the transition from what one performs into who one is. One chapter examines how role-playing facilitates (rather than hampers) loving intimacy in masochism; another traces how theatrical vocabulary underpins a suicidal gesture cast in the form of an eating disorder. In both, acting theory becomes a far more illuminating reservoir than assumed by theories of performative agency. Self-empowerment through role-playing, finding love through masks, entering, preserving, and establishing interpersonal values by theatricalizing self-other relations—all emerge as processes in which acting turns into a life-defining practice.

Self-shaping role-playing—self-theatricalization—comes in multiple forms and taps deep-seated needs: to be more than who one is by momentarily being other, to animate one's role and to thus understand the tendency to dis-inhabit one's own actually lived possibility, to enter into or withdraw from relations of care for another, as part of staged or non-staged role-playing, to momentarily bond with an inner object that underlies the discrete subject-effects that are agglomerated into what one is inclined to call identity—these are some of the processes of self-unmaking and self-remaking that this book attempts to delineate and understand. Its reader need not be an actor. Its reader need not be a philosopher. Anyone who looks at wide-eyed children staring bewitched at actors for the first time, and who wonders whether and how such fascination remains with adults, is welcome to join this odyssey.

*

Different readers may find their way into this book, and while it does aim to accommodate them, a few words of orientation are needed. In writing this book, I (genuinely) tried to preserve a style that communicates with actors, philosophers, and theater scholars. Attempting such inclusiveness will strike some as futile. When David Saltz (a former editor of *Theatre Journal*) presents the same argument to philosophers and to theater scholars, he prepares different papers.[1] Philosophers, he feels, demand arguments, clarifications, and take seriously objections that no practitioner or theater scholar is genuinely worried about. They also employ only skeletal examples when appealing to real performances. By contrast, theater scholars work closely with actual works (they would avoid calling these "examples"). Saltz adds that the use of "philosophy" in theater studies differs from the use of the term by philosophers: theater scholars tend to heuristically cite bits of philosophy that they find helpful—instead of themselves advancing philosophical claims. They are *using* theory rather than *doing* theory. His own practice is, thus, to supply much more argument when addressing philosophers, and to provide a much closer work with actual theatrical practice when addressing theater critics, mentioning the relevant philosophical labels, while shying away from the attempt to advance a thesis.

To compartmentalize one's audience in this way manifests a wise and respectful sensitivity to differences between expository methods among separate disciplines. This book, nevertheless, opts for a more hopeful stance regarding the ability as well as the desire of intellectuals to read outside their traditions. True, philosophers would find more description than traditionally provided in aesthetics, while theater critics would encounter a more exhaustive conceptual analysis than customary in theater studies. But the book does not require or expect a methodologically charitable reading from members of either discipline; it aims to abide by what each would regard as a rigorous inquiry.

It is the *kind* of philosophy practiced in the book, not philosophizing as such, that is likely to elicit the more substantive resistance from some theater scholars. Anglo-American aesthetics hardly appears in papers published in theater journals; nor does it influence books currently published by theater scholars. The dominant orientation in these remains a post-humanism underpinned by French philosophy. The post-structuralist critique-of-presence is one influential variant of this orientation. Another manifestation is political: a rejection of an ideologically-free aesthetic discourse as a mirage, one that is to be replaced by categories of analysis that tease out the interpenetration of experience with hegemony, pleasure with power. Both strands seem to be at odds with the kind of argument that will be developed here, and this may lead some readers to sense that it is politically or epistemically naïve to stitch together decontextualized categories of "experience" into explanatory schemes. The book responds to variations on this concern by simultaneously questioning this critique while aiming to absorb its genuine ethical contribution.

One visible expression of my attempt to communicate with actors lies in the size and number of footnotes—which have ballooned into longer and bulkier marginalia than is usually desirable. Relegating some material to the notes hopefully renders the main argument accessible to readers who may not urgently require a further conceptual clarification or an elaborate specification of the argument's precise deviation from partly overlapping theoretical predecessors. Academics (rightly) require the latter, actors do not. In addition, whenever possible, the sources that are directly cited are by actors. Philosophical claims are derived from these and are examined in relation to potential counterexamples featuring in the literature that performers themselves have produced. Such focus should not suggest that the book's method amounts to generalizing over testimonials: a philosophy of a practice is not merely a description; it undertakes to unearth the more abstract underpinnings of a practice, ones that even its best practitioners risk misrepresenting. What this method does promote is, however, a philosophical analysis that remains close to what practitioners say, and to the terms they use to formulate their abstract questions.

I will not pretend that the result constitutes an easy read for someone unaccustomed to academic work in the humanities. But it should be accessible to actors who are not philosophers. The gain promised them by picking up this gauntlet does not consist of improving performance skills (knowledge and ability are never neatly correlated). What a philosophy of art promises (and, sometimes, delivers) an artist is, rather, growth *as* artist: a greater insight into what one does. It responds, in short, to an identity-related desire: the dissatisfaction of being driven by a vocation without fully understanding it. I wish I could say that this book yields such complete understanding, exhaustively dissolving all of acting's mysteries. It does not. Yet actors who will be satisfied by less may find that it somewhat improves the vocabularies currently available to them when they articulate acting's risks as well as its magic.

PART I

LIFE ON STAGE

There are three general methods—descriptive, historical and conceptual—of explaining the acting process. Descriptive accounts focus on practitioners' own conceptualizations of their work. Historical explanations trace evolution and changes in conceptions of acting, embedding these in broader cultural contexts. Conceptual accounts pursue a psychological or philosophical depth-structure that underlies self-descriptions offered by practitioners.

To limit oneself to one of the three routes would yield an incomplete understanding. Relying on descriptions or accounts of historical evolution, means that one would exclude from the start the possibility of a normative perspective; by "normative," I mean a perspective able to *evaluate* a particular evolutionary turn within the history of acting—assuming that changes may manifest not only improvement, but also deterioration in the understanding of acting. A normative perspective allows for the possibility that—because the possession of a refined ability need not imply having a full apprehension of the more abstract underpinnings of one's art—an actor may be wrong in his grasp of his art. Equally dubious is the other extreme: relying solely on conceptual analysis. Armchair aestheticians, uninterested in what practitioners say or in how acting as an institution materialized in distinct cultural settings, are likely to miss the less obvious insights gained by the actual experience of the phenomenon they are attempting to explain.

Given the price to be paid by restricting oneself to one of these methods, a reasonable strategy for a philosophy of acting is to conduct a conceptual inquiry which is guided by, but not determined through, historical accounts or the testimony of actors. Such will be the method adopted in this section of the book. What actors say and have said about the acting process, about work on role, about good and bad acting, about its most important constituents and the like, will form the basis for a philosophical explanation of acting and its appeal for an audience. This account will explain issues such as inspiration on stage, the importance of an actor's voice, the audience's interest in acting, and the actor's need for an audience. In later sections, this account will also elucidate the interface between acting and ethics, as well as role-playing outside the theater.

The attention to acting—a neglected art-form in aesthetics—is prompted by recent shifts within the philosophy of theater. Like everyone else, philosophers assumed that theaters exist because people wish to watch plays. According to this conception, the best acting succeeds in making the performance itself a transparent vehicle, thereby communicating the literary merits of the play. Endowed with a sufficiently rich imagination, a sensitive reader of a play would not wish to watch it performed: such viewing can only fall short of what a perceptive reading yields. But this view—the belief that we look (or should look) *through* the actors—is now perceived as descriptively dubious and as normatively implausible. The reasons for dropping this view are both varied and compelling: it misdescribes actual viewing experiences (since the audience, typically, does explicitly think about the actors); it diminishes the aesthetic range of theater by ignoring what performers add to the literary values of the play; it cannot account for theatrical performances that are not based on plays; it is also selective, better suited for dramatized poetry (such as Shakespeare's) than for excellent plays that depend upon performers providing the subtext that breathes life into paper-thin dialogue.

An audience certainly does come to the theater to watch a play. But it also attends in order *to see people enacting* a play.[1] Moreover, since the play can be read without attending the performance, interest in enactment may be more central in motivating spectatorship than are literary interests. Here is an explanation which offers to show why this may be so.

WHAT ACTORS DO

"Acting is the process whereby people imaginatively become somebody else." This seems like a plausible characterization of acting. Regrettably, it is unsatisfactory. To begin with, it misses the embodied nature of imaginative transformation in acting—which differentiates acting from activities such as daydreaming, writing up a literary character, or whimsical role-playing. Secondly, such a definition runs together delusion and acting. As an oft-cited example shows, even at their utmost commitment to the role, actors preserve awareness of their actual surroundings and context:

> A famous tragic actor, Aesopus, was playing the scene of Orestes' madness. He had his sword in his hand. At that moment a slave in the theatre's employ crossed the stage and unfortunately stood in his way. Aesopus did not hesitate for a moment to kill him. Here was a man apparently so steeped in his role that he felt it to the point of madness. But why did he never kill one of the other actors playing with him? Because a slave's life meant nothing, whereas he was obliged to respect the life of a citizen. His rage was not then quite so true since it allowed reason to choose. But as a clever actor, he took the opportunity chance offered him.[1]

The actor's *control* over his imaginative transformation is the point highlighted by this anecdote: attacking a slave rather than a member of the audience gives the lie to the actor's "rage." Behind the sound and fury, there peeks a respect for social norms, a shrewd awareness of what will be tolerated, and what would not. Such (rather extreme) legal and moral checks on the actor's imaginative transformation bring out a range of milder manifestations of the actor's control: one's awareness of lighting, or of avoiding "back-staging" a partner, are routine indications of such aesthetically-oriented self-monitoring. Far more subtle variations of self-control are brought out by the following glimpse into acting's experience:

> That went well, that was good. Now, bring it up a bit. Now bring it down. No, that's boring. Now, do this. It will look good if you went like that. Now stay like that. Now turn like that." All actors have that. I think. Because that's how you act—somebody inside is directing you.[2]

The self-directing Michael Gambon describes involves the operations of a creative and highly selective consciousness. Choices are organized as part of an aesthetic offering.

The term *aesthetic* refers to attempted effects that result from particular prized powers or merits (capabilities, sensitivities, choices, insights) of the actor as creator. Some of these powers are rather basic, discernible by anyone in the audience (such as the actor's capacity to "move the audience," to elicit tears or laughter). More evasive merits would be accessible only to knowledgeable spectators (for instance, the actor's original characterization of a well-known dramatic character, or his manifestation of a mood through an unobvious feature, or the performance's moderation in a manner that respects the emotional range required by the part). Some highly subtle creative merits are likely to be noted only by fellow professionals (achieving depth of characterization rather than courting a more immediate effect, serving the play rather than the part, discovering rather than indicating, employing a versatile vocal range, giving focus, comic timing and the like).

An "aesthetic offering" refers, then, to establishing multiple relationships between desired responses (such as provoking the audience's laughter) and an achievement by the actress relating to her powers as creator (such as the exact timing of her fall). Superficial audiences would not consciously respond to such relationships, but merely undergo the established effects that these bring about. They would simply laugh. Their failure to note the art responsible for their laughter does not undermine the status of the act as an offering: for an actor to "be guided" by aesthetic control, means to constantly aim to establish such relationships on multiple levels, even if they are not acknowledged. A gratifying audience is, accordingly, not merely entertained by staged effects; it is aware of at least some connections between what it is moved by, and how such effects depend on particular constituents of the creative act.

This understanding of aesthetic control suggests the following definition of acting: Acting is an aesthetically-controlled embodied imaginative transformation.[3]

Embodied Imaginative Transformation

Two rival traditions argue over the precise meaning of embodiment. The first is mechanistic: the body is a tool—a more or less obedient vehicle for realizing the mind's will. The second is more holistic: the body significantly shapes the mind.[4] While unraveling the distinct nature of the actor's embodied imaginative metamorphosis seems to accordingly invite an exploration governed by the tensions between mechanism and holism, acting-theory is not really torn by debates between these, and happily combines elements of each.[5] The issue that does draw battle cries from acting theorists is whether or not an actor's embodied transformation necessitates fully experiencing the role: Stanislavsky-inspired approaches expect actors to perform as if the enacted state were personally happening to them, whereas rival methods stress projection, not inner experience.[6] The following story exemplifies the clash between these approaches:

> [Dustin] Hoffman is reported to have stayed awake for several nights before shooting the scene [in the film *Marathon Man*] in which Laurence Olivier, as the Nazi, tortures him by drilling his teeth. Olivier, whom I consider the greatest actor of our time, was there bright and early, ready to go to work despite several illnesses . . . Hoffman staggered in, bleary-eyed and chilled by nights of sleeplessness. "What's the matter?" asked Olivier. "Don't you feel well?" "Oh, I'm fine," said Hoffman. "I just stayed up a few nights so I'd be in the right shape for this scene." "Why don't you just act it?" asked Olivier.[7]

Hoffman is the "feeler" in this story, striving to recreate the conditions he incarnates; for Olivier, acting amounts to believable projection.

The feeling/projecting polemic is conducted on four levels: pragmatic, psychological, aesthetic, and moral. The pragmatic question is which method is likely to yield compelling acting, given the requirement (particularly in relation to stage-acting) to repeat enacted states. The psychological question is whether one can genuinely access one's past experiences, as if they were somehow available, patiently awaiting dramatic recycling. The aesthetic question is: a) whether one's own existing repertoire of responses can reliably guide the portrayal of significantly different situations; and b) whether experience-based acting is not better suited for some parts and genres, but unhelpful (and even damaging) in stylized theater or in some comic forms. The moral question relates to the moral dubiousness risked by expecting actors to conjure up charged personal experiences. This last question has been insufficiently discussed, and will be addressed in the third part of this book.

The experience/projection controversy is not empty: it influences training methods as well as our understanding of the acting process. But there is a risk of overstating the difference between these orientations and missing their overlap. The emptiness of the term experience (in opposition to what?) is itself symptomatic of an attempted over-polarization: practitioners neatly fall in two feuding camps, only one of which is "experiencing." In truth, these orientations are not far apart: experience-oriented actors would concede that identifying with a role differs from simply becoming another; projection-oriented acting of any real depth involves experiencing curiosity over the enacted state coupled with a detailed attempt to embody it convincingly. Such embodiment constitutes a very real form of experiential transformation, even if the actress is keenly aware of the difference between her own identity and the role (identification—here and elsewhere—never simply amounts to "becoming other"). Clearly, both parties regard acting as involving planned forms of embodied identification, while refusing to perceive such identification as existential merging. Both instruct and guide the actor on the ways to explore and externalize the imagined state.

Being in Another Way

Descriptions of acting by actors offer more fertile leads regarding the meaning of the actor's embodied transformation than those issuing from the feeling/projecting debate within acting theory. While some say that actors avoid such descriptions, or that acting lies outside the descriptive power of words, insightful testimonials of the acting process have been offered.[8] The following (Simon Callow's) is particularly rich:

> In all the anxiety over the show, worrying whether it was clear, whether everybody knew where to come on or go off, I had no time to think about my performance, no time to wonder about its effect on the group . . . or to ask, 'Was I funny?' or 'Was it clever?' I just did it. Suddenly, for the first time, I was acting. Not performing, or posturing, or puppeteering. I was

> being in another way. At a stroke the mask that I had screwed on to my face fell away. I was free, easy, effortless. For the first time since I'd arrived at the Drama Centre I understood what playing a character was. It was giving in to another way of thinking. Giving in was the essential experience. 'Leave yourself alone,' they'd been saying to us since the day we arrived. Now suddenly I was.[9]

"Giving in" to the part is Callow's characterization of real acting. Succumbing in this way to an alien power is echoed by others. "We speak of the actor playing a role," writes Richard Hornby, "but actually, the role plays him."[10] Charles Marowitz describes "a loss of consciousness on the actor's part—which is what engenders the alternative consciousness of artistic creation (the role)."[11] Surrendering to the character is also Antony Sher's experience of gradually absorbing Richard III:

> This has been a breakthrough. We work on through all the speeches, everything now that much easier. For the first time tonight I didn't feel frightened by the soliloquies; more than that, I actually felt comfortable in them. What's happening is that I am surrendering to Shakespeare's Richard. He is funny.[12]

Effortlessness, such is the quality shared by these descriptions of success. The actor relinquishes control, and witnesses the emergence of another way of inhabiting his body. The experience of the embodied transformation comes across not as one in which a rigid distinction between role and identity is maintained while "projecting." Neither does it boil down to losing sight of the self/role distinction and merely "experiencing." "Giving in" amounts to exploring a newly discovered experiential space, a visit into a previously inaccessible region; the actor becomes both a tourist and eavesdropper in the process.

Callow articulates this experience as "being in another way." Similar pronouncements pepper other writings on acting. In the eighteenth century, James Boswell claimed that, unlike the painter or the poet who offer us representations, "the player lives o'er each scene and, in a certain sense, is what we behold." Rémond de Sainte-Albine likewise asserted that "the painter can only represent events. The actor, in some sort, reproduces them."[13] A similar identification of being with acting undergirds the following description of Michael Chekhov's acting: "In the early part of his career, critics, who had never seen such a seamless and startling mix of deeply emoted realism within a portrayal of grotesque fantasy, even questioned whether what Chekhov did on the stage was actually 'acting.'"[14] The problem with these observations when contrasted with Callow's, is that they all blur the distinction between being and representing a fiction, a smudging which, as we already saw, cannot be accepted. The actor is not simply "reproducing" a scene, or "is" that which we behold.

Callow's phrasing is more careful than Boswell's or Sainte-Albine's. His actor is not simply *becoming* that which he enacts. But what substantiates the suggestive idea that the actor somehow *exists* in a different way?

THREE KINDS OF EXISTENTIAL AMPLIFICATION

Acting is a gateway to living more—such is a short version of what I shall now propose. *Existential amplification* will be the name given to such expansion of one's sense of being alive, and three ways through which acting puts such amplification into motion will be presented. The first consists of *accessing* fictional possibilities. The second appears in the *manner* whereby lived content is realized. The third occurs through the *withdrawal* from one's identity.

Content-oriented Existential Amplification

Personal existence is partly reducible to a set of possibilities.[1] A person is a cluster of possibilities, and actualizes a small portion of these. Graphically, our lives resemble a pyramid: we are what we can become, possessing numerous possibilities to begin with; these gradually diminish throughout our lives.

Thinking of existence in this way explains responses such as feeling pity for people born with radically fewer prospects, being charmed by a baby, or experiencing difficulty in meeting the gaze of the terminally ill: we react to possibilities or their lack. It also explains particular moral convictions (judging unjust, for example, a social system that systematically blocks the realization of some capabilities from some citizens), as well as specific educational intuitions (the parent or educator's attempt to open up new possibilities for the child). On an even more fundamental level, to identify existence with possibilities also discloses the evasive richness of perception, either of animate or inanimate objects: what the object is *just means* some of its possibilities. So while we may directly see only colors and shapes, we do not merely take in an object of perception as reducible to these. We look at its potential promise—what may be done with it, or what it may become. Sometimes, we take in what an entity can no longer become, or what it may have become, had it been placed in different circumstances.[2]

Spotlighting how possibilities are constitutive of existence also illuminates some kinds of fascination: We experience *fascination*—an experience of an incompletely understood attraction—upon recognizing a force that extends possibilities and is, in this sense, life-amplifying. Consider money or time. Both the noninstrumental fascination with money and the quest for the fountain of youth, disclose the allure of increasing one's possibilities. Having more life-time or far more money is tantamount to having more possibilities to enact.[3] The desire for more is not simply the instrumental craving for a specific this or that. It reaches into something that pertains to the structure of life as a set of possibilities, one that is enlarged by acquiring more time or money. True, the accumulation of money as an end may become pointless once the generating of more possibilities becomes disconnected from their actualization. The accretion of wealth is also self-defeating if it involves sacrificing other desirable possibilities that have nothing to do with what money enables. But given these qualifications, money and time still fascinate, and rightly so: both overlap with a metaphysical dimension of life as such. Both can be potentially enlarged—time in fantasy, money in reality.

How is dramatic acting connected to this view of subjective experience? Actors, I suggest, *amplify* their own lives by imaginatively embodying alien existential possibilities. Like the pining for the fountain of youth, or the aimless counting of hoards of money in literary money-driven heroes such as Spenser's Mammon, Eliot's Silas Marner, or Marlowe's Barabas, acting forges a link to a potentially unlimited range of new, hitherto unimagined, possibilities. It achieves this via the intimate identification required by theatrical embodiment and the momentary cooperation of others with this process when they validate it as audience. Some of these fictional realizations—falling in love, dying of a terminal disease, losing a friend—are genuine biographical possibilities for the actor, others—being the king of medieval France, being an evil wizard, being an alien or an "incredible hulk"—are not. Yet, unreachable though they might be in life, such remote ways of being remain experiential options accessed through a fictional realization.

"Liberating suppressed inner potential" is how this process was described in the past. But it would be reductive to conceive acting as a mere externalization of that which was pent up.[4] Acting is a detailed exploration of that which is being imagined, whether it happens to have been suppressed or not. The hold of acting over practitioners, be they amateurs or professionals, the effort and risk-taking that acting as a career choice mandates, are related to the fascination with this process of becoming other, with "being in another way." "Feelers" would typically attempt to plant their biographical selves in such imaginative expansions to a greater degree than supporters of "projection." Yet neither actually becomes the imagined character, and both patiently study and carefully embody the particularities of being other.

How does the unreal nature of the content of such amplification shape the experience of imaginative embodiment? Genuine amplification or diminution of who one is, surely carries its own import: education (or its lack), or the acquisition of a huge amount of money (or loss of the money that bare sustenance requires), are life-transforming changes that modify one's possibilities. But it would be a mistake to assume that a fictional metamorphosis is necessarily less substantive, insightful and satisfying than real amplification. To see why, consider another remark by Simon Callow, this time regarding his struggle to play Titus Andronicus:

> For me, the titanic emotions of the role were cruelly difficult to attain. I always felt false. The series of blows that befall Titus is very nearly comic in its relentlessness. . . . I felt myself too small, my voice too weak, my means too limited—and I was right. Only experience and the gradual expansion of one's instrument – oneself – can enable one to play such scenes. In fact, just playing them goes a long way towards it.[5]

For Callow, make-believe expansion enables the convincing acting of future fictional roles. This feat can be realized because fictional embodiment is not some fleeting daydreaming: it is an arduous process of progressively inhabiting an alien's world. "Inhabiting" is an important word here. The actor visits an existential possibility, occupying it in an intimate, repeated and planned way over time. It is precisely the distance between the actor and the space, them *not* being one and the same, that renders theatrical life-expansion unique in comparison to real expansion.

Three of the reasons responsible for this can now be stated. First, the ability to plan and rehearse the realization of the fictional possibility enables inhabiting it in a more intense, precise, and full way than non-fictional life might allow. This also explains how, by embodying Titus repeatedly and inquisitively, one can—as Callow says—*grow* as a person. Here, as elsewhere, art does not apishly imitate life, but, at its best, pursues and crystallizes a moment's meaning. The unreality of a fictional artistic representation is thus not opposed to truth (fictional statements are not simply false statements), but can sometimes tease truth out. What aestheticians have called "the paradox of fiction"—the mysteriousness of emotional response to unreal happenings—is met by denying that the responses experienced in a fictional context are the same as those triggered in genuinely-occurring analogous circumstances, but then adding that such responses to unreal events may still illuminate one's actual responses.[6] Secondly, real identity change typically mandates limitation and consistent fidelity to a relatively coherent narrative. Unlike real expansion through, say, money, acting is able to open up what *cannot* be experienced. Acquiring wealth may enable the exercising of life-changing generosity to many who need it. But, unlike thespian metamorphosis, wealth cannot render accessible the possibility of being a Viking warrior or coming to terms with one's homosexuality in thirteenth-century France. Thirdly, unlike real expansion, fictional amplification *protects* the actor from the consequences of a possibility, were it to actually occur. To be a Lear partly enables exploring the sense of losing a loved daughter *without* actually losing her; being a Lavinia enables approximating the experience of being raped and mutilated *without* genuinely being subjected to these. As person, imaginary rather than real amplification shields the actress. As artist, it establishes the creative distance that facilitates insights that may escape someone who actually undergoes such overwhelming states. This is why a careful artistic representation can be more insightful than a first-person report. To conclude, the fictional nature of the imaginative transformation establishes a form of imaginative existential amplification which can be more discerning, broader in existential reach, and also safer than genuine amplification. The actor's studied inhabiting of a previously inaccessible possibility is, accordingly, not necessarily a feeble substitute when compared to actual experiences.

There is, however, more. Precisely because his amplification concerns a fictional, rather than an actual, realization, the actor is able to explore and present a distinct form of amplification that relates not only to the realization of content, but to the *relationship* to lived content.

Existential Amplification as Self-animation

Performers, acting teachers and those who write for or about them frequently refer to the performer's *energy*. For some, the release of such creative energy is the heart of an entire approach to acting.[7] Yet, apart from drawing analogies to parallel notions—such as "inspired" performance, "presence," or having/lacking "it"—the machinery underlying the concept of energy is usually left unexplained.[8] Aestheticians have not proved more helpful: even the few who did discuss performance, shied away from grappling with the vitality that performers are after. The reason for their caution is obvious: one would either be obliged to dismiss "energy," regarding it as a vague and meaningless folk term requiring elimination (a move that too confidently brushes aside what practitioners know or say), or be forced to accept abstract features of situations (a move that militates against the implicit positivist bias of Anglo-American philosophy).[9]

The price of avoiding tackling such terms within the philosophy of performance is the likelihood of ending up with a distorted understanding of spectatorship. The attentive audience is restricted to a narrow focusing on plot and character-related aspects of the theatrical performance; they are explicitly or implicitly guided to be attuned merely to the literary dimensions of dramatized characters, who become "worthwhile to watch" because we care about them. This, in effect, amounts to saying very little about a performer's distinct contribution to a role.[10] To avoid this result, aestheticians sometimes explain performance as inviting a particular "kind of regard", one which is irreducible to enacted content, but consists of an ever-growing attention "to the vehicle."[11] While the emphasis on such attention is important, one would want to know more. To closely observe a performer never amounts to noting physical gestures, but extends to picking out a quality that animates how these gestures are performed: the same gesture can be moving and effective in one performance, dead and mechanical in another. What are these differences in "energy"?

Demystifying energy and its substitutes can assume two forms. The first is to identify energy with the resource that lifts acting above simple representation. Michael Goldman takes this route. "Acting is never simply mimetic," he writes; "it appeals to us because of some other or more inclusive power. We feel an energy present in any good actor's performance that goes beyond the demonstration of what some 'real person' is like."[12] This reduces energy to the mechanism of capturing and conveying the kind of *intensity* I will discuss in the next part of the book, which explores the relationship between the literary and the embodied aspects of acting. Literary intensity will be presented as the capacity of an insightful literary articulation produced by the playwright to reach and encapsulate lasting features of situations, and to thus transcend quotidian experience. When such encapsulations are fully experienced and communicated by the performer, the audience will sense "energy"—when they are not, the audience will merely be entertained.

A second possibility is to perceive energy not merely as another attribute of *what* one performs, but as manifested *through* what one performs. John Gielgud describes the following:

> I have a vivid recollection of Lucien Guitry's acting in a drama called *Jacqueline,* produced in London in 1922, in which he played an elderly roué who strangles his mistress in the final scene. It was the preparation for this denouement in the second act that impressed me the most. The scene was in a hotel bedroom where he had taken the girl for a weekend. Guitry stood over her as she lay on the bed, and she suddenly shrank from him crying, "Oh! You terrify me." For a few seconds he seemed to grow inches taller and become a towering and sadistic creature. Then, suddenly breaking the tension completely, he resumed his normally charming manner for the rest of the scene. I watched him most intently, and am convinced that in fact he did absolutely nothing, not moving his hands, his face or his body. His absolute stillness and the projection of his concentrated imagination, controlled and executed with a consummate technique, produced on the girl and on the audience an extraordinary and unforgettable effect. I knew I had seen a great actor.[13]

Can actors effect that which an audience perceives or imagines, without actually moving? Gielgud's answer would be "Yes!" This feature—an aspect of performance seemingly observed while bearing no obvious perceptible ties to the specific performed content—is unrelated to the larger-than-life aspect of acting on which Goldman focuses. Energy is located in a performer's *relationship* to content, not in *meanings* they happen to embody.

The term inspiration invites a similar analysis. Supervening above gestures that can possess or lack it, inspiration, too, seems to be unrelated to enacted content. An experience that definitively shaped Lee Strasberg's understanding of inspiration exemplifies this: Strasberg was abysmally disappointed by actor Jacob Ben-Ami in his performance in *John the Baptist.* Several days after dismissing Ben-Ami's acting as mechanical, Strasberg happened to again enter the theater in which the play was performed. The result, Strasberg tells us, had great consequences for his entire understanding of the acting process:

> Ben-Ami came through a gate onto the stage. He assumed the same stance that I had seen him take before, leaning against the wall; but this time there was something different—an indefinable, inner, feverish vibration; weary but excited. A character asks John why he will not recant. As he answered, Ben-Ami bent down as if he were listening to something, as he had in the earlier performance. It was a purely mechanical gesture. Then he spoke his line, "God tells me." The first time I saw this scene I had thought sardonically, "Yeah, God tells him." This time when he was asked the question, he again leaned down to listen. He started to say, "God tells . . ." and a shiver ran through my spine because this was something totally different. The gesture was the same externally, physically; yet there was an inner life. It was a kind of scenic communication that we in the theatre would call inspiration. It had been completely missing in the first performance I had seen and obviously in the performance the critics had seen. What I was now seeing was something ineffable.[14]

Like "energy" or "intensity," *inspiration* is a philosophically vexing concept. "Inspiration" harks back to archaic metaphysical associations between emotions and breath: the belief that courage and energy are inhaled and exhaled, and breathed into mortals by gods.[15] To resuscitate such beliefs is pointless. Yet some contemporarily valid variant of "inspiration" should be salvaged precisely because it denotes an all too familiar aesthetically significant feature of performing arts: the same performance by the same actor can possess or lack a crucial potency. Performances are criticized for being "mechanical" or "precise but lifeless"; actors experience this element as animating their work and as crucially determining its quality. Inspiration is neither a necessary nor a sufficient condition of good acting. Nevertheless, audience and actors look for this evasive quality in a performance.

Western thought has cultivated two approaches to inspiration. The first associates inspiration with an external, overtaking force that works through the actor (in the case of theater): it is transmitted to the audience, much like the force of a magnet (God) reaches a piece of iron (the audience) via a different intermediary piece of iron (the actor). The second account construes inspiration as an inner resource that rare individuals can sometimes command.[16] Both explanations regrettably say little about what inspiration actually is, telling us more about where it is situated and who ultimately controls it. They also push the term into theological territory, importing into art an unworldly force that ostensibly animates it.

Unlike these older conceptualizations, to regard acting as existential amplification enables seeing inspiration as synonymous with energy. In relation to both terms, amplification does not consist of a broadening of one's possibilities but of *a quality of inhabiting a lived possibility*. Due to the performer's familiarity with the performed content, its fictionality and (at least in the case of most live acting) the distinctive repetitiveness of theatrical performance, acting is, in part, an artificial mechanism through which a *suspension* of concern for lived content takes place. Through such suspension, a performer is able to probe and communicate stronger and weaker relations to lived content. Intense or inspired acting is powerful to behold since it conveys another human being's capacity to momentarily narrow the gap between moments and one's distance from them. Such effect has nothing to do with the interpretative, meaning-making activity of an attentive audience—how it comprehends the unfolding play, or its sensitivity to the relationship forming between the performance and the realization of the play's intent. Attending an inspired performance is *not* primarily a form of understanding something, but of witnessing an exemplary state of oneness with content for which understanding is no more than a crutch.

Such unification with content broadens the idea of existential amplification: We are what we can become, but such becoming also encompasses our ability to recede from our perpetual absence. "Living more" is not only to live in the quantitative sense of realizing more possibilities, but also to grow in one's capacity to possess one's own possibility in a more binding way (significantly, the biblical use of "inspiration" as a word denoting the literal act of breathing life into man—the Latin invokes the term in the *Vulgate* in Genesis II, 7—already suggests a linkage between the inspired and a sense of being alive, a crossing over from inanimate matter into life). Acting addresses this relational kind of amplification: it is a form of self-animation that presents the transition from mere functionality into agency, from incomplete being into "selfing," from part object into a fuller subject.

Existential Amplification as Disembodiment

An actor's work *into* an alien role is, simultaneously, a migration *from* his biographical embodiment. While both movements are parts of the same process, they establish distinct dimensions of existential amplification. Receding from her ordinary embodiment, yet remaining in control, the actress turns her body into puppet, a servant of a different mind. Sometimes this feat is experience by the audience as unification between actress and role; sometimes two personalities—actress and character—conduct an intense dialogue within a single body.[17] Either way, a process of withdrawal from daily embodiment is both undertaken and projected. "An actor of feeling," wrote Michael Shchepkin in 1848, "must begin with wiping out his self . . . and become the character the author intended him to be. He must walk, talk, think, feel, cry, laugh—as the author wants him to. . . . You may say that this is impossible. No, it is only difficult."[18] Acting exercises that dislodge self from body have been devised to help the actor overcome this challenge. Sanford Meisner speaks explicitly of the attempt to reduce actors into meaningless inhuman robots in order to later generate a truly personal yet untainted immersion in the role.[19] (Others go further than Meisner, but such positions will concern us once we turn to the relationship between acting and ethics).

To regard acting as disembodiment may seem puzzling for two reasons. The first is that many actors do not usually attempt a radically new incarnation. Employing their own body language when playing a character, such actors adapt the repertoire of their own gestures and quirky mannerisms to the role (Woody Allen is a well-known example). The second is that seeing acting as disembodiment is *not* how actors and actor-training programs typically present what they do: numerous drills that underline the body and enhance awareness of its expressive possibilities are performed; in body-centered programs acting is even cast as an odyssey into the meaning of incarnation—an unleashing of the body's creativity.[20]

But while actors frequently (in some cases exclusively) draw on their personal body language when creating a character, they do not thereby retain their own incarnation. The audience beholds gestures that are no longer the actor's own, but bits and pieces of body language that have been *given over* to the character. As for the second counterclaim, while it is true that acting exercises often aim to amplify awareness of the body and to expand its expressive range, the precise aim of this process is not a sharpening of one's capacity to embody, but an establishing of the plasticity required for receding from present embodiment: to "expand the body's range" is an attempt to free the actor from just one way of walking, talking, or sitting down.

I am not suggesting that the audience is merely aware of the actor's withdrawal from embodiment, but that such a feat is *precisely what they have come to watch.* The audience is looking at a fictional character, made up of mannerisms and gestures. Either these are not the actor's own, or they are, but are carefully stitched together and given over to a created fiction. The result is a person who puts his body in the service of some other controlling entity. Witnessing such an act touches the audience on two levels, both of which have been explored in the past. The first involves the resistance to identity, a resistance that has been alternatively conceptualized through various vocabularies (religious, psychoanalytic, aesthetic, erotic, or political). The gist of the idea concerns the prescriptive nature of authenticity: desiring to become this or that in the first place, to be a subject rather than an object, already entails limitation and self-coercion; the further leap into identities involves additional taxing obligations to become a self-determining, interesting, cohesive, accomplished personality. By contrast, the "actor toys with role, to help us temporarily rediscover rolelessness."[21] Unyoking oneself from the pressure of identity taps a desire for its undoing. Acting fulfills this for its practitioner. It also exhibits and nourishes it in its beholders.[22] Such is the first reason for an audience's attraction to disembodiment.

Solemn, humorless anti-theatrical polemicists have supplied the second: acting shows that the link between identity and embodiment is potentially revisable. John Harrop writes: "The actor, in putting on other faces, is embodying other souls and the Christian tradition tells us that only Satan does this."[23] The faithless adaptability of the actor's body, its ability to host radically different identities that fully and convincingly inhabit it, exposes a contingent relationship between body and embodiment, a flexibility that both alarms and attracts. The actor experiences this contingency; the audience merely witnesses it. Witnessing is not, however, detached observing. It is, rather, an active position from which the audience responds to this withdrawal and, for acting's opponents, is liable to be morally contaminated by it.

The first cause underlying acting's appeal for an audience is its capacity to voice a resistance to roles as such—the second, its exposure of the contingency of the roles that one endorses in life, by showing how some other role can be convincingly adopted. For our purposes, it is sufficient to recognize that the actor's movement *out* of identity constitutes a distinct form of existential amplification, *regardless* of his reaching towards some other identity.

Two Counter-Arguments

This tripartite account of acting as existential amplification illuminates several of acting's more evasive aspects. But before turning to these, two immediate objections need to be faced. The first is that not all acting readily manifests existential amplification. The second is that to conceptualize acting in such a way ignores important post-structuralist and post-humanist insights.

The first objection calls attention to non-realist theater or to traditions of non-Western theater, neither of which appear to be undergirded by existential amplification. Even within traditional Western theater, enacting types (a pantaloon or a Vice figure), or personality fragments that are choreographed into theatrical spectacles, performing as a member of a chorus in a Greek tragedy, or as a marginal character (say, *Hamlet*'s Marcellus)—does not entail existential amplification. To think of acting in such terms may even be pragmatically detrimental with regard to some roles: to act a Falstaff may be well-served by imaginatively accessing such a life—to act a Bardolph would not. Even roles that do involve amplifications may include long episodes that do not require this.

This objection is partly correct: not all acting involves existential amplification. But it is also overstated. While not all acting involves content-related amplification or holds the possibility for inspired acting, it is difficult to think up examples of acting that do not exemplify a receding from embodiment (we saw that even actors who "act themselves" are usually acting). Virtually all acting exemplifies at least this manner of being in another way. Moreover, the self-animation that acting sometimes involves does not depend upon realist theater or upon acting characters. It can appear in non-Western theater or when enacting types (the latter is, in fact, a far more complex process than the one implied by the objection). More importantly, when acting is thought of as a collaborative rather than a personal undertaking, incarnating roles that do not require content-related existential amplification often enables the amplification that goes on in the roles that do. Granted, performing a Bardolph need not demand imagining a lived possibility in detail. Yet a gifted performer may generate his performance of Bardolph's interactions with Falstaff, not out of his own speculations regarding the life a Bardolph may lead, but out of that which assists and empowers the existential expansion performed by the actor who is performing Falstaff. Being a Bardolph would be a derivative process, relating to what being a Falstaff consists of. Much of the brilliance of comic acting consists of the ability to imperceptibly focalize another character in such ways. Oblique forms of existential amplification may explain how this process transpires: one's acting, in such moments, amounts to actively facilitating another actor's existential amplification.

The second objection derives from arguments that may be found most explicitly in essays by Philip Auslander, but are implicit in much of the work published in theater studies.[24] It holds that the above account of acting—with its vocabulary of unrealized possibilities that can be imaginatively actualized—presupposes a questionable view of subjective experience. The death-of-the-subject tradition, from Nietzsche's elimination of the doer in *On the Genealogy of Morals*, through Derrida's critique of presence, to Butler's performativity-without-a-performer, invites pausing before accepting assumptions regarding some nuclear subjectivity. Metaphysical doubts aside, the emphasis on living and "living more" may also provoke ideological reservations. These will be underpinned by the political layer of post-humanist critique, from Marx to Raymond Williams, Foucault, and Althusser. All encourage unearthing the implicit ideological forces that underlie powerful presence-effects. Acting as existential amplification will be suspected of applauding episodes of pseudo self-empowerment and pseudo-liberation, as if these constituted the thing itself.

The view of acting as existential amplification—such critics would claim—entails turning a blind eye to the "post-dramatic" nature of contemporary theater: characters are no longer modeled on selves; they are fragments— identity-effects that need to be incarnated as such, rather than offshoots issuing from an integrated subjective core. Theater not only recognizes this, but has learned to write its scripts with such criticism in mind (as is exemplified in Beckett's plays). Theater has also learned how to disrupt default forms of identification (as Brecht advocates). For anyone sharing such an attitude to theater, the view of acting as "living more" will be suspected as regressive and partial. It would also prove pragmatically misleading for actors who are called upon to embody characters in plays informed by a less assured metaphysical stance with regard to character, self, presence, and the desirability of emotional ties between actor and character, between audience, and actor.

I wish to relate the actor's existential amplification in two ways to this critique. First, note that identifying acting with a realization of possibilities or with self-animation does not rely on a "metaphysics of presence." Nor does it require postulating that a robust subjectivity exists prior to its effects.[25] Such amplification harmonizes with conceptualizations that emphasize performativity and identity-effects: "energy" or "inspiration" will designate particularly potent moments of self-performance, in which a self-citation is strikingly achieved by experiencing or projecting a unique relationship to the enacted content; as for existential amplification as withdrawal from identity, such would be understood as a reification of the playfulness that was always already built into identity, exposing seemingly set-in-stone identities as a façade. The point is not merely that existential amplification can be harmlessly cast in post-humanist terms. It is, rather, that the distinct ideological and metaphysical underpinnings of post-dramatic theater do not annul the need for an account of inspiration: Beckett's or Brecht's theatre still include inspired versus trite acting. Existential amplification can explain the difference between these. Moreover, it can achieve this by infusing substance into the distinct moral objectives of the post-humanist critique.

This brings us to the second point. I have elsewhere argued why some of the epistemic and ontological moves on which post-humanist critique rests, undermine its moral motivations.[26] The "death of character," the caustic cynicism regarding truth-oriented self-talk, the categorical questioning of rationality standards (as if their partial ideological determination automatically invalidated them)—they all ultimately erode any politics that seriously wishes to eradicate injustice, or to correct the marginalization and silencing performed by hegemonic power-knowledge networks. The point is simple: any genuinely ideologically-motivated view of art, literature, and performance, cannot deny the subject-position of a *genuinely suffering* agent, situated across cultures and times, which is why taking marginalization seriously necessitates a belief in *some* valid version of truth-talk. Existential amplification explains the sensitivities upon which such cross-cultural identification and cross-personal empathy should rest, once human beings are no longer homogenized into accepted subject positions. It is precisely because selves are clusters of actualized and dormant possibilities, that spotlighting the processes whereby cultural regimes render such possibilities inaccessible and unimaginable acquires moral import.[27] Far from a regressive return, existential amplification (and the implied potential for existential *diminution*) thereby provides a palpable foundation for the moral thong of the post-humanist critique. And it does so in a way that explains theater's special role in promoting this: the actor's unique embodied bond with a lived possibility and the special relationship established between it and the audience turns the theater into a particularly powerful bridge through which denied forms of suffering may be experientially accessed.

THE EXPERIENCE OF AMPLIFICATION

A philosophy of a practice is required to illuminate questions actually posed by practitioners. In what way does the view of acting as existential amplification address puzzles raised within acting theory, and how does it elucidate the felt experience of acting? This chapter opens with the feeling/projecting controversy. I then suggest how existential amplification is able to expose misrepresentations of the acting process by leading actors who identify acting with lying. Finally, existential amplification will explain the particular role played by repetition in theatrical acting, bringing out an important source of the different experience of live versus filmed acting. Following chapters will turn to spectatorship and to the unique significance of the actor's voice.

Feeling versus Projecting

The inner experience of existential amplification is partly determined by the actor's approach. Consider the following anecdote, reported by Uta Hagen: "One night, after having received accolades for his performance from the audience, the nineteenth-century French actor Coquelin called his fellow actors together backstage and said: 'I cried real tears on stage tonight. I apologize. It will never happen again.'"[1] Here, by contrast, is John Barrymore's description of his acting of Richard III. It was, he says,

> the first genuine acting I ever managed to achieve, and perhaps my own best. It was the first time I ever actually got inside the character I was playing. I mean I thought I was the character, and in my dreams I knew that I was he.[2]

I previously claimed that "feelers" (like Barrymore) and "projectors" (like Coquelin) are both "being in another way"; they are split over the question of *how* to amplify and *what* it consists of, not over the question whether or not acting constitutes amplification. Even the Brechtian actor seems to mobilize a twofold process: amplification followed by commentary.[3]

What we are now able to recognize is how the feeling/projecting debate is actually an ill-formed disagreement over competing accounts of *identification*. These accounts are not mutually exclusive. They can even jointly enhance different aspects of identification with the same state. Once this flexibility is acknowledged, the feeling/projecting controversy disappears, remaining a problem only for someone who implausibly believes that there exists only one gateway for identification. Identification can be emotionally centered: feeling *with* a character or feeling *for* a character both exemplify such identification. But identification need not be emotional: thinking through a character's situation as if it were one's own; fully imagining a character's state and aiming to capture its embodied subtleties— such acts of body and thought do not stress emotional oneness. They consist, rather, of noting, discrimination and insight. They are, nevertheless, forms of identification. Generally, accessing a new possibility does not always require a maximal importing of selfhood into the imagined space. In fact, "being in another way" may sometimes depend precisely upon *leaving* a biographical self behind. Imaginatively becoming other is thereby unlimited by personal history or by biographical sensitivities. Here is Gielgud's realization of this point:

> Of course, all acting should be character-acting, but in those days I did not realize this. . . . I could not imagine a young man unless he was like myself. My own personality kept interfering. . . . In Trofimov for the first time I looked in the glass and thought, "I know how this man would speak and move and behave," and, to my great surprise, I found I was able to keep that picture in my mind throughout the action . . . and to lose myself completely as my appearance and the circumstances of the play seemed to demand.[4]

Sometimes acting mandates drawing on inner resources and on one's experience; sometimes it requires disengaging from these. "Method" techniques are excellent ways through which the imagination can be trained to fully take in another's state, even if one ends up projecting. In the other direction, to focus on convincing projection of embodied features is often an insightful key through which the character's unique experience can be penetrated and felt with wholeness. To exhaustively rely on unifying with the character is to accept a limited understanding of the actual scope of identification. To erroneously believe that the only alternative to emotional merging is externalized presentment of a character amounts to misdescribing projection-oriented acting, demoting it to a mere effective technique. On the contrary, such acting is a form of existential amplification that locates specific external manifestations of an imaginatively embodied state, using these as avenues through which the enacted state as lived possibility can be visited.

Both feeling and projecting are valid ways through which existential amplification can be achieved. Once their relationship to this overarching objective is realized, their antagonism is exposed as a sham. Feelers are guilty of relying upon a restricted understanding of identification. Projectors are guilty of believing that the only alternative to the feeler's position is a defense of hollow skill. When properly contextualized within the real scope of identification—broader than each of these is willing to allow—various combinations between them become viable. Actors need not choose sides in this futile argument (actor autobiographies suggest that most actors hardly feel a burning need to do so anyway, which itself indicates that there was something incompletely thought-through when the feeling/projecting debate was initially introduced).

Acting versus Pretending

Pretense too, is a form of imaginative embodied transformation. Does pretense amount to existential amplification? Is it the same as acting? Indeed, reducing acting to an elaborate pretending is precisely the position endorsed by no less an authority than Olivier: "For what is acting but lying, and what is good acting but convincingly lying?" Michael Gambon seconds this view: "Acting is very sophisticated lying, isn't it? Highly skilled lying."[5] Both significantly misrepresent acting: while acting can involve pretense, and while prolonged pretense can develop into acting, the two are distinct. Here is Declan Donnellan's more perceptive description of the relationship between acting and pretense:

> As soon as we show, we pretend. And pretending is not acting. Certain things cannot be acted; they can only be pretended. States can never be

> acted. . . . You cannot act being asleep. You can only pretend to be asleep. . . . This is not really acting. It is something else, but it may be theatrically crucial for the audience that you do it.[6]

When we pretend, we are involved in mimicking a state while maintaining a clear sense of who we are on the one hand, and of what we are pretending to be on the other (in Donnellan's example above, pretending to be asleep). Offstage, pretense is often negatively colored, associated with an objective to cozen someone else into forming specific beliefs. It is usually a subset of deception (Olivier and Gambon both talk of acting as lying). Pretense is typically instrumental: one desires to draw out a particular response from another, and little else matters; the elicited response is often subordinated to some ulterior objective, say, swindling someone into giving money by pretending to be a pauper.

Acting is different. Firstly, it educes fictional beliefs in the audience, not false ones: no one exits a performance of *Julius Caesar* feeling enraged at having been duped into thinking that the people onstage are Romans. Secondly, while dramatic role-playing is designed to draw out a specific response, it is also significantly dissociated from this goal, whereas pretense is thoroughly instrumental. Actors can drive an audience to laughter or tears, yet still be dissatisfied with their performance. Con artists who swindle their victims' money through fraudulent pretenses would hardly experience such disappointment; if they do, cheating has metamorphosed into an artistic outlet for them. Thirdly (and related to its noninstrumental character), is the different role played by curiosity. The con man pretending to starve is not interested in how hunger is experienced or projected, or in how he would personally feel and act if he were genuinely famished. Acting, on the other hand, is predicated on an artist's *inquisitiveness* regarding how states are experienced and manifested. Fourthly, pretense and acting are experienced by their respective addressees as different communicative acts. Such difference, in turn, affects the experience of acting by contrast to pretending. Pretense is manipulative: when deceived, we feel used and played upon. Acting, on the other hand, is an invitation to partake of another's experience. Such an invitation may occasion a response, and, if successful, it would usually induce it. But acting aims at an altogether different effect than the one elicited by pretense: an opening up to others—the actor to the character's predicament, the audience to the character, the audience to the actor, the actor to the audience—rather than a manipulation of them. To put the same thought differently: to the extent that acting involves lying and manipulating the audience, such is part of a broader gesture of *invitation*.

All four distinctions explain why pretense is usually experienced as aggressive while acting is not.

Nevertheless, while acting and deception are distinct, acting does involve four kinds of non-deceptive pretending. First, the actor may be called to act a character that pretends. To perform Iago demands gathering how Iago would dissimulate in various contexts. Secondly, acting (as Donnellan claims), may entail nondeceptive pretense, such as simulation of sleep or death. Thirdly, some actions require pretense because presenting a full fictional version of the act would carry genuine undesired consequences, or would be impossible: Othello pretends to kill Desdemona, and when Othello and Desdemona stroll on stage looking at the sea, they are clearly pretending to see something they do not. Actors usually pretend to have sexual intercourse rather than actually engage in it. Such actions differ from sitting on a chair, drinking or holding hands, in which the actor is able to fully perform a fictional version of the character's act. Fourthly, an actor's pretense may even seem deceptive: if an actor pretends to be a member of the audience, interrupting the performance as if he were an enraged spectator, this involves pretense vis-à-vis other audience members.

All of these examples involve nondeceptive pretending. The first is actually a form of acting: one pretends *in* character. The others can be situated in relation to acting on the one hand, and to deceptive pretense on the other. Unlike deceptive pretense, the second and third forms of pretense establish *fictional* beliefs rather than false ones. Unlike deceptive pretense, all four forms of pretense are not experienced by the audience as aggressive, but as part of an invitation: when a fellow audience member is discovered to be an actor, his act overlaps with deception, since he establishes a false belief rather than a fictional one. But the pretense does not amount to deception, because, as part of an aesthetic undertaking, it invites the audience to adopt a different attitude to the purposeful instilling of false beliefs, construing this deception as itself a constituent of art. Pretense in all these cases, even when overlapping with deception, does not collapse into it, because pretending is subordinated to the overarching aesthetic offering that acting involves.

On the other hand, *like* deceptive pretense, such forms of simulation seem to be largely or entirely instrumental. They are performed in order to induce beliefs in the audience. They are—as Donnellan calls them—forms of "showing," and, as such, are audience-related: the audience needs to believe that Desdemona is looking at the sea, or has been strangled, or is asleep. By pretending in such ways, the actress is merely enabling spectatorship to continue uninterruptedly: if *they* believe that she is asleep or dead, nothing more is required of her. To achieve this pretending calls for a skill that actors need to perfect; to learn to pretend in such ways does require, for example, the curiosity that differentiates acting from non-artistic deception. But while acting can require such pretending, they are, nevertheless, not the same. By pretending I try to get *them* to believe something; when acting, *I* attempt to *be* something. These processes are related, and may facilitate each other. But they are not identical.

It is at this point that the more significant implication for acting of these fine distinctions can be stated. While acting is an aesthetic offering to an other, and while actors need an audience (for reasons that will be presented in the next chapter), the difference between acting and pretending is that good acting may or may not correlate with its effect on a spectator. Whether projecting or experiencing, acting involves depth of imaginative embodiment communicated to another as part of an aesthetic offering. To reduce this process into showing or pretending is to miss the virtues that successful embodiment demands—curiosity, selection, control, subtlety—virtues that are, on their own, unrelated to an audience and what it would pick out. This is why actors are only partly guided by their audience's evaluation of their work: an unmoved audience may indicate that the actress has failed in accessing a role; a moved audience may indicate that she has succeeded—yet neither of these implications is necessary.

A different way of attempting to reduce acting to pretense is to take the examples of pretense presented above one step further, and claim that they are symptomatic of all acting in general. If it is true that an actor only pretends to strangle Desdemona (since the performed action cannot obviously be the projected one), such holds for more mundane acts as well. When Othello and Desdemona enthusiastically chat, the performed act of the people on stage differs from what is being projected; hence, such performed actions constitute pretense. Simulating to strangle another character merely bares the pretense that all acting involves. Moreover, acting a character may be aptly regarded as the attempt to *pretend* to be one: it may be said that, while not involved in deception, on some level the Othello actor nevertheless *pretends* to be Othello rather than "be" Othello or act "as if" he were him. It is not only impossible to *be* Othello; if one truly imagined what an Othello would do and act *as if* one were Othello, one would have to concede that Othello would not remain on stage, and would refuse to perform the story into which he has been scripted.

This objection correctly underlies how the actor's manner of being in another way does not amount to becoming the character, but to establishing an embodied fictional version of the character's state. It thus helpfully corrects the distorted understanding of Stanislavsky's "magic if" as advocating literally attempting to act as if one *were* the character.[7] But deducing from this that acting *is* pretending assumes an overly broad definition of pretense. True, if pretense simply involves intentionally establishing a gap between a performed act and its processing by another, all acting (and all role-playing) are forms of pretending. But this characterization leaves too little outside the sphere of pretense. Given the multiple discrepancies between what is projected and what is experienced, virtually all living and interpersonal interaction is, under this definition, a form of pretense: paying a complement, deceiving, withholding information, role-playing, politely refraining from voicing an opinion—all are different ways in which projected meaning differs from inner state. Acting is a very specific version of establishing this difference, one that needs to be set apart from the rest—not forced into some undifferentiated similarity to them.

The more interesting mistake this objection involves—both from the perspective of actors and that of philosophers—is not the blurring of categories, but running together the process of establishing fictional beliefs (acting) and that of generating merely false ones (pretense). False beliefs are opposed to true ones—fictional beliefs are not. The transition into fictional beliefs involves a deviation from that which actually takes place, but can be a means of capturing and presenting a more evasive dimension of the represented state. So, while the actor does present a fictional version of Othello rather than try to simply be Othello, his performance gives shape to the unfolding of lethal jealously. The actor does not merely move away from reality, but aims to distill and convey a lasting and accurate version of it. Like pretense, a gap between what is experienced and what is represented is introduced. But, unlike pretense, by establishing this gap, another gap—the one between the representation and that which is being represented—is, by acting, often *narrowed* down. Weaker and stronger versions of this connection between fictional representation and truth can be held, the weaker holding that actors sometimes present truth, the stronger claiming that some truths can only be accessed via fictional representation. But regardless of the specific version endorsed, to reduce acting to pretense is to ignore the complex relationship between fiction and truth.[8] (As will be explored in later parts of this book, some forms of role-playing outside the stage possess an analogous quality: a stepping out of identity sometimes enables accessing and realizing more intimate dimensions of who one is. There, too, characterizing such processes as "pretending" amounts to overlooking the manner whereby a deviation from reality can sometimes enable its fuller intake).

Theatrical Repetition

Repetition is intrinsic to live acting, rehearsing, and to the experience of existential amplification in the theater. It also constitutes a formidable psychological challenge to actors. Marlon Brando describes just how emotionally oppressive such repetition can become:

> What I remember most about *A Streetcar Named Desire* was the emotional grind of acting in it six nights and two afternoons a week. Try to imagine what it was like walking on a stage at 8:30 every night having to yell, scream, cry, break dishes, kick the furniture, punch the walls and experience the same intense, wrenching emotions night after night, trying each time to evoke in audiences the same emotions I felt. It was exhausting. Then imagine what it was like to walk off the stage after pulling these emotions out of yourself and waking up in a few hours knowing you had to do it all over again a few hours later . . . it was emotionally draining, wearisome, mentally oppressive, and after a few weeks I wanted out of it.[9]

Kenneth Branagh provides another indication of the taxing nature of repetition:

> Over the following weeks I learned about the uncomfortable phenomenon of playing Hamlet twice on Saturdays. The stomach-wrenching sick feeling that overtakes one as the first soliloquy begins is truly terrifying and it's impossible not to be aware of quite how far you have to go in this Everest of a role.[10]

But if it was merely a *difficult* requirement of theater, repetition would not provoke further philosophical scrutiny. Nor would such scrutiny be called for if repetition amounted to no more than a skill, mastered by good actors. Lee Strasberg asserts, for example, that "The real problem for the actor is how to create in each performance the same believable experiences and behavior, and yet include what Stanislavsky called 'the illusion of the first time.'"[11] When this claim is understood as a practical requirement, it raises no particular puzzles: actors should avoid disclosing awareness of what is about to occur, or refrain from projecting the outcome of a lived process before it has taken place ("Playing results, not processes"), or rush through a dialogue in an unrealistic pace. All of these indicate failures to suspend prior knowledge when repeating a lived process. Competent acting does not trip in such ways.

Yet the experience of repeating a fully-known lived sequence reaches into several additional layers that go beyond difficulty or mere skill. To access these, we need to first distinguish repetition from overlapping notions such as exercise or duplication. Drawing such fine distinctions can seem pedantic—splitting hairs over nothing. But this is one of those areas in which a refusal to attend these distinctions risks serious mistakes in one's entire approach to theater. Consider the following observation that aspires to communicate the heart of Artaud's theater:

> Here we touch upon what seems to be the profound essence of Artaud's project, his historico-metaphysical decision. Artaud wanted to erase repetition in general. For him, repetition was evil, and one could doubtless organize an entire reading of his texts around this center. Repetition separates force, presence, and life from themselves.[12]

In the passage above, Artaud is interpreted as associating deadness with repetition; his "theatre of cruelty" being designed to avoid it. Note how, at least in this description of Artaud's project, he indiscriminatingly runs together several distinct forms of performing the same act more than once (repetition, exercise, duplication); a blurring of categories that leads to adopting a particular philosophy of theater.

But repetition, exercise and duplication are distinct forms of reenactment. *Exercise* is a goal-oriented form of repetition. It plays a central role in honing a skill or in training, and it figures both in the arts and elsewhere.

A musician practicing his arpeggios, a singer going through voice drills, a weightlifter pushing dumbbells in a gym—they all repeat an action. Exercise is "goal-oriented" in the sense that it is a means rather than an end—happily dispensed with if a more convenient way of obtaining the desired result was found. Long-term exercise can be seen as intrinsically valuable, since it is indicative of character virtues such as endurance and perseverance. Such fortitude breeds the achievement we sometimes praise in sports or art: we admire the performer's devotion of countless hours of practice that enable reaching the level of prowess we witness. Some kinds of aesthetic pleasure are attuned to this dimension: musicians able to play difficult passages will be applauded for their virtuosity. But exercise is still valued only because it is symptomatic of an independently valuable character trait, or because it enables an autonomously valued performance of an independently prized piece of music; the mere capacity to play quick or difficult passages is a condition, not an end in itself. Censuring artists for being merely "technical" is related to this perception: such artists confuse means and ends by trumpeting their dexterity rather than offering a genuinely creative effect. Another defining trait of exercise is that, beyond the performer's grasp of it as goal-oriented, *its experience* is itself goal-oriented: one practices scales for the purpose of developing agility, or to master a particular instrument, or to facilitate improvisation. Repeating scales is an expedient route through which such objectives are promoted. On its own, there is nothing musical, emotional, or artistic in going over the scales; these actions may be carried out in a technical, uninvolved way.

Exercise differs from, but also overlaps with, *duplication*: the act of merely copying another's movements. Consider a forger creating an identical copy of an expensive piece of jewelry by recreating the formative actions in which it was produced. While unrelated to developing a skill, duplication of this kind resembles exercise in being goal-oriented. The process of duplication can exert some interest and poses challenges of its own. But in itself it is unimportant and may have been dispensed with, if possible. What matters is bringing into existence an identical jewel. Aside from its instrumental nature, such duplication also involves an attempt to work from an original sample: ideally, the forger would have been happy to produce the original itself time and again rather than go through the trouble of duplicating it.

There are other, slightly different, forms of duplication of actions. A child annoying his sister by mimicking her movements or echoing her words, a chef cooking a dish she has already often prepared, a scientist repeating an experiment. In these, it is less obvious that one is working from some original. Nor are such processes merely goal-oriented: the process itself can be experienced as meaningful and pleasurable. The child takes pleasure in annoying his sister in a particular way; the chef concentrates on getting the dish just right, perhaps modifying and trying to improve on what she has already made in the past; the scientist is genuinely interested in the experiment under examination now, regardless of past results. The child is repeating something that he sees or hears. The chef is recreating something that she knows. The scientist is assessing the validity of a claim. What distinguishes such forms of duplication is that, while pleasure or some other intrinsic value can be experienced, duplication remains largely a means for some *other* desiderated result: the child's actions are geared to annoy; the chef aims to bring into the world a new dish; the scientist establishes a hypothesis as true or false. To put this differently, if such results are not attained, the actions undertaken will have *failed*.

Such are exercise and duplication. Theatrical *repetition* is different. Suppose that I am acting *King Lear*'s Gloucester. Two minutes from now, Cornwall is going to gouge out my eyes. Yet I must enter the castle and socialize with Regan and Cornwall, withholding what I know of Lear's whereabouts. As Gloucester, I feel unthreatened. Only Lear is in danger. My own dire predicament will dawn on me only later, when Regan and Cornwall interrogate me. Even then, its severe and heinous outcome will escape me until it actually occurs. I berate Regan for plucking my beard, as if symbolic humiliation is what I should be fussing about, when it is mutilation and my son's partial orchestration of my blinding which will crush me in minutes. Yet up I come on stage for the umpteenth time to undergo this ordeal, experiencing each shock anew.

Throughout the five years in which I acted the part, I made some highly particular decisions: the differences between my screams when my second eye is plucked out, or the degree of my physical resistance. Our troupe also has the blocking meticulously worked out. But to avoid rote, I must be blinded tonight as if for the *first* time. In the past, these moments had induced in me rage, or pain, or shame, or numb inactivity. Yet instead of harping on what has occurred and mimicking my own past acting, believable live acting invites me to lay myself open to what such moments will spawn in *today's* performance. The new repetition need not register my previous visitations of the role. What is crucial is defamiliarization; discovering anew that which is previously already intimately known. "Feelers" would have to look for such differences in their present experiences. "Projection-oriented" actors would be obliged to convey a chosen incarnation freshly. The point is that neither approach to acting can rely on mere duplication of a previous performance.

Process-oriented versus Goal-oriented Repetition

John Gielgud believes that, unlike the painter or the writer, the actor cannot be satisfied with merely creating a fine piece of work, but is required "to repeat it with unfaltering love and care for perhaps three hundred performances on end."[13] But how does "love and care" in repetition of this kind differ from exercise or duplication? Although not a form of practice undertaken in order to perfect some skill, acting is surely goal-oriented in the sense of aiming to elicit a particular response from the audience. Yet, unlike exercise or duplication, such responses are not the be-all and the end-all of acting: as argued before, an actor may be satisfied with a performance even if the audience was sleepy or inattentive, or failed to acknowledge and be moved by nuanced choices. The actress might even be angry with herself for moving her audience in a way she deems cheap, crude, or sentimental. Sometimes, one's best acting may arise during rehearsals. It may appear when one is one's sole spectator. Acting is an activity that generates a response which may be internally pleasing or satisfying. Yet significant as such payoffs are professionally, or as forms of implicit participation with the acting process, they are not the *motivation* which underlies acting. The actor may persist in acting even if he suspects that he will never be happy with his performance.

While it leads to various desirable results that, in themselves, contribute to the aesthetic value of the performance as a whole, theatrical repetition is not goal-oriented. True, some acting repetition exercises are designed to instill an empty verbalization of a text in order to later facilitate authentic enactment. Drills of this kind are goal-oriented in the same way that other exercises are: they are performed in order to achieve the emotional clean slate from which histrionic discovery can begin.[14] A different form of goal-oriented theatrical repetition takes place when the performance explicitly focuses on repetition.[15] But unlike exercise (theatrical or other) or duplication, theatrical repetition is not a means for some other end. Whether rehearsed or performed for an audience, theatrical repetition is process-oriented: it is the act of living afresh the enacted sequence of events—an attempt to be.

Claiming that theatrical repetition is process rather than goal-oriented sets apart acting, firstly, from forms of repetition that are dispensable means for some other end. Secondly, such a claim distinguishes acting from modes of repetition that are "mechanical" in the sense of being *experienced* merely as a means. The difference between the two senses of instrumental activity is that a person may carry out an instrumental activity while undergoing a fully involved experience. "Mechanical" by contrast, captures a sense of inner hollowness that accompanies the performed action. Goal-oriented actions such as pushing weights may carry this additional dead quality. They are not valued in themselves and may be absentmindedly performed—what matters is that they bring about the desired result. Theatrical repetition differs from both kinds of instrumental activity: it is not a means; and it would be difficult to find actors who relate to it as a mechanical experience. If Gielgud is to be believed, even an actor who experiences nothing is obliged to conduct the repetition "with love." Acting can surely deteriorate into mimicry of what others did or what the actor has successfully pulled off in the past. At its best, however, acting projects, or, on more demanding versions, is a singular, first-time encounter. Third, the claim that acting is process-oriented distinguishes it from types of repetition that produce an independent object, like the ones produced by the chef or the forger.

Repetition and Existential Amplification

Through repetition, acting is able to amplify life not solely by forming a gateway into a range of new (fictional) possibilities, but by establishing a unique context in which numerous dimensions that are condensed into what appears to be a single possibility are discovered. The point is not quantitative or logical (the Heraclitean point that no two events, however similar, are one and the same). The actor is compelled not merely to intellectually acknowledge but to actively embody the experiential heterogeneity that an apparently identical moment contains. This is not merely a mode of "living more" through art in the familiar sense of entering fictionally enabled, usually inaccessible, realities. It is a study of intense, lived moments that the actor has an opportunity to examine and *re-examine*. Acting is an exploration of the hidden thickness of the present.

There are two distinct ways in which theatrical repetition is both discovery and embodiment of multiplicity in the seemingly same. The first is interpretative, and relates to minutely different choices of emphasis that the same lines are open to. The line "He . . . laughed at my losses, mocked my gains, scorned my nation, thwarted my bargains, cooled my friends, heated mine enemies; and what's his reason?" (*The Merchant of Venice*) can be successfully acted whether uttered quickly or slowly, whether implying sardonic irony, world-weariness, or deep-seated anger. The actor may emphasize the links between money and identity (my "losses," "gains," "bargains") or the ones between religion and self ("my nation"). "Cooled my friends" can be an expression of rage or an admission of irrevocable loss. This agglomeration of possibilities folded in Shylock's line entails not a mere numerical accumulation. It forms important differences in stress and meaning that surface if the actor succeeds in releasing them. Repeating such lines between performances, the actor—particularly if he does not limit his skill to projection—can delve and explore different interpretations of the line. Such differences in scansion can issue from a conscious decision. They may also materialize spontaneously. They are not, strictly speaking, repetitions, since they modify, however minutely, the previous mode of delivery, discerning and projecting novel nuances in what appeared to be known. Such new found differences need not improve the interpretation, and may even constitute a less compelling incarnation. Actor John Barrymore was criticized precisely for such inability to stick to a successful interpretation:

> As always, his [Barrymore's] first performance was his best. Some of his later were embarrassingly bombastic. He did not have the gift of knowing when he was right. . . . Once he had successfully created a part he was given to embroidering, and his embroidering was not good. . . . It was as though once he made the mold he proceeded to break it.[16]

But a criticism such as this, relates to performance from an audience's perspective; it misses precisely the living quality of the repeated process that Barrymore aimed for, even at the price of a slightly inferior interpretation. To freshly encounter the enacted state requires freedom in acting, and such free exploration of the seemingly same can be—as it evidently was for Barrymore—more important than the interpretative value that emphasizes the unique understanding of the text, worked out prior to the performance. Barrymore's critic reveals a misunderstanding: in hoping for a precise duplication of a performance that has worked before, he reveals that, in effect, he is dreaming of a film! Barrymore's understanding of live performance is opposed to this: the acting process presents an exploration, and the audience of a live performer is looking for such. The audience may even secretly wish that something would go slightly wrong in the performance—that a piece of furniture would accidentally break, that a line would be forgotten, that a comedian would be unable to maintain seriousness. Such a wish discloses a desire to attend a live, not fully-determined repetition of a known process. The fake analogy with object-producing arts is again instructive: no one wishes to find spelling mistakes in a book, or to watch a film in which sound and picture are momentarily out of sync. But slight slips in live performance possess charm that can enhance pleasure, suggesting that the fresh encounter of an actor with the enacted episode can sometimes prove as important to an audience as is the strength of the offered interpretation.

But there is a second, less obvious, sense of such an exploration of the present that unfolds when no interpretative discovery takes place, when nothing in the meaning of the line is highlighted. Such a discovery occurs within the rigid boundaries posed by repeating the same scansion in which a line is delivered. It relates to a qualitative spectrum that opens up through repetition, whether one experiences the enacted state or "lovingly" projects it. This spectrum concerns *how* one inhabits the same possibility. We have already encountered this dimension, the self-animation underpinning inspiration or energized acting. Differences in intensity, from the mechanically distant and empty to the fully absorbed make up this domain, which—to iterate—is not about the content of a lived possibility but concerns qualitative differences in inhabiting a lived process. The previously cited testimony by Strasberg regarding Ben Ami's inspiring acting involved Strasberg attending a repeated performance. Strasberg emphasized similarity of movement and voice that could, nevertheless, somehow establish dissimilar effects. The example is unique, since the import of repetition is here experienced by a spectator rather than a performer. But this dimension of repetition is usually open only to performers: they are the ones who would sense how theatrical repetition can become a powerful form of *suspending* one's involvement with overly-familiar embodied content, inviting exploration and projection of different relationships to content instead. Strasberg's attending a repeated enactment enabled him to similarly bracket the text, and access the *relationship* to known content instead.

Repetition (in both these senses) colors the actor's experience of existential amplification. Not only does the actor momentarily extend the range of his possibilities, he also *re*-visits familiar content, searching for multiplicity of meaning within the seemingly known. Simultaneously, the actor is also able to experience different ways in which the *same* lived possibility may be inhabited. The fascination of acting for practitioners is, I suggest, related to both dimensions of this experience.

WATCHING ACTORS

Acting is a form of existential amplification. But why is an audience drawn to watch it? This chapter takes up the relationship between spectatorship and the existential gesture performed by the actor. An important difference between watching live and watching filmed acting would thereby emerge.

The Audience

The concept of an "audience" is too varied to be encompassed by a simple description:

> One talks continually about "audience reaction" as if an entire horde of spectators touched by the same stimuli were simultaneously experiencing the same feelings to the same degree. This never happens. . . . The lowest form of audience attention is that mentally fugitive state where events on the stage are continually mixing with unrelated events in the audience's mind; commingling thoughts of the supper-to-come, the architecture of the house, the number of scenes still to be got through before the interval, the waste of money, the median state of interest is when characters and action possess enough sustaining power simply to interest the audience in the passage of time; creating an unpressured sense of wanting to know what comes next. The highest state of audience attention is that moment (and it rarely lasts for more than a moment) when a varied number of people of all ages and walks of life, unexpectedly discover a sense of unbroken communion as a result of a perception which has simultaneously infiltrated their minds.[1]

The challenge for a theory of spectatorship is to explain further the sense of a momentary "unbroken communion" described by Marowitz, given the heterogeneity of the audience.[2] Attempts to achieve this typically fall into two kinds: the first posits a sharp distinction between performers and audience, setting apart "the art of watching" from "the art of being watched," indicating that the audience is merely "spending some of its lifetime" simultaneously with the actors. When an attempt is then made to account for the bond between the performance and the audience, such theories underscore the response to the enacted *content*.[3] The second kind, while recognizing the difference between enacting and watching, and while acknowledging response to content, focuses on that which draws the audience to watch the process of *acting*.[4]

These options are not mutually exclusive, and are best thought of as differing in emphasis: most would (or should) agree that a comprehensive theory of spectatorship ought to incorporate *both* components complemented by a third : the audience's ability to respond to the performance as an aesthetic achievement (the addition is entailed by acting's previous characterization: an aesthetic offering in which relationships are established between projected effects and the actor's power as creator — an audience ideally grasps these relationships). By "grasping" I mean that an ideal audience is not merely mesmerized by a performance (since it would then only respond to effects); nor does it simply note and appreciate relationships between merits and effects (since its response would then amount to a cerebral observation of a skill). A rich combination of genuine response and appreciation for the creative merits that elicit these is what a performer hopes for. To be an audience is to accept the invitation to potentially respond in such ways to an actor's aesthetic offering.

But what I wish to spotlight is less the audience's attunement to aesthetic merits, but the relationship between the actor's existential amplification and the audience. Conceiving of acting as existential amplification that somehow reaches the audience belongs to the second of the orientations specified above: the audience perceives much more than a fictional role when watching an actor. That which is perceived behind the character is usually unrelated to the actor's individual biography—as Kendall Walton claims, the audience "cannot be expected to have a clear idea of an actor's personal thoughts and feelings while he is performing [since] that would require being intimately acquainted with his offstage personality."[5] Ignorance of an actor's personality does not, however, support restricting audience-actor connection to a response to roles. Rather than be restricted to content-related features belonging to the part, the audience's perception can apprehend the actor's movement into a character, thus tapping the process of existential amplification undergone by the actor. Identification, specifically in the theater, involves this twofold process: accessing a fictional character's state while simultaneously responding to a real person's experience (the actor).

To consider spectatorship in this way partly accounts for the view of involved theatrical spectatorship as a form of complex participation in what the actor undergoes. A multilayered *validation* of the acting process underlies such participation: in accepting the actor's metamorphosis, the audience responds to, empathizes with, and thereby *validates* the actor's existential expansion. *Validation* means that in a persuasive dramatic embodiment the audience is willing to ignore what it directly recognizes to be unfolding on stage—an artificial activity organized by professionals situated in its own culture and time—and to respond to it as an altogether different event.

The audience is not doing this for the sake of the actors. Spectatorship is not an altruistic act. Nor does the audience merely purchase amusement or a momentary escape from its own routine by a "willing suspension of disbelief." While such experiences may be felt, they are parasitical upon a second layer of response, which concerns the spectator's rather than the performer's needs: by allowing itself to respond to an enacted fantasy, the audience accepts—not just intellectually but in what it itself *performs*—the ability to actualize possibilities that lie outside the limits of one's identity. The audience, in effect, provides—in a way that perhaps only a collective of strangers can—a key through which existential expansion can be achieved. To put the same thought differently: by cooperating with the theatrical offering *by allowing itself to relate to the fiction*, the audience turns acting into a means whereby imaginative existential expansion occurs.[6]

Consider, in this context, Stanislavsky's warning against attempting to entertain the audience:

> The more the actor wishes to amuse his audience, the more the audience will sit in comfort waiting to be amused, and not even try to play its part in the play on the stage before it. But as soon as the actor stops being concerned with his audience, the latter begins to watch the actor.[7]

The insight is not developed by Stanislavsky. Nevertheless, it captures the idea that audience members wish to play a part in the theatrical process rather than be passive recipients of a creative offering, who, at their best behavior, exemplify the appropriate kind of focused attention. Actors who merely seek to amuse, prevent the audience from mobilizing a more fundamental form of participation in the event. On some level, the audience *completes* the act of acting by recognizing and responding to the actor as character.[8]

Four Further Puzzles

Understanding spectatorship in this way explains four further puzzles: the actor's need for an audience, the particular force of live performance, the need that the audience be a collective and the disproportion which often exists between the effort spent in preparing a theatrical performance, particularly in amateur theater, and the limited quantity of performances that are planned.

Actors need an audience because only a spectator is able to provide the external indication that the actor momentarily exists in this amplified form. Actors are certainly able to perform to themselves. Rehearsals are partly performances too, since a director and one's fellow actors also function as audience; sometimes an actress may even feel that she gives her best performance in a rehearsal. Ultimately though, actors need an audience—not in the sense of a logical interdependence between theater and a present audience, but in the psycho-existential sense of a body of unfamiliar observers, who provide the inter-subjective context of recognition by playing along with the process presented by the actors.[9]

Two aspects underlie this participation. The first is the audience's capacity to shape a performance, an effect that performers are keenly aware of.[10] The second is the validation provided by the audience to the actor, its ability to complete the actor's act, as described above. The first aspect explains a unique feature of live performance. But since audience response need not radically differ between two performances, the possibility of variation in audience response cannot account for the more fundamental significance of *live* performance for actors. The second aspect does. Through a sharing of space and time with the performer, the audience's attention constitutes and communicates an acceptance of the performer's creative act, a recognition of existential amplification as it takes place. Such validation will not materialize if the performance is watched only onscreen, since its occurrence, while it can be imagined by the performer, is no longer a *felt* part of the creative act. This is why an attentive and moved audience often *does* something to a performer: it tightens the embodiment and energizes the performance. As a member of such an audience, the viewer individually participates in this act. The desire for such participation in a particular theatrical event carried out in relation to particular performers partly explains a desire to attend a live performance and to become *its* audience in particular.[11]

A response to existential amplification also explains why the audience needs to be a *collective*. The actor's need for an audience resembles the spectator's need for each other: single spectators are unable to provide a validation for amplification similar in effect to the one granted by a conglomerate of strangers. The difference is not merely numerical. A "collective" or "an audience" performs something that is impossible for an individual participant to accomplish. Precisely because of its heterogeneity, an audience is a body which enables the *disconnection* of response from any particular member. To put this differently: a deindividuated "audience" constitutes an abstract authority that accepts the breaching of identity boundaries celebrated during a theatrical performance. Such validation is independent of the potentially contestable response of any particular spectator.

Finally, the view that the audience somehow completes the act of acting explains why amateurs, undriven by pecuniary motives, aware that the play they rehearse for will only be briefly performed, devote a disproportionate amount of time, money, and energy to a perfection of a play. Professionals too, may spend excessive energy on performances that they know would draw a small audience. But in their case, aesthetic considerations may underlie such a choice. Amateurs, precisely because they cannot rationalize the effort spent via appeal to aesthetic merit, unravel a dimension of the audience-actor relationship that is unrelated to content or aesthetic value. Amateurs wish to be watched, not because of the high artistic achievement they erroneously attach to what they present to friends and family, but because the existing audience would somehow participate and validate the process they have been engaged in. A prolonged rehearsal period which does not lead to a performance is dissatisfying precisely because without the acknowledgment of an audience, a particular dimension of living in an imagined space will not be realized.

To what extent is the audience aware of this process? Are the claims above presented as psychological observations regarding what the audience is genuinely experiencing and why it is actually drawn to theater? Are they, rather, prescriptive claims regarding what the audience should be attentive to? These questions suggest a false choice between descriptive and normative features. In reality, these intertwine. The audience is typically unaware of the process just described; theater, in this respect, does not differ from other art forms, such as music or dance, in which the source underlying the recipient's attraction is not readily obvious or given. Nevertheless, I suggest that the audience's interest in theater is rooted in this participation with the acting experience. To conclusively prove that this is so is obviously impossible. Like other proposals regarding the subliminal pull of this or that art form, one cannot appeal to anything more compelling than the explanatory power of the proposed explanation—in relation to the art form itself, to features relating to its practice, appreciation, and experience.

Cinematic and Theatrical Acting

Throughout virtually all of acting's complex history, the audience encountered only one kind of acting: the live kind. This is no longer the case. Cinema and television expose people to much more acting than they would have watched in the past. But the *kind* of acting differs too. A comparative dimension has now been added to our experience of acting—a capacity to think through the differences between live and filmed acting which was unavailable to past philosophy of theater. The pervasive existence of theater reveals dimensions of meaning found in live acting that we are now better positioned to identify. We can be surer than before, for example, that acting is not merely an attempt to achieve perfect mimesis. Why? Because the most obvious difference between live and cinematic acting is that filmed acting is more lifelike; it allows the actor to deploy subtle gestures and minor changes in body language; it enables employing the volume of actual spoken or even whispered voice; an actress can merely think herself into a state and the camera will pick this up; her subdued nuances powerfully communicate her character's inner state. The camera, in short, permits tiny inflections of facial and bodily tension to become a rich expressive vocabulary that resembles actual forms of interaction and response. Amplifying these, as theater requires, detracts from the mimetic realism and from the absorbing potential of the fiction—which explains why theater is initially experienced as artificial to many viewers who are accustomed to filmed acting.

The familiar rebuttal of this complaint is to reverse the charge of artificiality: unlike filmed acting with its repeated takes and non-diachronic shooting, theater assures us that the process we are witnessing is (usually) structured according to the chronology of the enacted event. The stage unfolds the witnessing of a complete embodied process. Cinema, by contrast, offers a recording of a fragment of a process that is not part of a complete experience that the filmed actor has fully undergone. Accordingly, the film actor's momentary embodied forays into imagined space, stitched together by an editing team to be later presented to an audience, are not an obviously more authentic presentation of a fictional world.

Determining whether live or filmed acting is or isn't more truthful is not the interesting issue. My point is, rather, that live performance's capacity to consistently attract spectatorship given its (at least strongly sensed) failure to be as truthful as its filmed rival, may be symptomatic of distinct needs to relate to (or to enact) experientially distinct processes that remain unfulfilled by cinematic acting. To regard acting as existential amplification can explain live acting's survival: cinematic acting consists of an ability to fully enter a fragment of a process, and to interact effectively with a camera—the film actor's most significant partner. This is surely an art form in its own right. It is also a kind of embodied existential amplification. Such an acting process is, nevertheless, categorically different from theatrical embodiment, in which a live performer undergoes (and an audience simultaneously validates) a process of identification with a character's fuller story.

A similar thought arises when considering why theater's overstated expressive vocabulary turns it, for some, into a "less absorbing" medium relative to cinema: rather than effortlessly drift into the fictional world of cinema, in the rougher world of theater one is constantly aware of watching actors. Yet here too, the objection brings out the subliminal pull of attending live acting: the flawless migration into the fictional realm in filmed acting is more akin to the experience of reading literature—not to the particular response to existential amplification that one perceives in and responds to in live actors. Rather than constituting an interference, the mimetic friction of theater—by contrast to the over-verisimilitude of cinema—is an important enabling condition of the event an audience wishes to attend. Instead of smoothly moving into the world of the characters via a technology that enables the audience to altogether forget that they are watching an actor, the audience is repeatedly reminded of the actor-role relationship that mobilizes the existential amplification they have come to witness and participate in.

Such a view of the mechanisms underlying spectatorship also explains a third frequently mentioned difference between live and filmed acting: the relationship between artistic action and the artist's work. Live acting is "the work of art"; it is inseparable from the actor, and disappears when the performance ends. John Gielgud describes his envy of painters or writers.

Precisely because their work forms an independent object, such artists are able to look at their past creations: "I have often wished that I were able to rise in the middle of the night, switch on the light, and examine some performance of mine calmly and dispassionately as I looked at it standing on the mantelpiece."[12] Filmed acting, by contrast, is precisely geared to create such an independent object.

Here one should distinguish between filmed performance and cinematic acting. Both are captured on film and can be repeatedly watched. But whereas a taped performance of a play records a moment which would have existed regardless of its filming, cinematic acting is *intrinsically* linked to its filming. By "intrinsic" I mean that cinematic acting depends upon another art form (actually, a set of art forms) responsible for transcribing the acting into an independent object. Such acting differs from a recording of a performance. When a live theatrical performance is filmed, it retains all of its distinguishing features as theatrical acting. Although an object will be extracted from this performance via an interaction with a camera, a recorded live performance does not thereby metamorphose into an object-making activity; the performance would have taken place even if it was not being filmed.[13] In filmed performance, the dialogue that cinematic acting conducts with the other artistic functions that go into the making of a film is radically curtailed—the cameras merely *record* the event rather than actively *shape* the aesthetic object by modifying the acting. A taped theatrical performance does not turn theater into an object-creating art.

Such a difference with regard to the object-oriented goal of the acting modifies both the experience of acting—in cinematic acting one's subtle dialogue with the camera becomes at least as important as imaginative metamorphosis—but also the experience of watching such acting. In cinematic acting, one is presented with an object rather than a performance: one does not share or partake in the process undergone by the actor.[14] In fact, any identification with the acting process on the part of the viewer is bound to impose on actors a comprehensive metamorphosis which they did not experience, since their acting never followed the fictional chronology in the first place. The bridges connecting spectatorship with the acting process are, in cinematic acting, a fantasy. Creator and spectator are drawn apart: the former focusing on fragments of incarnation and a dialogue with the camera, the latter absorbed into the fictional layer, in a viewing experience that is calculated to render the acting process invisible.

The philosophical debate over the importance of live performance should be related to these differences.[15] If theatrical spectatorship validates the process of existential amplification undergone by the actor, the audience importantly participates in the live actor's act. While acting may sometimes be dissociated from an external audience, actors nevertheless need an audience to complete their act. Live performances enable the unfolding of this interpenetration and mutual dependency: *one presents a process rather than a work*, inviting another to validate it by relating to the fiction; both performer and audience cooperate in existential amplification. By contrast, to watch a digitized recording of the same performance is to invite the audience to relate to the fictional events and (at least in the case of filmed performance) to relate what the actor has experienced *in the past*. The audience is not invited to implicitly participate in the act, but to enjoy and appreciate it, and be absorbed by *the story*. Gone is the interpersonal interaction constituted by the performer's invitation and the audience's participation.

Finally, since, unlike theatrical acting, cinematic acting is designed to create an autonomous object, filmed acting and watching such acting lacks a vital relationship to repetition. If a filmed sequence of acting is artistically successful, it will be retained, even if the sequence was only acted once. The repetition of the sequence is time-consuming, expensive, and, on its own, would have been happily dispensed with had circumstances allowed; repetition, in such a context, designates dissatisfaction and uncertainty. For the purposes of cinema, an ideal actor would be one who never needs to repeat. Theatrical acting is, by contrast, independent of the art forms applied in cinema in order to produce an autonomous object. It is intrinsically and importantly linked with repetition. The duration of the repetition too, differs in movies and in the theater: filmed repetition rarely lasts more than a few seconds or minutes, and the sequence of shooting is itself unrelated to the presented fictional chronology; theatrical repetition is of the entire play and follows its chronology.

This is not merely a difference in the acting process. The audience in the theater is *aware* of attending a repeated act; audience members know that the actor now crying has wept in last night's performance too. The audience relates to a revisiting of a familiar experiential possibility, bonding not just with the actor's transcending of identity through the role, but with his capacity to freshly embody the experiential structure, finding variety, intensity, and (rarely) inspiration in a lived process when its content is fully familiar. Such subliminal awareness is part of theatrical spectatorship, dormant, but, nevertheless, feeding an audience's engagement with the acting process. It does not play a role in cinematic spectatorship.

LISTENING TO ACTORS

Striking, memorable acting is often bound up with effects created by modifications of the actor's voice. Stanislavsky summons Salvini's testament on the point: "When Tommaso Salvini, the great Italian actor, was asked what one must have to be a tragedian, he replied: 'Voice, voice, and more voice!'"[1] Salvini is not alone in singling out the voice as a crucial tool for potent acting. Chaplin repeatedly declined offers to make his tramp talk. "This was unthinkable," he writes, "for the first words he ever uttered would transform him into another person."[2] John Barrymore's groundbreaking performances of Richard III and Hamlet in the 1920s—his transformation from a lightweight comedian into a great Shakespearean actor—involved a thoroughgoing metamorphosis of his vocal technique.[3] Simon Callow presents vocalization as no less than the key, authenticating, role-establishing component of a believable theatrical characterization:

> I had installed the play into my brain. Only one thing was missing: I had no idea how Molina should speak. I believed I knew him, as a man, his speed of thought, his camp vivacity, his neatness and would be daintiness; I saw, too, the emotional openness, the sexual need, the instinct for subservience, for service; and I had a most vivid sense of his dream life, filled with the myths he had drawn from his obsession with the screen, and especially with love goddesses. . . . I saw all this, and felt it in my bones and in my muscles. I could become Molina at a moment's notice. Except for one thing: how the hell did he talk? The voice is almost invariably the starting point for me: until I hear the right sound coming out of my mouth, everything sounds false, out of tune, and my body ceases to behave as it should. I feel awkward, blocked.[4]

Callow conceptualizes voice production as if it somehow emanates from an external entity, in his need to "hear the right sound coming out of [his] mouth." Producing an imprecise voice is rendered problematic in several distinct ways: Callow feels false, unexpressive, distorted, out of synchronization. The stress is less on the mechanics of vocalization—tonal range or smooth diction—but on a linkage between genuinely inhabiting a character's world and mastering its voice. Intriguingly, since there is no preexisting voice that the Molina character simply possesses and which the actor aims to discover, "hearing the right sound" seems to appeal to authenticity that is *not* predicated on correspondence; an unspecified criterion of adequacy underlies Callow's own assessment of his success.

Callow subsumes the import of voice to a vague distinction between authentic vs. inauthentic fictional embodiment. He is not alone. When RSC voice trainer Cicely Berry speculates why otherwise hardworking actors shun intense work on their voices, she writes:

> I think many young, interesting actors shy away from working on voice because of this restrictive attitude. Quite understandably they do not want something so personal interfered with and sounding well produced; they distrust it for the fear their individuality will be lost, and in any case it is not relevant to what they feel.[5]

Fearing the loss of authentic expression, actors avoid experimenting or refining such an intimate part of their being. Rather than capture their feelings, the trained voice threatens the performer with artificiality; a "well-produced" voice is not only removed from the realm of raw, unembellished life, but dooms everyone to sound like everyone else.

Why is the voice singled out, and what is its precise relationship to compelling acting? The response echoing from both Callow's and Berry's remarks is that, like eyes, voice is intimately associated with an access into another's "interiority." But interiority is a concept that needs to be unpacked: why and in what sense does the dramatic voice tap a highly intimate dimension of another mind?

States and Thoughts

The following remark by Stanislavsky hints at what may be misleading in the authentic/inauthentic schema:

> When an actor with a well-trained voice and masterly vocal technique speaks the words of his part I am quite carried away by his supreme art. If he is rhythmic I am involuntarily caught up in the rhythm and tone of his speech, I am stirred by it. If he himself pierces to the soul of the words in his part he takes me with him into the secret places of the playwright's composition as well as into those of his own soul. When an actor adds the vivid ornament of sound to that living content of the words, he causes me to glimpse with an inner vision the images he has fashioned out of his own creative imagination.[6]

Unlike Berry and Callow, Stanislavsky does not refer to realistic characterization or to non-artificial embodiment. He conceives of the voice as disclosing a relationship with words. The voice reveals "secrets" of composition; it betrays unvisited recesses of the actor's "own soul." The voice conjures for the auditors some imaginary scene. It also envelops them in the *rhythm* of words. Rhythm, that mysterious aspect of language that is unrelated to content—but has everything to do with a relationship to content—is here highlighted. Stanislavsky would probably not object to Berry's or Callow's claims regarding the contribution to verisimilitude made by the voice. But his remarks invite us to investigate friction or harmony with linguistic content that the actor's voice somehow captures and conveys. Judgments regarding authentic/inauthentic voice actually issue from an altogether different perception: the actor's capacity to penetrate the character's attitude to words or thought. It is *this* capacity that authenticity in acting amounts to.

The previous discussion of acting as existential amplification and self-animation brings out the abstract underpinnings of Stanislavsky's observation: if embodying a fiction means allowing one's body to take possession of the character's physical appearance, vocalizing a text means allowing one's voice to take possession of the character's *thoughts*. The actor's voice is, in this sense, essentially a complete second actor, *an actor within an actor*. This is why the voice is one of the most intimate and crucial encounters between actor and role. To miss this encounter by careless or merely competent acting discloses an incomplete inhabiting of the fictional world, a falling short of a fully realized existential amplification, thereby blocking the audience's attempt to bond with the actor's process.

It will be objected that embodiment expresses mental states as well. Nervously tapping one's knee, for instance, is not some mindless activation of the merely physical, but indicates agitation. How plausible can it then be to argue that language and voice are singularly linked with "thoughts"?

A distinction between states (what one undergoes, experiences, feels) and thoughts forms a response to this objection. On the one hand, body language typically conveys states (nervousness, anger, dissatisfaction, happiness), and is able to do so in a nuanced way. Spoken language, on the other hand, externalizes particular thoughts. Thoughts differ from other mental operations by being linguistic entities not merely conveyed through language, but themselves made up of words.[7] States, on the other hand, often include words, but not necessarily and not all the time. Happiness, for example, may include the verbalized awareness of the reasons underlying one's feeling. But it can also encompass substantial gaps, in which no thought is being consciously formulated, or in which only half-thoughts surface.

Unlike states, bodily gestures (such as shaking one's head to express "no" or extending one's hand for charity) can also externalize specific (linguistic) thoughts, without using the voice. But theatrically powerful gestures are, nevertheless, usually related to states—to that which is irreducible to language. Brando writes of the magical effect of Chaplin's tramp nervously nibbling a flower as he is recognized by the (previously blind) flower girl.[8] Simon Callow describes the effect of Charles Laughton's Quasimodo, covering his face when attempting to tell Esméralda of his love ("It is almost impossible to watch the scene").[9] Such gestures can be exceedingly touching precisely because they articulate a powerful conflict of states (hope and fear in Chaplin's case, hope and shame in Laughton's): the thrust and counter-thrust of two opposing states overwhelming a single mind. Such hopefulness is irreducible to a desire fully captured by a linguistic description. Sometimes the desire is itself incomplete or inconsistent (what is it that Quasimodo wants when hiding his face but, nevertheless, not leaving?). Sometimes the desire amounts to more (or less) than what gets formulated as a thought (is Chaplin's tramp thinking verbally while studying the expression of the previously blind girl as she recognizes who he is?). Such distance from articulation is different from the vagueness of ambiguous linguistic descriptions. It captures the strength of a moment as consisting of preformed thoughts, or of the manner whereby a character resists allowing desires to become articulate thoughts (fear of expected rejection is the force behind this resistance in Quasimodo or in Chaplin's tramp). An actor's voice, we shall later see, can sometimes capture analogous disjunctions between what is experienced and what can be said.

The distinction between communicating thoughts and expressing states does not correlate with a distinction between success or failure in achieving particularized acting. Actors have to express both states and thoughts in an accurate, personal, and vivid way. The distinction relates, rather, to the unique intervention made by language: when this intervention occurs, we are usually accessing a character's thoughts; when it does not, we are usually made aware of its state. Sometimes, we are mindful of both.

The Seven Operations of Voice

Seven possible dimensions mediate the meeting point between an actor and a character's thoughts through the voice. The first three relate to the content of the specific verbalized thought. The fourth, fifth, and sixth concern the relations between character and thinking at large. The seventh covers the potentially rugged transition from private to public. Common to all seven dimensions—which in reality overlap, operate independently, or interlock in various ways—is a unifying idea: since the audience attends an act of existential amplification, failures of voice betray an incomplete incarnation, one that remains ever so slightly outside the lived possibility which the performer undertakes to realize. The listening audience is obviously not explicitly aware of these as distinct components; the audience is, on the whole, either moved or left unresponsive. The point of offering this sevenfold distinction is that it may explain what underpins the experience of being "moved." I shall now describe these dimensions, specifying how they can determine effective, non-effective, or merely competent acting.

The three dimensions relating to content do not require detailed elaboration. The first carries the specific semantic meaning conveyed by the words. The second expresses an attitude with regard to this meaning (irony, hope, relief, and so forth). The third accesses the specific degree through which the attitude—say, anger—is experienced (whether or not the anger is mild or fierce, for example). All three layers jointly comprise the dimension of content as conveyed by the voice. When Lear says to Cordelia, "Nothing will come of nothing," his meaning (first layer) is clear enough: "Persist in saying nothing and nothing is what you will get." His attitude vis-à-vis the warning he issues (second layer) may differ: it can involve anger, or a lighthearted pretense that his warning is not (yet) serious; it can even be delivered as a plea. The Lear actor then needs to choose the precise degree—of bitterness/dissatisfaction/anger—in which this attitude manifests itself (third layer).

The next three dimensions (four through six) relate to the relationship to the verbalized content. The fourth dimension concerns the intensity with which the actor succeeds in infusing the first three dimensions (the ones concerned with content). While "intense" acting will be explained in the next part of the book, essentially such intensity consists of the variation and degree by which the actor inhabits enacted moments. Intensity concerns the shades discovered and the capacity to convey these to the audience. We often sense it through the actor's eyes, darting, searching, taking in aspects of the situation and the multilayered response to it, thereby disclosing nonverbal abrupt transitions of focus in the character. When exemplified in the actor's voice, intensity is not merely bound up with the sheer strength of the voice, but with a variety of minute transitions of inflection infused into a brief moment. Qualitative differences between actors arise from their mastery of this particular ability. A compelling Lear is able to inject intensity into his anger; seething under the surface of the line are different facets of it—disappointment, impotence, speechlessness, choking rage. By contrast, inferior Lears capture no variety in the anger. Their creative shortcoming is the disclosure of a lack of observation with regard to the structure of anger, an inability to convey its different nuances. The audience would likely remain unmoved, since the actor has not fully migrated into the character's world. Had the actor achieved such migration, the result could not amount to a monolithic emotion—some static lump of anger.

Amateurish acting often consists of failures related to this fourth dimension: while the amateur successfully conveys to the audience meaning, attitude, and degree, the lack of vocal intensity (single attitude, single degree) leaves the performer outside the role and the audience unresponsive. The audience knows what it is supposed to think and feel; but the incomplete transition of the amateur into the lived moment is betrayed by the simplification of an experience: undergoing or envisioning the embodied state in a careful creative attempt would have revealed a far more complex and unstable experience. The amateur *tells* the audience what the embodied character thinks and feels (a fault that professionals call "indicating"), but fails to fully plunge into the character's state.

The opposite case is when the content is largely irrelevant or, even, not comprehended at all. Responding to masterful acting in a language one does not understand exemplifies this. Here is Chaplin on Duse:

> When Duse came to Los Angeles, even her age and approaching end could not dim the brilliance of her genius. She was supported by an excellent Italian cast. One handsome young actor gave a superb performance before she came on, holding the center of the stage magnificently. How could Duse excel this young man's remarkable performance? I wondered. Then from extreme left upstage Duse unobtrusively entered through an archway. She paused behind a basket of white chrysanthemums that stood on a grand piano, and began quietly rearranging them. . . . When she had finished, she slowly walked diagonally downstage and sat in an armchair by the fireplace and looked into the fire . . . After his impassioned address, she spoke calmly as she looked into the fire. Her delivery had not the usual histrionics; her voice came from the embers of tragic passion. I did not understand a word, but I realized I was in the presence of the greatest actress I had ever seen.[10]

Chaplin's written orchestration of this moment of watching what he calls the greatest acting he had ever witnessed includes several elements—not just the vocal. But the realization is presented as crystallizing only upon hearing Duse's voice. Unable to comprehend the content, Chaplin responds to a character's relationship with language.

Intensity also involves the actor's infusion into the vocalized text the character's history: a past relationship to the spoken words. Elza Radzina as Goneril—in the division of the kingdom scene in Kozintsev's 1971 *Karol Lir*— and Adrian Lester in Rosalind's banishment speech in Cheek by Jowl's *As You Like It*, both capture a painful past in their respective utterances.[11] Radzina's Goneril makes yet another attempt to prove her commitment to an indifferent father. Lester's Rosalind suppresses agonizing rage at the injustice done to her father by the person questioning her. Voice stands out in these performances, because it does not merely reveal a present relationship to content, but also subtleties connected with past events that are implied but are not presented in the play. Voice carries over deep scars, the hold exerted by the past on the present. Capturing such inflections is part of vocal intensity.

The fifth dimension concerns the voice as embodied thought.[12] The kind of voice-training associated with Kristin Linklater emphasizes the self-empowering potency of vocal training. Taking on some other voice becomes a vehicle for self-realization; it constitutes a fuller release of one's possibilities.[13] The voice also instances and conveys inhibitions of self-realization. Freeing the voice may unblock these inhibitions as well:

> To free the voice is to free the person, and each person is indivisibly mind and body. Since the sound of the voice is generated by physical processes, the inner muscles of the body must be free to receive the sensitive impulses from the brain that create speech. The natural voice is most perceptibly blocked and distorted by physical tension, but it also suffers from emotional blocks, aural blocks, spiritual blocks. All such obstacles are psycho-physical in nature, and once they are removed the voice is able to communicate the full range of human emotion and all the nuances of thought. Its limits lie only in the possible limits of talent, imagination or life experience.[14]

One need not accept wholesale Linklater's catalogue of "inhibitions" and the vocabulary of "unblocking" to recognize the distinct facet of voice that her approach underscores: the actor's work on a role can extend to encompass the ways in which the character's body *takes on language*. The fifth dimension concerns the voice's capacity to register *inhibitions* hampering this process. "Finding the right voice" means that formative aspects of the character's sense of self have been accessed.

To prevent this from sounding overly abstract, we need not imagine an actor such as Callow, when searching for Molina's "right" voice, to be consciously thinking about Molina's inhibitions as these are disclosed by his voice; the process is more intuitive. The point is that in a successful "intuitive" choice of voice for a character, the "right" voice embodies language in a particular way, possessing and conveying a specific uneasy history with language. The actor's voice thereby forms a gateway into an entire dimension of depth in existential amplification, where one embodies not only the character's thoughts, intentions, and emotions, but encompasses the character's rough relationship with language. This, incidentally, brings out an important difference between actor-oriented voice training, and the voice training directed at singers. For singers, conveying inhibitions of vocalization never seems to be a desired objective—for actors, such inhibitions constitute the spine of a compelling performance.

An example is John Hurt's portrayal of John Merrick in *The Elephant Man* (1980), of whom Vincent Canby wrote the following:

> The key sequence in the movie is when Dr. Treves, played with humane, quirky compassion by Anthony Hopkins, brings Merrick home to tea with Mrs. Treves in a perfectly ordered Victorian drawing room.
>
> Merrick, looking like the fastidiously dressed Walrus in the Tenniel illustrations for "The Walrus and the Carpenter," is a most dainty guest. He speaks in the acquired accents of an English upper-class gentleman's gentleman, and has the same sort of manners. "They have such noble faces," he says of the Treves family photographs on the mantelpiece, and then shows his hosts a picture of his mother, a very pretty woman. "Yes," he acknowledges, "she had the face of an angel," adding so delicately that one can only suspect what depths of feeling are being ignored, "I must have been a great disappointment to her. I tried so hard to be good."[15]

Canby calls attention to a spoken sentence and a chosen accent. What he does not mention is the crucial dissonance between the polished accent and the rough and slightly distorted voice that Hurt lends his creation. Hurt's part becomes particularly moving by his adoption of a voice that has been infrequently used as a vehicle for articulating language. It is a voice for which language is an achievement, its use thus constituting an assertion against the dehumanization imposed upon its bearer. Each act of articulation by Merrick entails a poignant attempt to belong. The upper-class accent captures an overeagerness to be an equal partner in a society that regards him as a monstrous spectacle.

The sixth dimension relates to the manner whereby the voice may expose a character's relationship to thought and thinking. Gaps between selves and thought are of two kinds: the first is a resistance to articulate experience through words, a refusal of language as such; the second concerns varying degrees of estrangement from words (unaccompanied by the more radical withdrawal from language that characterizes the first kind). Paul Scofield's Lear exemplifies the first kind. Scofield's Lear (in Peter Brook's 1970 film) initially projects a lifeless, slow voice. It matters little what he plans to say: whether he discusses his plans for England, or (joylessly) calls upon his "joy," Cordelia, his voice remains hollow, uninterested, forced.[16] Scofield's zombie-like demeanor and lifeless voice masterfully communicate a wall separating character and thought—a state effectively established through a verbalization dissociated from the energy of articulation. Dramatists sometimes invite actors to convey such drops of energy. A character's experience might be so overwhelming that it fails to be translated into words as such—

for example, when Lear enters howling after Cordelia is dead. A character may be so lost that words refuse to come—for instance, when *Macbeth*'s Macduff, upon hearing of the massacre of his family, fails to respond to Malcolm.

The second kind of gap is unrelated to a *disinterest* in articulation as such, but to the unsmooth relations between personal experience and words, even if the desire to articulate is keenly felt. Philosophers typically present such ideas of comfort or distance from language either through architectural metaphors (language as "the house of being"), or via economic figurative clusters ("possessing" or "owning one's language"). Both image clusters capture the capacity of words to possess either a welcoming, intimate texture or a harsher, alien one. When language is a "house" inhabited by a subject, it acts as the inner-outer divide: a shelter, a mere instrumental building or, alternatively, a home. When, by contrast, language is there to be owned, it can be taken away; it needs to be claimed and reclaimed; and the degree of its possession can itself become the focus, disclosing how entrenched or nonattached subjects can be in relation to their words.

Again, this is not as abstract as it sounds. Memorable acting often consists of capturing this dimension, and dramatists can write in a way that invites the actor to search out and reveal uneasiness with language. Shakespeare's foreigners—Othello, Shylock, or, in a different sense, Caliban come to mind—have an alien quality built into their language, soliciting from the actor's delivery, if it is within his range, linguistic homelessness and/or unsure possession. An example of foreignness vis-à-vis language is Meryl Streep's much-acclaimed performance in *Sophie's Choice*.[17] Streep adopted a Polish accent which succeeded in realistically capturing the voice of a refugee, but also in inflecting her character with a nomadic quality that permeates her story. Her voice thereby acquires the shades of the psychic ramifications spiraling out of her tragic choice. Language is, among other functions, a vehicle of socialization. Distance from words can thus reflect an aspect of trauma, a resistance to socialization once society can no longer be trusted. The gap captured by Scofield is the resistance to forming thoughts as such; in Streep, the wish to speak is there, but a friction that will not be smoothed away surfaces whenever an articulation of experience is attempted. Unlike Macduff's momentary loss of words, Streep's character inhabits a space in which words are slightly out of reach, a placing induced by a momentous self-shaping past event. The difference between this hiatus from language and the one conveyed by Hurt's "elephant man," is that the latter's does not reveal a distance from articulated thoughts as such, but *lack of practice* in using them;—Merrick's tragedy, in one sense, *is* this gap. Streep's voice, by contrast, reveals a distance not from expression, but from that which may be *thought* by a mother forced to choose which of her children will die.

Finally, the seventh dimension concerns the relations between selves and their *public* appearance through talk. This aspect is unrelated to distance from words, but to making one's inner state known to others. Outside the theater, fast-talkers and stutterers provide two polar instances of malfunctions in relation to such transitions from private to public. The fast talker may provoke envy, because the appearance of the self in language seems unhindered: words materialize on command; no gaps arise between intention and action. But it is precisely this overconfident smoothness that may also trigger resistance and suspicion from the fast-talker's hearer, due to a sensed failure to experience the pauses that selecting one's words necessitates. The stutterer inhabits the opposite extreme: the self-consciousness of public speech (which is frequently attributed as a cause of stuttering) leads to a highlighting of the shift from intended to public articulation. Stutterers and those listening to them are forced to inhabit the twilight zone that lies between planned and actual appearance in language.[18]

Exceedingly smooth plunging into language as opposed to a lingering in the state of transition into it—such are the extremes. Outside the theater, we look for a manifestation of identity in language. Yet a meaningful appearance also involves a level of resistance in relation to this process. No resistance (the fast- talker) conveys an appearance of *language* rather than an identity in language. Excessive resistance (stuttering) implies, by contrast, a desire to altogether *avoid* an appearance as such, a disinclination to turn the private public. While most roles actors are called upon to embody fall between these extremes, voice remains a primary bridge between the character's inner life and its public identity. Thoughtful acting inquires how easy such a transition is for the character at *that* particular moment. Actors who embody fast- talkers or stutterers can create moving effects when the set pattern is broken: a stutterer who suddenly becomes fluent (I have in mind Colin Firth's "I have a voice" in the 2010 film *The King's Speech*); a fast- talker who is compelled to pause (here, I am thinking of a stage performance I watched of Nicholas Lindhurst in *The Dresser*, or of Nick Nolte's pauses before he speaks about being raped in the 1991 film *Prince of Tides*, and Nolte's inane attempt to return to lighthearted joking immediately after this disclosure).[19]

Such examples bring out an ideological implication of this analysis as well. Brechtian alienation-effects invite actors to mobilize political resistance by withdrawing from the fictional space. But we can now perceive how actors may establish effective ideological interventions *internally* to the embodied act. They may achieve this by inserting various gaps between what characters say and how assured their inhabiting of their voice actually is. A failure to conjure up the right words, a failure to utter them, discomfort when they are used, a sleekness that intimates some deep evasion—breakdowns of such kind communicate homelessness in language, or a resistance to be exposed, or being overwhelmed and momentarily out of touch with discursive expression. Through capturing distinct failures of voice, a thoroughgoing act of existential amplification conveys distance between characters and their social settings. Showing uneasy relationships with the voice they are meant to possess according to the gendered or class-based configurations in which they happen to be embedded, constitutes one of the more powerful tools available to actors for introducing and registering resistance to a norm.

PART II

STAGING FICTIONS

This part of the book investigates diverse ways in which fictions are animated. Two chapters explore the relationship between literary and theatrical fictions. The first chapter traces differences and points of overlap between embodying a fictional character, and the writing of one as author or the identification with one as reader. All three have all been perceived as "life-amplifying" at one time or another. Setting them apart without missing the subtle links between them enables understanding what distinguishes the actor's work with a literary text.

The second chapter identifies the networks that link the *act* of acting to literature specifically written for the stage. Drama is not merely enacted literature, nor is it simply a subcategory of literature, as has been traditionally assumed by literary theory. Drama is, rather, a unique form of composition in which projected animation by actors implicitly informs creative literary choices, themes, and motifs. Both chapters reject the older hierarchical model which used to dominate these discussions, in which theater was simplistically subordinated to literature. But these chapters also avoid subscribing to newer views that advocate thoroughgoing dissociation between theater and literature when theater's autonomy is being defended. Instead, a position stressing aesthetic synergy between literary value and theatrical potency will be developed.

The third chapter discusses animation as such. It performs this by examining puppetry, a mode of animating fictions in which an object—rather than an embodied linguistic entity—is the medium. Puppetry thereby provides an oblique entry point into an aspect of the actor's act—the performance of animation—without it being entangled by other features of embodied animation. Apart from manifesting pure animation, puppetry is also a unique medium which enables performers to externalize identity-role relations. The puppeteer-puppet dyad structurally duplicates the process that is inherent in all acting: the manner whereby something that is not alive becomes animated through the joint imaginative work of performer and audience.

I will suggest that puppetry playfully destabilizes the subject-object divide that underlies "animation" as such. It unearths a broader form of personal experience than the more limited self-as-possibilities model so far advanced in this book. The actor's self-animation will thereby be extended to encompass not only the relationship between self and the possibility it happens to inhabit, but also episodes of "un-selfing," or "re-selfing." In these, the subject emerges from an insuppressible object. "Animation" will emerge as a constitutive, repeatedly performed aspect of nonacted life, one that puppetry is able to hyperbolically mirror to its audience, but that acting, too, constantly presents in a subdued form.

STAGING WORDS

Any comprehensive philosophy of theater and acting is rooted in a conceptually prior understanding of the relationship between theater and literature. Two extreme versions regarding such relations are currently on offer. The first is Aristotelian: theater exists in order to enact literature. The second holds theatrical performances to be autonomous (aesthetically, ontologically, conceptually) from literature. Neither of these theories should be accepted.

To relate to theater as an instantiation of literature overlooks several vital features of theatrical performances. Firstly, some theatrical performances do not rely upon prewritten scripts. Secondly, responsible for some of the most memorable theatrical moments is a *deviation* from the script (and seasoned viewers will be aware of this). Judy Dench provides the following example:

> Donald Sinden was quite brilliant as Malvolio and he invented a wonderful moment on one entrance. He was just about to speak his first line when he looked at the sundial, looked up at the sun, then he took out his watch, looked at his watch, looked back at the sundial, put his watch back, and then moved the sundial round. It used to bring the house down.[1]

Thirdly, some of the most absorbing theatrical moments involve bodily expression—not verbal delivery. To some of these, there is no analogy in the written script. Much face and body work in comedy has nothing to do with the script or its merits; the performance of an identical sequence by a lesser comedian can become bland and merely funny (consider silent comic figures—Chaplin's tramp, Atkinston's Mr. Bean—acted by weaker talents). Fourthly, there is no correlation between the literary value of the enacted work and the artistic merits of the performance: a superbly written text can be disastrously enacted by excellent performers; hackneyed plots can be masterfully performed. Excellent actors have even felt that high-quality texts draw from them mediocre performances.[2] Even within the same work, a role that is inferior to another from a literary viewpoint can be more powerful to watch as realized drama. Granted, at times a striking experience in the theater is the outcome of the *combined* effect of a well-written play being masterfully performed. Yet the capacity to attain an outstanding achievement when a play of high literary quality is staged by gifted performers does not mean that a performance is not an autonomous work of art. Nor should such achievement suggest that theater exists merely to enable a palpable accessing into what is, primarily, a literary work.

Fifthly, some of the most potent writing for theater is specifically designed with actors in mind, relying on their capacity to infuse a rich subtext to paper-thin dialogue (Pinter's work often exemplifies such writing). Not surprisingly, such texts may lack those literary qualities expected in works that are specifically designed to be read. "When a poet, thinker, or philosopher writes a dramatic work, he knows what he is doing," claims Ermete Zacconi, "if he wanted to write literature he would have written a good book instead of a good play."[3] To regard theater merely as enacted literature is thus to err, not only by ignoring the various arts that make up a performance, but also by distorting the manner in which the written play itself needs to be approached as a distinct kind of literature. Rather than being conceived as a participator and catalyst for performance, the play gets distorted into an independent entity. Even the plays that can be read as literature (dramatized poetry of Shakespeare's kind serving as the prime example) contain many episodes that altogether lack literary merit, and that effectively work only when imagined as realized drama.

Theater is not reified literature. Yet the other extreme—altogether disengaging theater from literature—is farfetched as well.[4] To hold that theater is autonomous from literature is to both overstate and understate the relations between the two. By "overstating," I mean that the term *autonomy* suggests an overly neat dissociation of theater from literature. It risks missing the role of theatrical performances—at least those based on plays—as potentially insightful *interpretations* of these plays. To interpret a play—whether as a troupe of actors or as a literary critic—is to reach a set of decisions regarding the work's meaning: its sections, sentences, and words. Interpretation also sometimes implies a stance regarding the relevance of the play for a contemporary audience. In both these senses, a theatrical performance constitutes an interpretation: a claim as to the meaning and significance of a work.[5] To conceive of theater as categorically autonomous from literature erects an artificial divide, concealing from view the overlapping endeavor shared by performers and literary critics.

By "understating," I mean that to merely defend an "autonomy" of theater (in the sense of its being nonparasitic on literature) is to miss a possibly far more radical and interesting position: literature written for the stage might be parasitic on theatrical interests rather than the other way round. From this perspective, traditional drama theory has erred by looking at the situation the wrong side up. Rather than engage with tragedy and comedy from a plot-related lens, emphasizing, say, the fall of a formidable character due to some character flaw or a plot device aimed at generating a particular emotion in its beholder (pity or fear in tragedy, a sense of superiority in comedy), we should begin by addressing genres as deriving from *the way successful (repeated) plot combinations tap the audience's interest in the act of acting*. A substantiation of this idea will be undertaken in the next chapter.

The relationship between literature and theater is multidimensional, and will not be captured by neat models of subordination or dissociation. Two such dimensions will now be discussed. The first is a proposed stipulation of the relationship between plays and theatrical performances. The second concerns the actor's *work* on a character as distinct from an author's *creation* of one or a reader's imaginative *engagement* with a protagonist.

Play, Interpretation, Performance

A relationship between a performance and a written play (if the performance is of a play) can be presented in several ways. I favor the following tripartite distinction between the "play," its "interpretation." and the "performance" of the interpretation. The *play* is the equivalent of the notation in music or the choreography in dance—the (usually written) masterplan for that which will be performed. Apart from rare improvisational forms, virtually all theatrical performances are based on plays.[6] The *interpretation* is the specific "take" to which the director and actors subject the work; their attempt to enact a particular view regarding the meaning of the play. Decisions to modernize the play, or to situate it in a surprising location, to experiment with its original gendering of the cast, or with its politics (for instance, to have a white Othello amidst a black cast), to inventively recontextualize the play in a manner that would infuse it with fresh potency (for example, having Macbeth acted by a convicted murderer), selecting a specific blocking—such are the constituents of the interpretation: the set of creative decisions making up the ensemble's collective response to the play. The interpretation is not merely a detailed execution plan, but implies a claim as to the significance of the play. Such a claim can relate to the play alone. But in the case of canonic works that are frequently produced, such a claim may encompass a creative response to the production history of the play. An ensemble, thereby, may combine a claim regarding the potential meaning of the play with a claim regarding that potential being missed by past interpretations. Finally, we have the *performance*—the particular enactment of the interpretation at a given time. As we saw, different enactments of the same interpretation may significantly differ in artistic quality, ranging from the mechanical to the inspired.

This distinction lends itself to a three-part breakdown of the constituents of aesthetic response in the theater (as well as in some other performing arts): a brilliant play can be interpreted in a predictable way and yet be exquisitely performed; an inferior play may be wittily interpreted and deftly performed; groundbreaking texts and interpretations can be amateurishly performed, and so on. As audience, we look for and are affected by the *combined* effect of all three elements: the quality of the play, the thoughtfulness of the interpretation, and the skill and vitality of the performance—categories that themselves result from numerous features that, when articulated, underlie theatrical criticism.[7]

The misconception underlying some discussions of "ideal performance" is that performances are implicitly regarded solely as *realizations* of the values inhering in the scripted work (an ideal performance being one in which all such values are ostensibly realized). Sometimes this paradigm surfaces explicitly, when the relationship between a play and its performance is likened to a "recipe" and its instantiation by the performance.[8] But, in a less hierarchic modeling of the performing arts, performers are co-partners in an aesthetic offering. They thus present a *dialogue* with the aesthetic values of the work—*not* a realization of it. Such values are patiently teased out and respected. Then, a response carrying its own values is generated from the director and performers. Such creative rapport requires an attentive engagement with the focal point of the work (rather than a superficial impression that serves as basis for a quick response). It may include growth and a re-creation of the performer's own ways of reading and thinking. The audience looks for indications of this kind of dialogue.

"Realizations" can be ideal, since they can be complete: one realizes all that was supposedly contained in the script. Dialogues, by contrast, are never ideal. They can be merely rich, surprising, amazingly deep, patient, insightful, daring, multi-dimensional, challenging, and so on. To think of performances as dialogues is preferable to the paradigm of realization, because all that is contained in the alternative value-realization model is present in the dialogical model as well: the performer is urged to unearth the values of the script in a careful and sensitive manner. But the important addition made by the dialogical model is the different implication regarding the performer's art and its status. To think of one's performance as a dialogue with the work urges performers to bring into their interaction with the work shades constituting their singular response. To put this differently, an ideal performance—in the sense of realizing all the values of a script—can be conceptually possible (ignoring the problem of determining how *all* such values have been noted). It may, nevertheless, be aesthetically inferior relative to a nonideal performance that includes imported elements that are at least as interesting as those infused into the work by its creator. To always have in mind written masterpieces that a performer can only struggle to capture well, misses the opposite possibility: performers whose enactment is far more creative and artistically interesting than the work they happen to enact.

The manner whereby the three constituents in this distinction are linked to each other through genitives—a play, *its* interpretation, and the performance *of* the interpretation—is important. Genitives bring out interconnections between theater and literature that are masked by alternative typologies. Within Anglo-American aesthetics, proposing such typologies is motivated by three ontological questions: the status of the performance as an independent work of art; the conditions that turn a performance into an enactment of a specific work; and whether or not one can stipulate conditions for the ideal performance of a work. The problem with thinking of the play-interpretation-performance distinction primarily through the need to answer such puzzles is that they conceal other issues relating to aesthetic pull, evaluation, and interconnection. To regard individual enactments as "tokens" of a "type"—the performance—which is itself a token of a broader type—the play—(a view adopted by several aestheticians), or to set apart the play as a "thing" by contrast to performance as "event" (Paul Thom's view), tells us very little about aesthetic evaluation or about the creative process invested into such performances.[9] Such typologies can also mislead us into enfranchising performance from plays, since they turn performances into distinct works of art. By contrast, the above tripartite distinction between a play, its interpretation, and the performance of an interpretation does not aim to address the ontological questions, and can harmonize with various ontological accounts. Concomitantly, employing it advantageously preserves and accounts for the strong case that can (and should) be made on behalf of performances as standing in a unique dialogic relationship to plays.

One implication regarding the second of these ontological questions does arise from adopting this proposed typology. It relates to the conditions that determine a theatrical production as a performance of a particular play. The performer's intention to enact a particular play is virtually always a sufficient and necessary condition for determining that the performance is *of that* particular play.[10] The endorsement of an aesthetically-oriented rather than an ontologically-oriented vocabulary enables to see that, as interpretation, the performance can be superficial, idiosyncratic, or silly. It, nevertheless, remains an interpretation of a specific play. Sometimes an outraged academic dismisses a modernization of a canonic play as unrelated to the original, and as simply hiding behind a respectable façade when it actually enacts a different play. But the dialogic model helps explain why the complaint is actually different: instead of attending a patient creative dialogue attuned to the merits of the play, one witnesses a superficial exchange; neither work nor performance inform each other. To hold that such failures undercut the production's presumption to offer an interpretation *of* the play is to misdescribe the specific aesthetic flaw. When the sense and meaning of an important work are ignored by a performer, one does not watch a different play (which, on its own, would not necessarily be considered an aesthetic disaster), nor would one complain of having been deceived. The complaint is far more serious: it is that the performance exemplifies a failure in understanding the *dialogical* nature of performance. In engaging a rich work yet hearing nothing but herself, the performer misunderstands a core feature of her art.

Existential Amplification: Acting, Reading, Writing

Writing literature or reading it attentively, are also sometimes conceived as expanding one's life. Milan Kundera writes:

> The characters in my novels are my own unrealized possibilities. That is why I am equally fond of them all and equally horrified by them. Each one has crossed a border that I myself have circumvented. It is that crossed border (the border beyond which my own "I" ends) which attracts me most. For beyond that border begins the secret the novel asks about.[11]

Kundera describes a process of imaginative exploration that issues from the writer's non-actualized possibilities through the creation of literary characters. A parallel argument has been made in relation to readers of literature, who are also said to "live more" through empathic involvement in relation to unfamiliar contexts. We read Ishiguru's *Never Let Me Go* and visit a new experience of systematic exploitation; Banville's *The Sea* invites us to partake in the hidden undercurrents of grief; Egolf's *Lord of the Barnyard* will probably extend our experience of revenge. "Expanding" and "extending" mean that literary fictions familiarize worlds that are only dimly and fragmentarily perceived in life. Literary works thereby become gateways to other lives. In particular, and in contrast to many other arts, literary fictions render intimate the first-person perspective of another, encouraging intimate involvement rather than detached eavesdropping.

Before turning to the different ways in which writing and reading facilitate existential amplification, it is important to first determine their points of overlap in relation to this process. To begin with, like reading a literary work, watching fictional events on stage presents the audience with unfamiliar lives, states, and conflicts. These turn from abstract possibilities into vivid, detailed, and personalized instantiations. We might, for example, suppose that we know what jealousy means. Yet engaging with a character such as Othello or Leontes either on page or on stage takes us into the internal rhythm of such a mind: the rationalizations, jarring suspicions, the thrust and counter-thrust of hope gnawed away by image-driven doubt. Actors are less important when considering this particular life extension. The reason is that while, unlike the audience, actors fictionally live through the situation portrayed, the audience—as far as this particular function is concerned—basically sees *through* them into the play and the world it discloses.

A second point of overlap relates to the *manner* whereby an aesthetic representation shapes a fictional possibility when contrasted to actually lived experience. Expansion through immersion in a fiction—whether such immersion takes the form of writing one up, reading it attentively or embodying it on stage—does not amount to merely adding more of the same lived experience that one possesses in life—the kind one accesses through reading nonaesthetic reports documenting actual lives. As Richard Shusterman claims, to "dramatize," both in English and in German, means "to treat something as, or make it seem, more exciting or important."[12] Dramatization is intensification. Acting a well-constructed fiction permits the actor to release, explore, and experience intense possibilities with which an audience can then engage. It is not merely the movement into a different biography—a queen's, a beggar's, a drunkard's, an adulterer's, a murderer's, a miser's, a god's, a saint's, an animal's, a courtesan's, and so forth—but into specific configurations of such states, when they have been well-written. This part of theatrical experience is (again) attuned to the *literary* dimension of theater. It is accessed by a reader without recourse to theater. In the theater, this dimension of theatrical pleasure arises from the audience looking through the actors and taking in the meanings of the words.

To avoid vagueness, let me provide examples of such intensity. In dismissing a Rome that cannot accept his heroism and banishes him, an enraged Coriolanus bursts out: "You common cry of curs, whose breath I hate as reek o' th' rotten fens, whose loves I prize as the dead carcasses of unburied men that do corrupt the air, I banish you" (III.iii.127-31).[13] A soon-to-be dethroned Richard II tells his company:

> Throw away respect, tradition, form and ceremonious duty, for you have but mistook me all this while: I live with bread like you, feel want, taste grief, need friends: subjected thus, how can you say to me I am a king? (III. ii. 172-77).

A torn-to-shreds Lear beseeches his dead daughter: "Cordelia, Cordelia, stay a little" (V.iii. 245). In such moments the actor is not merely regurgitating a mental state or hypothetically placing himself in the staged situation, but is, rather, allowing the words to elevate him into an emotional intensity that life usually falls short of. The same holds for the involved reader of the text, who accesses not some simple description of an inner state, but a distillation of its essence. "Essence" does not here imply linguistically formulated necessary or sufficient conditions that hold in all states of outrage, depression, or grief—culturally independent concepts that ahistorically hover above human life. "Essence" means, rather, the surfacing of a stable encapsulation of an evasive meaning, one that lies at the heart of many overlapping appearances of these states (often in distinct cultures and times).

Essences are proposed crystallizations of the meanings of states. They can inform when reapplied. They illuminate a nonobvious feature that appears in many manifestations of grief or disappointment. Poetry, literature, and the visual arts offer many such encapsulations—which is partly why we find them insightful, and why we utilize the vocabulary of epistemological growth to assess their merit.[14]

"Intensity" is not tantamount to strength: non-fictional experiences are stronger than fictional ones. By "strength" I mean that when events such as those featuring in the examples above take place non-fictionally, they are more personally significant, bear life-changing practical ramifications, entail central interpersonal consequences, and carry an altogether different emotional impact than fictional situations. Intensity means that the literary articulation of such experiences enables that which typically remains vague or overwhelming when personally undergone to be illuminated through two interlocking operations. Firstly, rather than merely name or categorize, intense linguistic articulations render intelligible and accurately convey the underlying complex makeup of a state that, when directly experienced, may appear deceptively monolithic. Secondly, the language provided by gifted authors may succeed in capturing the essence of the expressed moment in the manner just described: literature—in the examples above—is not merely modeling itself after reality, but offers a distilled articulation of a life-defining experience. A well-written fiction is intense in this sense, and—either as an engaged reader or as spectator—one responds to such intensity.[15]

Fictional texts of high quality enable actors to experience what they undergo in a particularly potent configuration. The predetermined nature of the states portrayed and the carefully moderated build-up established by the play's language enable the actor to access, vocalize, and embody such intensity. It is precisely this ability of a well-written text to shape and intensify experience—not merely to restrict the actor's fancy—that explains why actors are drawn to an art-form that solicits *cooperation* with a dramatic text, rather than to free-form improvisation. They do not merely wish to participate in an elaborate game of make-believe, but to embody intense possibilities, carefully crafted by another artist—the playwright. Spectators, in turn, are able to behold and respond to these dimensions of existential amplification—dimensions that are perceived by looking through the actors at the fictional events and by absorbing the words by which the import of these events is being communicated.

This is why the refusal to perceive performance as a mere ancillary vehicle for a literary play should not be confused with the cruder idea that performance, because it is artistically autonomous, is independent of the need and expectation for faithful communication of (and with) the play's literary values. It is precisely these literary values that facilitate unique, qualitatively intense forms of existential amplification for readers, audience, and actors by making it important to relate to a specific character's world because of what *this* character has accessed.

But what does such "relating" mean? It is here that, after acknowledging their points of overlap, we can articulate more carefully the difference between the manner in which an actor animates a fiction, and the imaginative life rendered to a literary fiction by its reader or author.

Acting versus Reading (I): Identification

Although reading and acting both partake of hypothetically "placing oneself in another's shoes," spectatorship (or readership) differs categorically from theatrical embodiment. The difference is both qualitative—in terms of the level of commitment and compenetration with the character—and quantitative—in terms of the degree of detail sought, the sheer time spent by the actor-as-character, and the attempt to interrelate body, language and inner state (rather than merely imaginatively try to fathom another's interiority). Such differences should not be taken to imply an evaluation, an identification of acting with a superior form of reading. Acting is certainly a highly committed form of reading. But the transition from reading to acting also carries interpretative costs: some distinct merits of reading may be lost by the transition into acting.[16]

In specifying such differences, consider first the different role played by identification in relation to theatrical embodiment, as opposed to its looser connection with involved reading. Literary critics spend weeks, months, even years, furthering their understanding of a character. But such understanding is not the same as "identifying," and the latter is not necessary for the purpose of effectively interpreting a literary work or for deeply responding to it. Much literary criticism does not rely on or mention identification. Many find it a somewhat rudimentary and unschooled response to literary characters. Even when identification takes place in more demanding literature, it is not ubiquitous: some complex characters lend themselves to identification—others do not.

The ability to avoid incorporating identification into literary theory is fortunate, since "identification" (or, for that matter, "empathy") is, at best, a theoretically dubious concept that critics eschew for many good reasons. Here are some of its problems: identification misleadingly suggests identical emotions between empathizers and their object. It risks collapsing the distinction between understanding characters and justifying their choices. The term is indiscriminately used in relation to real people in multiple contexts (friends, patients) as well as to fictional characters in plays and novels. Accordingly, the danger of using the term in aesthetics is of blurring the distinction between distinct attitudes—ones that we allow ourselves as part of response to art—with altogether different empathic operations that we depend upon in non-fictional contexts. Finally, there is a difference between the distinct shape assumed by identification in a variety of states (sadness, happiness, fear, hope, depression, love, joy); conceptually and emotionally, diverse processes and capacities appear to be involved when identifying with each of these, contributing to altogether different mental states within the identifying individual.[17]

And yet, while it may be a dispensable attitude when theorizing literature, identification cannot be avoided when reflecting on acting. Theatrical incarnation is the most powerful form of identification imaginable. It is a meticulously planned act of identification, in which the actor undertakes to imagine and assume an alien existence, and to convincingly project it. The actor cannot afford to endorse some merely sympathetic attitude towards a character: to act is to create and inhabit another person's physicality, dress, body language, belief system, emotional sensitivities, and so forth. Unlike cinematic acting, theatrical acting involves undergoing this comprehensively and repeatedly, sometimes through years of performing the role. Actors can and often will maintain a critical distance from their roles (identification—in art, literature or life—should not be confused with acceptance).[18] Sometimes, as in Brecht's theatre, actors project this distance. But to act is to identify. An actress may achieve this by attempting to approximate another's state (identification as importing another's state into her own identity—for instance, feeling another's pain). She may attempt this by perceiving the character's circumstances as a state that could befall her (identification in the sense of feeling *for* another's pain). She may also try to patiently grasp what her character's state involves (identification in the sense of identifying what another's state is genuinely about—fully taking in another's pain). Yet since all of these forms of identification can be part of engaged reading of literature, a pinpointing of the distinctive features of *embodied* identification is still needed.

Acting versus Reading/Writing (II): Embodied versus Literary Particularization

Whichever form of identification it takes, what distinguishes the actor's identification is that it is *embodied*. Here is Stanislavsky's unfolding of what such embodiment demands:

> Every invention of the actor's imagination must be thoroughly worked out and solidly built on a basis of facts. It must be able to answer all the questions (when, where, why, how) that he asks himself when he is driving his inventive faculties on to make a more and more definite picture of a make-believe existence. . . . To imagine 'in general,' without a well-defined and thoroughly founded theme is a sterile occupation.
>
> On the other hand, a conscious, reasoned approach to the imagination often produces a bloodless, counterfeit presentment of life. That will not do for the theatre. Our art demands that an actor's whole nature be actively involved, that he give himself up, both mind and body, to his part. He must feel the challenge to action physically as well as intellectually because the imagination, which has no substance or body, can reflexively affect our physical nature and make it act.[19]

What, then, sets apart the embodied imaginative partaking in a fiction that Stanislavsky describes from a mere imaginative engagement with a literary character? Consider Dorothea's disenchantment with her bloodless marriage to Casaubon in George Eliot's *Middlemarch*. When we empathize or imagine Dorothea during the reading, we access a range of highly particular feelings that are brought out by what she thinks and what she does not allow herself to think, by what she does, or by her attempts to come to terms with her dissatisfaction. All this is not obvious. It requires a patient and highly sensitive literary analysis to expose the multiple and complex insights that Eliot infuses into this state. But at no stage is the reader compelled to imagine what shoes Dorothea wears, or how she brushes her hair, or how she conducts herself physically in the presence of her husband, or how her body language alters when Ladislaw enters the room.

Eliot, and not only her readers, may refrain from imagining such matters, too. The author's imagination does entail following a character through in a highly particular way. J. M. Coetzee's Elizabeth Costello (a fictional author) is described by her son as follows:

> My mother has been a man. . . . She has also been a dog. She can think her way into other people, into other existences. I have read her; I know. It is within her powers. Isn't that what is most important about fiction: that it takes us out of ourselves, into other lives?[20]

The author is committed to particularize an imaginative possibility, to patiently pursue it. In discussing Kafka's role in relation to a fictional character (the ape in "An Account for an Academy"), Elizabeth Costello (the same fictional author mentioned in the citation above) says:

> Kafka had time to wonder where and how his poor educated ape was going to find a mate. And what it was going to be like when he was left in the dark with the bewildered, half-tamed female that his keepers eventually produced for his use. . . . That ape is followed through to the end, to the bitter, unsayable end, whether or not there are traces left on the page. Kafka stays awake during the gaps when we are sleeping. (ibid., p. 32)

Authorial imagination is here powerfully contrasted to reading: the author is pictured as an involved guardian of his fictional creations, even at points ignored or "slept through" by readers. We can, nevertheless, still note how—unlike Stanislavsky's guidelines to his actors—the authorial imagination, even here, at its most conscious commitment to particularize and follow a character through, is free from the need to provide a consistent physical rendering of what the author has only partly imagined: Kafka probably did not envision the precise cage size in which the ape is cooped up, or the ape's specific accent when uttering particular words in his speech to the academy.

Authors may watch their characters while readers are asleep. But authors watch characters as mental constructs. They exercise a form of particularization that is at once specific and open-ended, refined but not fully defined. By contrast, theatrical embodiment requires that the actor master the various insights that can be culled from the text, just as a careful literary critic would proceed. But from that point on, an entirely new dimension of particularization (and existential amplification) opens up: a simple act—

sipping tea—differs when Dorothea performs it with Casaubon at different stages of the story. When Eliot's novel is transformed into an enacted work, the actress becomes accountable for such changes—weighty on stage, imperceptible on the page. Creatively, the actress becomes accountable for every aspect of Dorothea's worldly manifestation: clothing, movement, gesture, body language, voice, the *hows* and *whys* of each moment of her fictional existence, as well as the fine details involved in projecting the transitions between such moments.

Another sense in which the actor's particularization differs from the specificity of the literary imagination is rooted in the necessity to select and actualize a single possibility out of the numerous ones implied in the text. "And if you poison us, do we not die?" asks Shylock of his Christian antagonists. This question can be abstract and rhetorical, just like the ones preceding it. "Poison" could, however, alternatively refer to the elopement of Jessica (her "spiritual poisoning" by Lorenzo's suit, convincing her to escape her Judaism). The sentence can even be elocuted—as actor Warren Mitchell did—as a joke.[21] The line on the page will merely suggest these interpretative options, whereas an actor will commit to and particularize one of these, turning it into Shylock's specific meaning by, for example, looking at a portrait of Jessica as he asks the question. A line such as "[l]et him look to his bond" (in the same speech) can be uttered as a warning relating to Antonio. But it can also be played—as Olivier did—as expressing the dawning realization that Shylock can now genuinely pursue Antonio's flesh (which, in turn, implies that the original contract was, as Shylock insisted, in face of their disbelief, a genuine act of trust and friendship rather than some premeditated diabolical plan on his part).[22]

Immersion in literary fictions involves a loose form of specificity. Its power is acquired from the freedom of *not* particularizing certain textual possibilities. By opposition, the actor's form of embodiment is concrete: it is necessarily circumscribed to particular selections of tone, movement, and positioning. Specificity brings to the audience's experience a sharpness and vivacity that is missing if the play is merely read.[23] Concomitantly, specificity also detracts from the play's open-endedness as a literary text. Such delimitation—the inevitable abandoning of some exciting interpretive options that cannot be held together in a single coherent performance—explains why, for spectators who are deeply familiar with a literary work, even strong performances can be somewhat dissatisfying. We have already delineated the grain of truth in the belief that acting is sometimes unnecessary, since some aesthetic merits can be readily apprehended from the page. The mistake of such views did not consist in their identification of some performed merits as literary ones, but in needlessly restricting attention to a limited pool of aesthetic values at the expense of many others that are brought out in a performance. Sometimes such claims lead to a stronger position, according to which a theatrical performance is not just redundant, but may positively *detract* from the aesthetic values of a play, even if it is performed well. This view was asserted by Charles Lamb in relation to some Shakespearean plays. "Shakespeare's *Lear*," Lamb claimed in 1811, "cannot be acted."[24] We are now able to perceive the strand of truth in this stronger position as well: the point this time concerns not so much the redundancy of acting in relation to the literary value of the text, but the *limitation* that a performed interpretation necessitates relative to the hermeneutic openness of the written work. Lamb can imagine several inconsistent Lears. He may wish to hold on to this plurality, feeling that any selection among them diminishes the play's richness. A performance compels him to momentarily accept the necessarily limiting choices of a production.

Acting versus Reading/Writing (III): The Role of the Fictional Past

How many children did Lady Macbeth have? In literary circles, L.C. Knights' famous question has come to exemplify critical confusion. Readers do not have to know whether or not Lady Macbeth had children. If they preoccupy themselves with such matters, they conflate a response to a real biography with the distinct act of literary appreciation. Yet, for the actress playing Lady Macbeth, such a question matters, and deeply so. The answer determines how she will deliver:

> I have given suck, and know how tender 'tis to love the babe that milks me: I would, while it was smiling in my face, have plucked my nipple from his boneless gums, and dashed the brains out, had I so sworn as you have done to this. (I.vii.54-9)

The actress will probably make a decision respecting whether or not her fictional character had any children, whether they are alive or dead, conceiving even the manner of their death. She might prepare herself through detailed pre-play improvisations in which loving transactions between her and them are played out (directors sometimes initiate such improvisations in order to establish a believable pre-play to which a character refers as her past). Her goal would be to reconstruct and create a believable biography, one which is not merely intellectually deduced by her audience, but experienced by them in a moving and rich way.

References to the past modify, particularize, or create new dimensions of meaning for the work. When Othello tells the Venetian duke and council how the narration of his life story won Desdemona's heart, he goes into details:

> Wherein I spake of the most disastrous chances . . . and of the Cannibals that each other eat . . . and men whose heads do grow beneath their shoulders. This to hear would Desdemona seriously incline. (I.iii.134-46)

Some Othellos deliver these lines solemnly, introducing something of the wild imaginary world simmering beneath Othello's calmness. Other Othellos convey them jokingly, stressing the "seriously" above; Othello is thus able to defuse the explosive potential of his questioning by inviting the male Venetian council to enjoy the tricks with which an experienced suitor allures a beautiful young woman. By selecting one of these, the actor, in effect, *decides* whether or not Othello genuinely discloses a painful biography or is merely boasting—a choice left open when one is reading the play. Such a participation in and embodiment of a fictional life beyond the temporal boundaries specified by the written fiction differs from the looser engagement required by literary imagination, even when the latter is involved.

Acting versus Reading/Writing (IV): Focused versus Relational Identification

Another discontinuity between identification as reader/audience and as part of theatrical embodiment relates to the general difference between enjoying art and producing it, a difference I have so far ignored in comparing the identification experienced by the recipient of a work (a reader of literature) and its performer. Whereas reading and acting are both forms of participation in a game of make-believe (to borrow Walton's terms), some of the differences between them affect existential amplification.

Some dramatic genres depend upon their readers' or audience's experience of empathy (tragedy); others often rely on its withdrawal or suspension (comedy). But in opposition to spectators, the actor has to intimately embody the fiction, even when the dramatic effect intended for the audience is one of detachment. Here, for instance, is a terrified Falstaff mulling over his narrow escape from drowning after being unceremoniously ditched into the Thames:

> Have I lived to be carried in a basket like a barrow of butcher's offal, and to be thrown in the Thames? . . . . The rogues slighted me into the river with as little remorse as they would have drowned a blind bitch's puppies. . . . And you may know by my size that I have a kind of alacrity in sinking. If the bottom were as deep as hell, I should down. I had been drowned but that the shore was shelvy and shallow—a death that I abhor; for the water swells a man; and what a thing should I have been when I had been swelled! I should have been a mountain of mummy. (*The Merry Wives of Windsor*, III.v. 4-14)

Floating down the river is an immense, bloated corpse. Such is the image filling the mind of a mortified Falstaff. Conjuring the repulsive appearance of his dead body had he drowned, he unites with the audience in his imaginary self-spectatorship. Yet it is the disjunction between his and his audience's response that mobilizes the humor: his horrified shame contrasting with the audience's delight. Comic effect here depends on the actor experiencing or projecting utter dread—decidedly *not* what the audience experiences upon hearing this confession. A successful performance of comic roles (or of villains, shrewish wives, fools, or bullying husbands) sometimes depends upon actors insulating themselves in such ways from the radically different response that they draw from their audience.

The example shows how different the actor's embodiment of a character can become from its spectatorship by others. Unlike the reader, the actor is not only delving into the experience of a character, but into a compound one that will be simultaneously perceived and responded to by an audience. The actor will not simply empathize with Falstaff, but will embody Falstaff's horror and shock *while* the audience is laughing (hard). Theatrical embodiment is, accordingly, *relational*. It engages in a constant dialogue with something that lies outside the boundaries of the work: an audience's response that exists simultaneously with the actor's act. Reading, on the other hand, entails a gravitating into the fictional character's world, but remains confined to the parameters established by the work. As for the writing of a comic character, while the author, like the actor, creates in relationship to predicted responses, unlike the actor, he or she need not fully inhabit or even empathize with the state that elicits the ridicule.

The comedian's loneliness consists of his inhabiting the state that makes everyone else laugh. In inferior comic acting, the actor seems to join the audience in mocking the ridiculed character. This pushes comic acting into the spheres of tragic acting, in which the actor can usefully draw on his own pity and compassion for the character he embodies, and, to some extent, bond with an audience's response. By contrast, comedy allows actors to reveal the extent to which they become other through the role. It compels them to fully suspend their own biographical inclinations and responses. Comic "genius" is rooted in this capacity to evoke the audience's disidentification with the character, and to simultaneously exhibit the actor's ability to fully lose himself in a situation he himself would have laughed at in other circumstances. It is this achieved dissociation that can elicit not merely the audience's admiration, but its fascination with the actor behind Falstaff, who exhibits a distinct form of existential amplification.

Reading about Falstaff's imagining of his drowning—even an involved reading in which one enters another place and time and thus "lives more through literature"—will never create this response. One will only respond to the fictional Falstaff rather than to the combined dyad of a fiction inhabited by an actor. The uniqueness of responding to a comedian consists in relating to a spectacle of insulation, a feat of identification with an imagined state. The performer is able to be in another way while freeing himself from his own purported response as spectator. Once again, it is to *the acting process* and not merely to the enacted content to which the audience responds.

STAGING LITERATURE

From Aristotle on, genres such as comedy or tragedy have been understood solely in terms of the content or the emotional structures they are meant to convey. Tragedy is (still) said to instill a sense of waste, or of estrangement or homelessness, or to induce a combination of pity and fear, or to bring into collision a conflict of mutually exclusive values. Comedy, by contrast, is understood as establishing an experience of momentary superiority, or as fostering reconciliation among controlled and unruly aspects of one's life, or as facilitating an interruption of senselessness into the ordered world of sense, or as deflating human pretense, or as exposing the mechanical within the human. Yet the previous analysis advises against approaching drama in this way. If neither interest in fictional plots nor care for fictional beings constitute the primary motivation underlying spectatorship; if a significant reason for our choice to become an audience is watching, experiencing and validating *the act of acting*; if such participation subliminally communicates with structural features of subjective experience and its limitations—these abstract concerns may plausibly percolate *into the written role* that is being enacted.

The bias built into traditional genre theory was natural: since, as spectators, we process content and plot *and* undergo powerful emotions (much as we do when reading a work of fiction), a *correlation* between what we watch and what we feel was confused for a *causal link* between these. The Aristotelian approach to dramatized genres thus mandated overestimating our interest in experiencing and sharing the feelings articulated by the plots and characters. Literary dimensions of theatrical experience were privileged. Such misplaced attention became more ingrained because some of the most influential theater theorists were authors or literary critics. Keenly attuned to the literary sides of drama, such theorists would naturally emphasize the use of characterization in a dramatic work, its powers of meaning-making, and the figurative potency of well-composed language.

Doubts may have been entertained by readers of such theorists: if the audience is interested in the words or fictional interactions presented by successfully depicted characters, why bother watching a play when it is less time-consuming (and cheaper) to read it? But if this objection was voiced, it was suppressed by the highly influential philosophy of theater mentioned earlier (itself also an Aristotelian paradigm): theatrical performances are merely an enactment of an effective plotline and compelling characterization.[1] According to this philosophy, acting compensates for our imperfect imagination; it merely communicates literary values. As we saw, such a position cannot be defended.

Exciting implications for the understanding of drama follow from the refusal to regard theater as instantiated literature. Once genre theory ceases to be determined solely by the idea of conveying literary content, there emerges an intricate web spreading between established dramatic genres—or repeatedly used plot patterns within these genres—and the experiences that the beholding of acting sets in motion. Literary theory has missed these because genre theory was implicated in that other Aristotelian heritage, for which theatrical spectacle is secondary to the plot or to some overarching emotional objective (of the cathartic kind). The major exception to this bias within literary studies is Michael Goldman's sustained and complex perspective on the experience of drama as a response to the acting process.[2] Goldman's approach to acting differs from the philosophical framework advanced in this book, stressing a particular account of identification, recognition, and a host of other features that are too detailed and varied to summarize here. Nevertheless, his central insight is one that I would like to draw on in what follows: if we attend the theater to watch the acting process, one would expect actor–character dynamics to find their way into recurring plot structures in drama.[3]

Tragedy and comedy both articulate themes that relate to features that draw us to acting as such. I shall first present six such general connections. I then provide two examples in greater detail. My exclusive choice of Shakespearean examples stems from my preference for discussing instances in which my own sense of the works that I actually study and teach has altered upon realizing the connection between theatrical and literary patterns. Moreover, the focus on tragedy and comedy is not meant to restrict the proposed thesis to these genres or, indeed, to genre at all. "Genre" is here used as a shorthand term denoting repeatedly used plot combinations of a roughly similar kind. Genres thus lend themselves easily to the type of examples I shall present. But the dramatic elements that underpin acting may appear in plays of other genres, or in plays that altogether fail to neatly belong to any single established genre.

(1) Comedy and tragedy often involve a loosening of the relationships between individuals and their identities. Both tragedy and comedy feature the theme of losing one's identity altogether, of being possessed by some other entity, or of selling one's identity to a demonic power (the Faustus theme), of losing one's sanity, of being wrenched out of one's place in the world through banishment or by being stranded, or by being compelled to don a disguise. The analogy between this and the actor's disembodiment is clear: acting is precisely an act of forgoing one's identity, allowing it to drift away, and then reclaiming it. The actor is stranded, banished from his identity for the duration of the play. He is, in a sense, possessed by some other entity inhabiting his body. The experience of dissolving into dew or dissipating into a cloud (Hamlet, Antony), or of having one's personality overtaken by some inner alien identity (Lear's madness, swelling from within, Angelo's emerging sexual violence in *Measure for Measure*), are ways whereby episodes of identity loss in the plot correspond to the audience's sensations vis-à-vis the actor's own disembodiment. We relate to loss of selfhood on the fictional level as we *simultaneously* witness an extended disengagement of personality from body.

(2) Role–character tensions within the fictional domain may mirror actor–role tensions. When a disguise is finally discarded (for example, in *As You Like It* or *Twelfth Night*), the ultimate return of a character into its undisguised identity parallels the anticipated return of actors to their identities at the end of the play. (Could the applause of an audience be partly a response to the need to know that such a return has been successfully accomplished?) Plays may also unleash the anxiety that reconciliation between role and actor will not take place at all, that one may lose oneself in the role: in *As You Like It*, Rosalind struggles to control Ganymede, her faked identity; *Twelfth Night*'s Viola is almost killed in a sword fight she becomes entangled in because of her mask. Acting is indeed a liberating form of existential amplification. Yet it is also risky: the road back to identity might become blocked. In fact, the next section of the book will explore how some forms of performed amplification may *take something away* from a performer (the disturbing possibility that such a process is itself attractive to an audience is an option I leave open).

(3) Consider, next, the theme of self-transgression. The aspiration to

transcend one's limits characterizes tragedy and comedy alike. Tragedy often highlights *hubris*; comedy center-stages the overreaching braggart. These characters are then crushed or humbled. Such deflation is, again, not isolated from the process enacted by the actress: the creating actress overcomes her own existential limits through the acting process.

Such structural similarity affects our understanding of endings in these genres. Tragedy is heartwrenching not only due to the predicament of its heroes. In tragedy, the actor's aspiration to be more than he is expires with the destruction of that creation. The fantasy inhabited by him and acknowledged by the audience ends when the character dies, implying an irrevocable separation between actor and character: the character will not go on whereas the actor will. Comedy, by contrast, is uplifting not just because it ends in marriage, reconciliation, a reaffirmation of life, or some other momentary overcoming of a conflict, but because its ending suggests that the characters will carry on with their fictional lives when the play is over. Comedy encourages the fantasy that the actress's existential amplification is unbounded by the theatrical context. Tragedy contains the termination of such amplification within its own bounds.

(4) Heroes of drama, particularly its war heroes, constitute another example of a subliminal dialogue between our (usually unarticulated) experience of actor–role relations and the construction of the fictional character favored by theater. A hero, such as Titus Andronicus or Coriolanus, is an identity-formation in which fusion between self and some socially endorsed narrative is achieved. Heroes may evoke envy (but also criticism) precisely because of their unreserved merging with an ideal. Another way to put this is that heroes are those for whom all resistance to being subsumed under a socially prized narrative disappears. Heroes live as if such absorption into a valued narrative were necessary—in truth, it is merely contingent.[4]

A profound irony emerges here when we shift attention from literary events to theatrical occurrences. The presentation of a contingent narrative as a necessary one (heroism) is performed by someone who is *simultaneously exhibiting* the contingent ties between who one is and the role one performs (the actor). The irony is that acting is, in a sense, the antithesis of heroism: acting exposes contingency; the hero experiences and conveys a felt necessity. The actor thereby instances an ideal but also its opposite, at once inviting the audience to be other while reconciling them to who they are. Plays that feature heroes sometimes annul this irony: the titular hero realizes that a narrative he hitherto considered necessary is really contingent. Titus and Coriolanus discover that their past military achievements in the service of Rome and their unparalleled social status as a result of these achievements can be easily overturned. The rapture formed between them and Rome entails the emergence of an identity that no longer does its best to serve Rome, but becomes animated by a different agenda. The transition from unification to antagonism replays, on the fictional level, the possibility of multiple embodiments presented by the actor.

The failure to sustain pretentious role-playing—such is comedy's equivalent to tragedy's presentment of a painful emergence of a gap between desired performance and reality.[5] In comedies that spotlight such failures, laughter results from an unintended exposure of the gap separating people from the appearances they uphold. Comedies often celebrate the inability to control the difference between personality constructs that are presented as necessary and the far more flexible, varied, and (often) less commending reality. Try as one might to fully be one's role, the freedom to be other, indeed, the perception that one *is* also other, was always there to begin with.

(5) If acting is a form of "un-selfing," a movement out of one's role and out of one's ordinary embodied agency, such can manifest itself not only in the form of "re-selfing," a movement into a fictional identity, but as a more thoroughgoing receding from altogether being a subject. Some dramatic forms are keenly intent on suspending a character precisely in such a space. Farce could be construed in this way, as suggested by Bergson's "new law" of humor ("we laugh every time a person gives us the impression of being a thing"). Farce thus touches a form of "un-selfing," in which the actor presents a character's discovery of its own irreducibility to its formal identity. This time, the irreducibility does not consist of becoming other, but by collapsing into one's being as object. Since the damage in farce is mild, such exposure is benign and pleasant to digest. Horror themes, stressing as they do the capacity of humans to become nutrition or targets for cruel violence, bring out a grimmer side of the discovery of one's ability to become an object (how victims die in horror frequently involves subjecting them to tools or processes that are usually reserved for objects). Comedy and horror themes thus overlap, highlighting pre-subjective experience and one's being-as-matter. Through the comic situation, the actor can thus present (but also be mildly punished for presenting) a more encompassing sense of existence than the one stressing subjective experience.

(6) A different correspondence between theatrical interests and literary content is established by tragedies of fate—for example, *Oedipus*, *Macbeth*,

or *Romeo and Juliet*. Such plays present human weakness in the face of a powerful, usually hidden, external force. Such fate-governed plot structures mirror the character's total subjection to the actor. To watch an accomplished actor is to witness a character formed by the artist–actor, a puppet mastered by a puppeteer. Actor Michael Gambon was already cited earlier in relation to the experience of acting as one in which "someone inside is directing you."[6] The actor presents to the audience both an externally controlled creation and an externally determined fiction that, like a puppet, touchingly believes in its own freedom. In this way, tragedies of fate manifest coherence between theme and medium. They are gripping because they present characters that are multiply determined, once as scripted authorial creations, twice, as being fully governed by a force working within the fictional domain, and thrice, as embodied fictions.

Objections

The preoccupation of drama with heroism, reconciliation, homelessness, disowned and reclaimed identities, fate, and illusive freedom is no coincidence. Such themes are profoundly connected to the act of acting that the audience has come to witness in the theater.

The most immediate objection to adopting such a perspective on drama is that it does not square with our felt experience in the theater. Spectators are hardly ever conscious of actor–role relations. Most are totally absorbed in the fictional events, in what characters say or do. To posit a unitary reaction that "the audience" universally undergoes is, moreover, a distorting simplification.

There is a standard response to objections of this kind: mechanisms underlying aesthetic responses are seldom explicit. Counterpoint in music elicits pleasure without it being obvious that it is employed; energy sensed in poetry need not involve awareness of its arrangement in iambic pentameter. In going beyond conscious responses, the above thesis does not deny that our focus of attention revolves around plot, around figuring out what comes next, and around the emotions and interactions between characters. But here, as elsewhere in art, our conscious interest is not the most useful key through which the meaning of theatrical practice (in contrast to the meaning of the *play*) should be unlocked. Our plot-related interest may even hamper our capacity to recognize our genuine motivations for opting to watch a play rather than read a book.

A related objection is that there is something dizzying and over-sophisticated about the connections presented above. It seems overly complex to assume that Viola's unmasking is, for instance, somehow linked to the actress's return from the role to her own identity. We do not really think or respond in such manner to theatrical action unless they are explicitly thrust in our faces (as happens, for example, at the end of *As You Like It*, when Rosalind directly addresses the audience when taking off her disguise—but such is the rare exception, not the rule).

The response to this criticism calls attention to other art forms, for which we possess a no less dizzying theory:

> When analyzing recorded [jazz] improvisations [students] begin not only to grasp formerly impenetrable patterns whose components had eluded them aurally, but to name them in theoretical terms: 'I have heard that before; that's just a descending seventh scale with a half step between the one and the seventh, run down to the third, and diminished up from the third.'[7]

Sophisticated categories and highly elaborate mechanisms are here employed to illuminate aesthetic effects without themselves resembling the felt experiences of musical pleasure. The relative complexity of the above-mentioned claims regarding drama—far less indigestible than this snippet of musical theory—should not dissuade us from endorsing them as an account of our response and attraction to particular dramatic patterns.

A third objection to the above is that the themes I have highlighted are popular in nondramatic literature as well. Heroic characters that evoke feelings such as disillusionment, for example, feature in literature without any connection to a tacit interplay with theatrical embodiment. If they are sufficiently interesting in one aesthetic domain without being embodied by an actor (literature) why should we suppose that they are underpinned by a radically different structure in another (theater)?

There are two replies to this objection. The first is that although the fictional strength of such themes is independent of theatrical incarnation, this does not imply that when they *do* feature in theater, they are processed in the same manner as in literature. Heroes are interesting in one way when embodied, and in another when read about. A more interesting reply to this objection is that the distinction between literature and performance implied by the objection is itself not as rigid as it seems. What we call "literature" is itself historically indebted in many ways to drama and to oral performance. The widespread phenomenon of Ancient Greek rhapsodists—performers who, according to Plato's *Ion*, basically recited in public the epics of Homer and Hesiod—suggests a tight linkage between epics and oral performance. Arthurian romances such as *Sir Gawain and the Green Knight* rely on acoustic rhyme patterns that facilitate oral delivery by enabling the audience to aurally differentiate the transition between stanzas. Examples such as these suggest that some potent literary themes that are capable of generating autonomous interest without any relation to theater have been imported into unperformed literature. In some past context, they were tied up with a vivid storyteller: a performer.[8] Instead of discouraging our curiosity regarding theatrical interests, the objection above prompts us to look for them outside the formal bounds of drama as well.

A fourth objection is the claim that the above proposal is selective. Implicit dialogues between "literary" and "theatrical" interests (that is, between text-related interests and needs attuned to actor-role relations) may indeed mobilize the response of spectators to protagonists of the drama. Yet most acting is of minor characters who rarely instance the kind of themes mentioned above. Some characters, even when they do exemplify such themes, do not invite a rich engagement from the audience, simply because the latter's attention is directed elsewhere. Take, for example, Orlando in *As You Like It*. Orlando does not put on a disguise. Nor is he disillusioned or governed by fate. Is our response to him related to our reaction to Rosalind's predicament (since she does invoke theatrical interests by donning a disguise)? And what about our response to Rosalind *prior* to her assumption of a disguise? Does she elicit only literary interest at this stage, but not a theatrical one, beginning to tap the latter only when she dons the disguise? Portia in *The Merchant of Venice*—an important character but surely not a major protagonist—is disguised only in the fourth act. Is her disguise central enough to account for our overall response to the play?

To begin with, what I have just called "theatrical interests" are not supposed to animate all episodes in each and every play. They are merely meant to account for the recurrence of some central themes in drama. To catalogue numerous examples in which theatrical interests do not underlie the staged action is, thus, not a substantial counter-argument. A more interesting response is that when episodes of the abovementioned kind are closely probed in their contexts, possible theatrical interests *do* begin to surface. Is it negligible, for example, that Rosalind—a character who epitomizes existential amplification through her metamorphosis into Ganymede, a character who, moreover, discovers fresh forms of creativity and love under disguise—is placed in relation to Orlando, a character who issues forth nothing but hackneyed clichés when he is left to his own devices? If this opposition between them is one of the strands that make up the beauty of the play's humor, Orlando's detachment from theatrical concerns contributes to an emerging disjunction that has everything to do with theatrical interests (amplification versus remaining locked into one's identity). And what about the relationship between Portia's transgression when she enacts a man learned in law (thereby presenting an illicit form of amplification through acting) and the actor who plays Shylock's own potentially self-damning embodiment of a Christian-hating Jew? To marginalize Portia's play-acting risks missing the extent to which her overreaching in the fictional domain captures a central dimension of a Christian audience's response to this play in relation to the *acting* of Shylock.[9]

Reading Drama

There are two kinds of practical rewards involved in accepting the idea that substantial links connect drama's leitmotifs with aspects of the acting process. Understanding why particular motifs and plot devices repeatedly emerge as part of some dramatic genres such as tragedy or comedy is the first of these. Achieving a fuller appreciation of particular episodes within specific plays is the second. Rewards of the second kind will appear as part of detailed interpretations. Literary critics would allow sensitivities to an interlacing of fictional and theatrical elements to inform their readings. The following three examples suggest how such interpretations differ from familiar forms of metatheatrical awareness long ingrained within literary criticism.

Seeking shelter in a hovel, Lear is in the company of the Fool, Caius (Kent in disguise), and Poor Tom (Edgar in disguise). At the peak of this scene, Lear will undress (in some productions, the undressing becomes literal), inspired by something that Lear recognizes in Poor Tom: a sense of what unaccommodated, naked man is all about. In context, the undressing is the culmination of a movement that began the play—Lear's withdrawal from possessions, status, and power. The hovel scene is also the point at which Lear is enveloped by the unconditional love of those who have nothing to gain from tying their lot with his (which is, ironically, precisely the kind of love that was mere lip service paid by his eldest daughters). If only he could experience it as such.

A metatheatrical analysis of the episode would underscore the links between literary elements and theatrical reality: Lear is surrounded by characters who are play-acting; Edgar is pretending to be a poor, deranged beggar; Kent is acting a servant (Caius); and the unnamed Fool is, from first to last, playing a role that is part profession, part identity. Alone among this sorry company, the Lear character stands out as the only non-actor. The scene builds up to a discovered truth. At the same time, undressing, moving out of hypocrisy and becoming "the thing itself," is *performed* by a *hypokrites*—an actor playing Lear. The scene thus combines the wish to completely "overcome theatricality" (to borrow Michael Fried's terms) with a simultaneous undermining of this fantasy: unconditional love is expressed by and through characters *who act*, who we know to be other than they seem. It is the Lear *actor* who is calling on us to envisage a state beyond all pretense, who is not what he seems even when he is down to his naked body, ironically screaming away that he is the thing itself.

But we can go beyond such familiar metatheatrical patterns. If, as elaborated above, acting involves an exposure of the contingent bond between body and identity, the hovel scene bears more subtle and profound links to the audience's interest in the act of acting. In the scene, the body's ties to an established identity are undone through the tearing of the shards of official attire, providing a thematic analogue to the actor's ability to free his body from his identity. Lear's mounting madness in the scene is another aspect of the disintegration of identity within the parameters of the same body. In "madness," a new voice emerges from an old body.

A monarch withdraws from his position as king, then from his identity as father to Cordelia, and then discards his clothes. We watch him in the process of losing his sanity. He is profoundly tragic, not only because of his fall from power to the utter dispossession of an old banished father who is locked out of shelter by his own children, but also because he embodies an actor's nightmare: evacuating what one is, yet being unable to infuse one's body with a new self. By placing him among those who do manage to both recede from who they are and also become someone else, Lear enacts *a failure in re-embodiment*, a body that is not animated by an embodying soul. Rather than present an act in which the self is successfully amplified, in which the connections between body and identity are exposed as elastic, playfully revisable options, the play shows how disembodiment need not pave the way to further reincarnation; the gateway that opens in disembodiment hurls one out into limbo. The references to "nothing" and being a nothing that pepper the play—Marvin Rosenberg counts thirty of them[10]—thereby articulate a tragedy of withdrawal without self-reinvention.

If we watch plays not merely out of interest in plot, but also because we wish to respond to self-amplification as well as to disembodiment followed by incarnation, a "tragedy" can be a plot pattern in which such needs are thwarted in various ways. Unlike familiar metatheatrical patterns that typically mobilize double references (highlighting words that refer both to fictional elements and to real aspects of the dramatic situation), some highly charged theatrical moments relate to a corroborating or a stifling of the fantasy that draws us to acting in the first place. The Lear *actor* succeeds in infusing his body with another's governing identity. Yet the *character* being embodied, Lear, experiences an aborted metamorphosis; his disembodiment takes him nowhere.

Tragedies have other means of undermining the audience's unexpressed wishes regarding nonrigid bonds between body and identity. In such tragedies, the actor's freedom to become someone else is implicitly undermined by the fictional plot when overwhelming circumstances rivet bodies to identities. In the famous "balcony scene," Romeo is willing to be newly baptized should Juliet call him her lover. Throughout the play, the lovers will systematically underestimate their social identities and the extent to which these determine their future. "What's in a name?" is the most touching expression of such underestimation—the lovers' tragedy is, after all, *precisely* one of names, of the inability to turn names and the familial contexts for which they stand into mere arbitrary signs. *Romeo and Juliet* is a play about two souls yearning for a little more flexibility in the relation between their socially accepted identities and their innermost being. Intimacy, for them, is the establishing of momentary bubbles of space, time, and language in which they can insulate themselves from the rival families' animosity. The lovers will not prevail. Their identities will not be shaken off.

Romeo and Juliet is a tragedy of acting: it exposes the rigid connection between body and name, which is the precise inflexibility that acting relaxes. Anyone who undertakes the act of acting with some commitment is, on some level, asking with Juliet: what's in a name? Are our identities inescapable? The actor conjures a world in which names and identities are replaced, in which one identity is discarded whereas another is self-determined (precisely as the lovers wished it could). The actor also inspires other human beings—the audience—to play along with such an act of taking on another identity, acknowledging and validating it (precisely as the lovers cannot). None of this is metatheater: theater does not here reflect on itself in a manner audible to those trained to catch self-reflexive metatheatrical remarks. Yet the themes that dominate the play echo the concerns that create an interest in acting in the first place. These themes do not merely duplicate these theatrical interests, but (tragically) prevent the transcending of personal limitations that acting promises. Deflating the audience's hopes regarding the escape acting might be able to deliver, such themes morbidly color the play's specific sadness.

In contrast to tragedy, comedy kindles rather than quenches the transcending of personal limitations that acting allows. Comic protagonists who thrive by putting on a mask are usually put at some risk. Yet when they are punished for pretending to be other than they are, their punishment never amounts to annihilation. Comic characters will be humbled, but, unlike their tragic counterparts, they will survive. Comedy thus acknowledges the dangers of self-overreaching and turns these into a source of pleasure. But, unlike tragedy, it presents such obstacles as surmountable.

Consider the moments in *Twelfth Night* in which Malvolio (the pompous, prudish servant) fantasizes about marrying Olivia (the lady of the house). The disclosure of the fantasy takes place when Malvolio intercepts a fabricated letter in which Olivia supposedly eggs him on to aspire to be her husband and to act accordingly. He then dreams up scenes in which, once married, he haughtily orders about other members of the house (who are currently his seniors). These other members are actually eavesdropping on Malvolio (they are the ones who have composed the letter), and are enraged by his arrogant fantasies. Malvolio unhesitatingly takes up the idiosyncratic, bizarre behavior advised by the letter, irredeemably disgracing himself in the process.

The comedy of this episode revolves around overhearing someone's dream. The episode externalizes a particularly crass version of the need to be more than who one is. Malvolio is mentally conjuring up a scene in which, after his marriage to Olivia, he casually censures the drinking habits of one of his seniors. If, as proposed above, acting touches the audience's own preoccupation with self-transcending, Malvolio allows the audience to behold *this very process*. There are more and less dignified ways of experiencing this need, and one should grant that Malvolio's brand is not particularly endearing. Nevertheless, he mirrors something back to the audience. He becomes a caricature of the fantasy of overreaching which is also the audience's, a fantasy triggered whenever its members sympathetically follow through *any* actor they are watching. To put this differently, to listen to Malvolio's dream of attaining control over his seniors—the expression of his own resistance to the limitations of his biography—permits the audience to overhear itself at the very moment in which it attends and validates the self-transcending that theater presents. And while the Malvolio *actor* succeeds in this feat, the *character* he embodies does not.

A multilayered moment is being orchestrated: the verbal content articulates self-overcoming (Malvolio's words) while the theatrical event simultaneously and contrapuntally presents both the fulfillment of that self-expansion (the actor's successful acting of Malvolio) and the impending failure of this fantasy (Malvolio's predicament: his eventual confinement due to his "madness"). Theories of comic humor will differ over the cause of our laughter here; whether it issues from superiority and the establishing of an unbridgeable distance between us and Malvolio's secretive wish for greatness, or whether Malvolio enables us to reconcile ourselves to our own shameful sense of self-consequence. According to the first theory, comic laughter is the outcome of anxiety. According to the second, it stems from reharmonizing one's soul. The relevant point to the argument advanced here is that, whether we stress distance, superiority or inner peace, the moments in which Malvolio's private dreams are embarrassingly exposed articulate the wishes that draw us to watch acting in the first place and that our laughter is, on some level, a response to *these* wishes.

We should read drama for such connections. After all, it is only to be expected that the best dramatists possess a keen (though often unarticulated) awareness of acting and of the motives behind the audience's wish to witness it. To grant them less implies that they miss a central aspect of their medium. To grant them mere autonomy from literature overlooks subtle ways in which literary features interlock with the acting process, the act directly beheld by the audience whom the playwright is addressing. Literature and theater should not be separated from each other due to some defense of their alleged autonomy. They are mutually enforcing art forms that combine in multiple and unique ways as part of a theatrical offering.

STAGING OBJECTS

Acting is the process of animating a fictional role. Puppet theater, a medium that celebrates the animation of that which is manifestly not alive, reifies this process. Since, in puppetry, such animation is purified of many aspects involved in an actor's performance, puppetry opens for the philosopher of acting an important gateway into the aesthetics governing both creation and reception of this distinct strand of the actor's art.

Two additional reasons justify taking a less than cursory look at puppetry. The first relates to self-role tensions that are played out by the acting process, and that are mimicked and externalized by the puppeteer-puppet relations. In a sense, the "actor" in puppet theater is the puppet and the puppeteer conjoined.[1] Some of the favorite themes of puppetry include darker anxieties relating to this process: being overcome by a fiction, attempting to be liberated from a fiction, an inability to control it, or being destroyed by it. Puppetry is thus an art form that is able to structurally stage tensions between actors and roles: the threat of losing oneself in a role, or of the role attaining too much power. The quasi-paternal relations between actors and roles also acquire an external shape in puppetry — puppeteers often create their puppets, allowing these to develop as one does with a child.[2] True, unlike (most) actors who generally animate a single role in a play, the puppeteer usually operates several puppets. Sometimes—as is the case of the Japanese Bunraku theatre, the gigantic puppets utilized by *The Bread and Puppet Theatre* or special plays, such as *Warhorse*—several puppeteers operate a single puppet. It is likewise true that often the puppeteer does not merely occlude his presence, but also becomes another role. Yet these observations underscore, rather than modify, the general isomorphism between the actor-role relations and the aesthetic and psychological unit encompassing puppeteer and puppet: the possibility of one body inhabiting several roles, or of one body participating with others in forming a collective role, enriches this visual analogy and its implication for the spectators' own sense of their identity.[3]

The third reason for turning to puppetry is that due to its visible manipulation of an *object*, puppetry solicits response to a unique form of self-amplification—one that is unrelated to living more as this or that (as acting does), but to a subjectless mode of being. The selfhood-as-possibilities model that I have so far employed in this study will, thereby, be embedded within more complex horizons of subjective experience. "Being in another way" need not necessarily mean being another personality.

Pinocchio

The scope of the category of a "puppet" is easy to specify: glove puppets, shadow puppets, rod puppets and marionettes. Nor is puppetry difficult to define: a "replica of a human, animal, or other form moved by artificial means."[4] Yet a host of questions surfaces when one ventures beyond mere designation. What kind of object is a puppet and what modes of spectatorship does it mobilize? What manner of art is the puppeteer presenting? What is the source of puppetry's prevailing charm? What underpins "charm" as an aesthetic response?

A useful entry point into such issues is provided by the following, highly potent presentation of the relationship of a creator (who is not even a puppeteer) and his puppet:

> As soon as he reached home, Geppetto took his tools and began to cut and shape the wood into a Marionette. . . . After choosing the name for his Marionette, Geppetto set seriously to work to make the hair, the forehead, the eyes. Fancy his surprise when he noticed that these eyes moved and then stared fixedly at him. Geppetto, seeing this, felt insulted and said in a grieved tone: "Ugly wooden eyes, why do you stare so?" There was no answer. After the eyes, Geppetto made the nose, which began to stretch as soon as finished. It stretched and stretched and stretched till it became so long, it seemed endless. Poor Geppetto kept cutting it and cutting it, but the more he cut, the longer grew that impertinent nose. In despair he let it alone. Next he made the mouth. No sooner was it finished than it began to laugh and poke fun at him. "Stop laughing!" said Geppetto angrily; but he might as well have spoken to the wall. "Stop laughing, I say!" he roared

> in a voice of thunder. The mouth stopped laughing, but it stuck out a long tongue. Not wishing to start an argument, Geppetto made believe he saw nothing and went on with his work. After the mouth, he made the chin, then the neck, the shoulders, the stomach, the arms, and the hands. As he was about to put the last touches on the finger tips, Geppetto felt his wig being pulled off. He glanced up and what did he see? His yellow wig was in the Marionette's hand. "Pinocchio, give me my wig!" But instead of giving it back, Pinocchio put it on his own head, which was half swallowed up in it. At that unexpected trick, Geppetto became very sad and downcast, more so than he had ever been before. "Pinocchio, you wicked boy!" he cried out. "You are not yet finished, and you start out by being impudent to your poor old father. Very bad, my son, very bad!" And he wiped away a tear.
>
> The legs and feet still had to be made. As soon as they were done, Geppetto felt a sharp kick on the tip of his nose. "I deserve it!" he said to himself. "I should have thought of this before I made him. Now it's too late!" He took hold of the Marionette under the arms and put him on the floor to teach him to walk. Pinocchio's legs were so stiff that he could not move them, and Geppetto held his hand and showed him how to put out one foot after the other. When his legs were limbered up, Pinocchio started walking by himself and ran all around the room. He came to the open door, and with one leap he was out into the street. Away he flew! Poor Geppetto ran after him but was unable to catch him, for Pinocchio ran in leaps and bounds, his two wooden feet, as they beat on the stones of the street, making as much noise as twenty peasants in wooden shoes. "Catch him! Catch him!" Geppetto kept shouting. But the people in the street, seeing a wooden Marionette running like the wind, stood still to stare and to laugh until they cried.[5]

What comes across powerfully in the above passage is the uncontrolled and uncontrollable nature of matter. The marionette's insolence surfaces before it becomes fully alive. Geppetto feels slighted by the mere stare of Pinocchio, before a word has been exchanged between them. He next fails to limit the size of Pinocchio's nose, which seems to have an endless capacity to grow. Upon completion, each body part either attacks or mocks Geppetto, yet he persists in making Pinocchio. Collodi is subtle. No one is *forcing* Geppetto to go on. He had originally planned to make a marionette for financial reasons—he was not creating a son. Yet, throughout this process of relinquishing control and manifesting a curious inability to desist, Geppetto experiences profound sadness, "more than he had ever experienced before." Scolding the marionette, he refers to himself, for the first time, as its father.

Geppetto does not merely carve a puppet. He is reciprocally made—in some sense, reciprocally fathered—by it throughout the scene. This paternal seam of the connection between Geppetto and his creation is introduced into the novel when the old man experiences the surprising freedom and resistance of matter, the inability to control that which appears to be unproblematically owned.[6] Beyond the linkage between the experience of paternity and that of dispossession (the piece of wood belonged, belongs, to him), the creation of Pinocchio involves a waning of the creator's autonomy—we note how compelled, even (ironically) wooden Geppetto's own agency and work become in contrast to the exuberant license of Pinocchio; the latter's growth in freedom seems to be proportionately sucked out of the former, who becomes steadily deflated of volition throughout the scene. Paternal sentiment is born, not out of the endearing nature of the puppet, but out of the sadness induced by the creation's mocking dumb commentary on its creator, coupled with some unexplained compulsion to proceed. Geppetto hones and perfects the object/puppet/child-in-wood, endowing it with an even greater resilience, indeed, enabling it to actually escape by teaching it how to walk, when everything indicates that the puppet would misuse this capacity as soon as attained.

Collodi emphasizes the sense of a rebellious creation by opening not with the puppet, but with the wood out of which it would later be made, which already shows signs of resistance: "Once upon a time there was a piece of wood!" so begins the novel. A piece of wood all of a sudden talking to Master Cherry—startling the latter when he intends to fashion it into the leg of a table—presents the reader with the hybrid nature of a living object which Cherry, in dread, will hastily jettison. He passes it on to Geppetto, who will allow it to transform him into a father. By the end of the scene, the man who had set out to fashion a marionette finds himself controlled by the fleeing puppet, rushing after it into the bustling streets.

A plausible explanation for Collodi's choice to avoid simply beginning the novel with Geppetto, is that Cherry's more ordinary response to the living wood provides a potent foil for Geppetto's extraordinary state of mind in response to the same stimuli. The difference in attitude between Cherry and Geppetto is telling: both discover that the wood is alive. Yet while Cherry wants nothing more than to pass it on, Geppetto will not stop his carving and, throughout this process, will tighten his unhappy bond to it. Collodi's opening invites us to ponder whether the different function allotted to the piece of wood by Cherry and Geppetto (a wooden table leg for the former; a puppet for the latter) may be foretelling. Unlike Cherry, whose prosaic design on the wood involves letting matter remain what it is, Geppetto's manipulation of the wood is aimed at turning it into a puppet: a pseudo-human child. In Geppetto, the initiation of the process of make-believe animation encounters the all-too-real animation of the wood. His active participation in a play of pseudo versus genuine animation, natural production as opposed to supernatural creation, somehow disables Geppetto's ability to stop. Unlike Cherry, merely horrified by the abnormal ("His face had changed; fright had turned even the tip of his nose from red to deepest purple"), Geppetto does not experience fear at all. The two movements between which he is caught—mock-creation and actual animation—trigger the strange mixture of anger and profound sadness that Geppetto undergoes.

Why this specific combination? The anger is easy to explain: it seems no more than another manifestation of Geppetto's raspy nature. The sadness is more intriguing. Pinocchio's plucking off Geppetto's wig induces it. The wig—mock hair, a body part which is not a body part, matter which seems to organically belong but does not genuinely belong, a non-living replacement, a detachable chunk of the body that can all of a sudden be possessed by another—sets in motion Geppetto's deep sadness. To wear a wig is to pass off as someone else. By snatching it, the marionette exposes Geppetto's own theatricality, his own constitution out of detachable parts. Sadness, the experience of loss, issues forth from the unplanned exposure of the intermixture of nonliving and living matter in Geppetto's own body. Taking control of the wig is the culmination of the process in which Pinocchio becomes animated as Geppetto is de-animated. By pinching the wig and putting it on its own head, the would-be puppet unmakes its human creator, overturning the relations of creation between things and agents. By wearing the wig, Pinocchio also mockingly dons the shame of baldness and the need to hide it, reflecting back to Geppetto, in his very first "performance," not the dexterous fencing and acrobatic somersaulting that Geppetto had in mind, but rather aging, the body's betrayal, and the pathetic effort spent in hiding it.

Subjects and Objects

Pinocchio is not really a puppet. He is more of an actual child inhabiting the puppet Geppetto had planned to make. Yet much of what puppetry sets in motion is encapsulated in this snippet. The very medium of puppetry captures both an essential feature of life qua momentarily resuscitated matter—as well as the illusiveness of freedom and the disturbing autonomy of one's creations.

On the one hand, puppetry questions the autonomy of a seemingly spontaneous entity (the puppet-character, visibly operated by an external agent). The allure of puppets surely partakes of the fascination with tragedies of fate such as *Oedipus,* or *Macbeth*, which highlight the illusion of self-determination. Puppets can also be used in order to explicitly stage the collapse of this precise fantasy, as in Philippe Genty's profoundly moving piece, *Pierrot*. On the other hand, puppetry also steadily undermines the puppeteer's control over the animated fiction which the puppet becomes. Adult puppet theater often spotlights the puppeteer's capacity to be manipulated by the puppet, tricked, attacked, even killed by his own creation. The effect of this oscillates between the comic and the downright horrifying. The Israel-based "Gertrude Theatre" presents a piece in which the power relations between puppet and operator are overturned; their puppet is situated behind the puppeteer, who is lying on a trencher while the puppet offers him to another character as food. Duda Paiva's piece, *Bastard*, involves a scene in which the puppeteer is coerced into offering the use of his legs to an aging unappealing puppet that wishes to dance. Less comic and more disturbing is a piece in Theatre Meschugge's *Metamorphoses*, in which the puppeteer (Ilka Schoenbein) is assaulted by a puppet spider virtually growing out of her own body. Hadass Ophrat discusses Nicole Mossoux's *Twin Houses*. There, the puppet simply decapitates her operator.[7] The latent theological undertones of a betraying creation are familiar.[8] But betrayal/freedom also structurally mimic a more general existential preoccupation with the unfaithfulness of ostensibly controllable matter (body)—the vexing autonomy of which erupts at surprising moments.

Prior to its apprehension as an uncontrollable character, releasing conflicting dimensions of freedom within its spectators, the puppet is first and foremost an *object*, a thing. "Object exists only because we are deceived into being subject," writes puppeteer Peter Schumann, intriguingly destabilizing the object-subject opposition: from a descriptive distinction, the subject-object divide turns into a defense mechanism through which our dread of being an object is evaded. Schumann's observation presents the object as an internal constituent—*not* some alien entity from which we are set apart.[9] Schumann addresses, in an original way (as far as I know), a recurrent theme in Western thought, whereby the ambit of human subjectivity was understood either through setting it apart from the domain of animals, or by contrasting it with the sphere of objects. For thinkers such as Simmel, Mead, or Marx, the crystallization of subjective experience is intertwined with the differentiation from a realm of objects. "Will," "freedom," and "intention" as core constituents of subjectivity were and are repeatedly articulated by contrasting them with the causal (often deterministic) realm of mechanical and animalistic natures.[10]

Perceiving objecthood as Schumann does, not as an ontologically distinct external category, but as an internal possibility into which one may dissolve, is not foreign to Western thought. But such a collapse is unanimously perceived as a threat. Like countless Geppettos staring in dismay at their dangling wigs, philosophers regarded objectification as a fall, a refusal of freedom, or of self-determination, or of moral responsibility, or of authentic self-shaping. Horror stories like E.T.A. Hoffmann's *The Sandman* are sometimes structuralizations of such discoveries (in Hoffmann's story, external automatons set off a complex mixture of attraction, repulsion, and dread in a protagonist who fears that he is himself an automaton). Even when individualism is being criticized, becoming an object is nevertheless perceived as a danger. For Dostoyevsky's narrator in *Notes from the Underground*, one of the most fundamental desires of all human beings is *not* to become a well-regulated object. Accordingly, people would perform counter-productive or even self-destructive acts, as long as such acts can validate their non-thing-like nature: "it seems to me that the meaning of man's life consists in proving to himself every minute that he's a man and not a piano key. And man will keep proving it and paying for it with his own skin."[11] Driven by the need to prevent a relapse of the human into the world of things, acts of this kind become explicable: each one of the characters surrounding Dostoyevsky's narrator is ardently striving to be this or that. He despises them for it, declaring that only silly people become something. Rather than take pride in not being like them, he relates to himself as a horrid creature, presenting a stance betwixt two unbearable options: the first is to follow others in becoming "this or that"; the second consists of turning into a thing. From such a perspective, our art, philosophy, much of our activity, indeed, our interest *in* interest as such—all form part of a gigantic gesture of refusal on our part: a resistance to the irrepressible thingification that will eventually triumph.

Given such background, the uniqueness of Schumann's remark stems from its positing internal objecthood not as a danger to be averted, but rather as an invitation to be embraced. What would it mean to be an object *and to like it*? The association of subjectivity with deception ("we are *deceived* into being subject") presents subjectivity not merely as an imposed and contingent structure, but situates the histrionic dimension of the self deeper than we might acknowledge: instead of subjects Goffmanesquely role-playing as this or that, subjectivity itself—the as yet unspecified set of possibilities constituting a person—becomes a role that we are deceived into playing and maintaining. The roles we play and their relation with that which we take ourselves to be are instances of a more general discrepancy between some brute, internal thinghood, and the desire of being dissociated from it through the leap into subjectivity.

Art, philosophy, or literature rarely touch upon such "thinghood." Literary and philosophical articulations would rather flatter us into misconstruing subjective experience into some continuous chain of mental events, an uninterrupted stream of consciousness that can be harmonized into more or less cohesive narratives. While we are now familiar with nonlinear articulations of the self—by thinkers such as Bersani or Laplanche—which conceive of the self as an unstable construct, created but also undermined, tentatively constituted only to be unmade,[12] even in these descriptions self-negation appears to be a form of *activity*, a manifestation of a death-*drive*. But how about those yawning gaps in experience? Moments in which nothing occurs, in which nothing is taken in, perceived, integrated, registered? Minutes, hours of non-thought, in which one turns into (or returns to a state of) some barely perceiving, undifferentiated mass? Such episodes cannot be distinguished apart or individuated in some poetically exciting way; they are not even instances of boredom. And so their very uninteresting and uneventful nature—to repeat: we are not discussing the *activity* of not doing—disconnects them from standard or aestheticized formulations of self-experience. An apprehension of this drift into the thinghood that takes place within the gaps of subjective experience must not follow some lamentable "withdrawal from subjectivity." A sense of regret would merely disclose our bias in favor of individuality. Such apprehension should, rather, involve acceptance of an essential aspect of our condition as things. The unique attraction exerted by puppets as animated objects results from establishing rare moments in which the possibility of such acceptance takes place.

Dolls

The thought cannot be warded off: on some unerasable plane, puppetry involves an adult playing with dolls. Adults surely indulge in many different games they have played as children. But they hardly ever return to playing with dolls, which are such a pivotal dimension of childhood play. An explanation for this refusal, suggested by the discussion so far, is that dolls are particularly suited to accommodate pre-individualized experience.

Dolls facilitate not only the child's need to identify with a fictional character, but its desire to relate to an unindividualized object. Childhood is partly an experience of not being sharply divided from the world of things, a separation that is constitutive of adulthood. The transition into adulthood involves the introduction of "heroes"—character-formations that are so fully attached to a particular prized configuration of personality, that they would lose all in order to preserve it. Heroes are foreigners to early childhood. They supersede dolls. The resistance to returning to play with dolls thus intimates a forceful divorce from an attachment to objects. The refusal is not of the tool-like nature of objects, nor is it a rejection of the imaginary characters imposed on dolls. The empathic experience being evaded is a prior affinity with the doll as object. The child's identification is analogous to the structure of drama as discussed in the previous chapter, in which the fictional layer enables reaching into processes that relate to real structural relations between actors, identities and roles. The characterization of the doll to which the child seemingly relates is secondary; it excuses and enables a prior unarticulated attraction to an object endowed with a face.

I would accordingly disagree with theorists such as Max von Boehn, who account for the links between adult puppet spectatorship and childhood solely in terms of a return to some early games of make-believe facilitated by a manipulation of dolls:

> The child that occupies itself with its dolls is playing, without knowing or desiring it, at a theatre, and thereby is poetically and dramatically active. It puts itself in the place of the doll; it is artist and public in one person; it cre-

> ates the object of art and appreciates it at one and the same time. Herein lies the basis of the puppet theatre, for the first child which played with its doll as if it were a living being may be regarded as the originator of the marionette stage. When and where this happened we naturally do not know, even as little as we know where and at what period adults first perceived this tendency of the child's mind and created an art form out of its naïve play.[13]

For von Boehn, the "basis of puppet theatre" is a wish to repeat early theatricalization: in child-doll play, the child empathizes with the doll and interacts with it as character. Von Boehn is, I think, missing the *specific* regression to childhood that puppetry invokes as well as a more complex understanding of early theatricality: puppetry enables revisiting a different relationship with objects and with oneself as object; a relationship that was available in early childhood. For the child, the doll is not merely a space for imposing illusory subjectivity and empathy, but captures the child's own unclear allocation between the subject (which he is called to become), and the disorganized—not always experiencing—entity (which he is). The child is surrounded by loving and less loving adults who, through the pressure of affection and naming, impose on the child a rudimentary sense of self. Dolls furnish an escape; they capture a mode of being in which animation and personalization is momentarily put on, and is then suspended when the doll relapses into an object. The empathy von Boehn sees is real enough. Yet it is targeted less at the specific character the doll is fancied to be, and more at the transition from object to subject that is so seamlessly achieved by the doll.

This experience is beautifully captured in one of the final conversations between Christopher Robin and Pooh, just as Christopher is leaving the world of his early childhood to go off to school:

> ". . . what I like doing best is Nothing."
>
> "How do you do Nothing?" asked Pooh, after he had wondered for a long time.
>
> "Well, it's when people call out at you just as you're going off to do it, What are you going to do, Christopher Robin, and you say, Oh, nothing, and then you go and do it."
>
> "Oh, I see," said Pooh.[14]

The capacity to *do* nothing, to fashion oneself not as actual or potential agency (which is what Rabbit is all about), but as something that does nothing, is here being unearthed through Milne's light touch, situating childhood experience neither as agency, nor, significantly, as "play";—the adult category that all too conveniently lumps together any disorganized, undefinable childhood state. It is this capacity to linger in and enjoy a non-structured experience that removes the child out of the reach of subjectivity's demands, aligning him with the undifferentiated, depersonalized world of non-agency. Milne's moving closure of the book promises that "wherever they go, and whatever happens to them on the way, in that enchanted place on the top of the Forest, a little boy and his Bear will always be playing," suggesting that such dimensions of experience are somehow not lost to an adult (Collodi ends *Pinocchio* with a similar implication: the puppet is allowed to remain near the newly formed child, who eyes it thoughtfully).

The ubiquity of the death theme in adult puppet theater notwithstanding,[15] the resistance to objects we are touching on here should not be assimilated into anxieties set off by acknowledging one's mortality. The trace of a life that was, a Yorick's skull, induces a significantly different response than the one occasioned by entities that have never lived.[16] The hollowness of puppets, a hollowness that, nevertheless, forms a substrate for a character, presents the audience with an artistic medium which, in its very form, mocks our recoil from the object within. Indeed, triggering and assuaging such resistance becomes an internal dimension of the language of puppetry through underscoring the object-character transition.[17] Memorable puppetry often involves the puppeteer abruptly leaving one puppet in order to operate another, but to return to the one that had been momentarily cast aside and deflated of stage life.

Puppets are objects fictionally and momentarily endowed with life. But they are objects only in the subversive sense of a term, undermining its own usage, since it is the very subject-object divide that puppets problematize. To be (a subject) is to undergo repeated acts of animation. The virtually universal association of puppet theater with a culturally low form of entertainment which befits children is linked with this evasion of a more fundamental insecurity that puppetry touches. It is as if puppets *must* be taken as nonserious theater.[18]

Pygmalion

By proposing a unique relationship with objects, puppetry redefines subjectivity: the self is not only its possibilities, but includes a repeated collapse into inner "thinghood." When Western imagination traveled down this particular path, it was haunted by a sense of its own perversion. Consider Ovid's *Pygmalion*. Ovid does not begin his tale with Pygmalion carving the would-be Galatea and then falling in love with her, but introduces a man who turns to celibacy due to his revulsion at the corruption he perceives in women. Ovid, then, lavishly describes Pygmalion's dawning eroticism through a blurring of boundaries between fetishism and love:

> Pygmalion looks in admiration and is inflamed with love for this semblance of a form. Often he lifts his hands to the work to try whether it be flesh or ivory; nor does he yet confess it to be ivory. He kisses it and thinks his kisses are returned. He speaks to it, grasps it and seems to feel his fingers sink into the limbs when he touches them; and then he fears lest he leave marks of bruises on them. Now he addresses it with fond words of love, now brings it gifts pleasing to girls, shells and smooth pebbles, little birds and many-hued flowers, and lilies and colored balls, with tears of the Heliades that drop down from the trees. He drapes its limbs also with robes, puts gemmed rings upon its fingers and a long necklace around its neck; pearls hang from the ears and chains adorn the breast. All these are beautiful; but not less beautiful is the statue unadorned. He lays it on a bed spread with coverlets of Tyrian hue, calls it the consort of his couch, and rests its reclining head upon soft, downy pillows, as if it could enjoy them.[19]

"Fetishism" fails to adequately capture Pygmalion's love. The logic of synecdoche does not really apply: nothing in the object *stands for* anything else. It seems to be itself loved, and not merely sexually.

The main thrust of this apparently quintessential story of solipsistic love—an externalization of a dumb ideal of chastity that comes nearest to what Pygmalion can bring himself to love—surfaces upon contemplating the ending of the tale. Ovid devotes no time to Galatea after she comes to life. The story is over by then. We merely hear that after she opens her eyes and looks at Pygmalion, they marry and have a son. Ovid tells us nothing about the woman that Galatea becomes. In effect, she remains a walking statue. The Pygmalion story thus pushes the fantasy of loving an object to its logical end: a desire that the object would come to life. At the same time, by rendering Galatea's interiority void—by omitting any description of love between the couple *after* she comes alive—Ovid, in effect, situates Galatea in-between inanimate and animate. She is more memorable due to "her" previous effect as an object adorned with the tears of the Heliades—

women who, incidentally, had themselves receded from the human into the vegetative—than in her later coming to life.

Disinterest in the emerging human is brilliantly built *into* Pygmalion's love. Note Pygmalion's specific prayer to the gods:

> Pygmalion, having brought his gift to the altar, stood and falteringly prayed: 'If ye, O gods, can give all things, I pray to have as wife---' he did not dare add 'my ivory maid,' but said, 'one like my ivory maid.'

What is it, specifically, that Pygmalion does not dare ask for? The answer seems easy. *He wants her to come alive*. However, such a reading is too smooth. Why wouldn't he "dare" ask for that? Why would such a wish seem impious or particularly infuriating to the gods? (It certainly does not affect the gods in such ways in this story). But the tale suggests a different reading of "dare." In Ovid's (possible) sources for the story, the statue does not come alive at all.[20] Ovid's addition of the statue's vivification to the story could be read not as the blissful fulfillment of an impossible wish, but as a perplexing case of a god *misreading* the human.

What Pygmalion does not dare ask for is divine validation of his love. He desires to marry the statue. He wants to live with her/it as man and wife; to push the boundaries of the social and theologically sanctioned institution of marriage, so that it would include more than a bonding between living human beings. What he craves is for some authority to make the unconceivable thinkable. "If you gods can give all things," he says—in effect challenging the gods to grant this impossibility. Yet he cannot bring himself to verbalize his wish, replacing it for another (note how the text indicates a substitution in the precise formulation of the wish: the sculptor does not dare say: "the ivory maiden," but rather "one *like* the ivory maid"). According to this reading, Pygmalion is *not* asking that she would come alive. The actual wish that he dares not put into his explicit prayer is different: he asks that she, as statue, would be his wife. Pygmalion, it seems, does not really want Galatea at all. He wants the ivory girl, the unmoving one; she whom he may dress and undress at will, adorn, compliment, shower with gifts. But he cannot bring himself to ask for that. He does not dare. What he can ask for (and only from a god) is that the sense of secrecy and perverseness would be lifted. Not "daring" to ask the gods for that, Pygmalion prays to have someone "like" her. The sculptor is granted his manifest wish: Galatea is *not* the ivory maiden—merely someone *like* her.

What we recall from Ovid's story is the metamorphosis of a beloved statue into a woman of flesh and blood, a move from perversity and solipsism into mutual love, as these are registered in the tactile shift from touching cold stone to kissing warm lips. We insist on remembering the story as a paradigmatic tale of wish-fulfillment: an insurmountable obstacle for consummating one's love is auspiciously lifted through the superior knowledge of a god. Until we return to the subversive text, to the way in which it tacitly posits a middle ground between fetishism and ordinary love, a love for stone that strives to be sanctioned and retained, not exchanged for flesh.

Fueling our resistance to endorse the text's undermining of the subject-object divide are deep-seated moral sentiments—the refusal to be objectified, instrumentalized, the wish to be acknowledged, known, reciprocated and so forth. But the text is rougher; and its outcome is not unequivocally happy. Why does Ovid rush to wrap up the story? Could it be that giving vent to an expression of regret on behalf of Pygmalion would be going too far? Could the story be a tragic one? A fall from the uniqueness Pygmalion seeks to preserve with stone into some unremarkable experience created by the limitations of a god's understanding, limitations that arise precisely because, unlike humans, gods are not themselves a mixture of inanimate matter and life, lacking an inner "objecthood" that their identity is in a dialogue with?

Ovid's story touches on the unintelligibility of loving an object. Pygmalion is easily interpreted as merely sexually responding to the statue. It is the *love* that is harder to fathom, the desire for a subject-object union and erotic bonding that is broader than sex. Pygmalion wants *the statue as a wife*. Marriage is thus dissociated from its financial or reproductive dimensions. It is this form of erotic union that Ovid invites his readers to imagine. Herein resides the genuine perversion of the story, when perversion is understood as a deviation from erotic relations based on reciprocal acknowledgment.[21]

The story of *Pygmalion* is haunting; it reaches out to a different relationship with objects and the object-within-another, a relationship which is concomitantly offered by puppets when they are presented as objects for identification, or dialogue, or compassion. Unlike living actors and our relation to their experience onstage—as characters, actors or both—the puppet remains an object in the audience's mind. Any invitation to partake of its experience is, to some slight degree, a luring of the audience into the position of a Pygmalion.

Reversed Puppetry

The story that comes closest to genuinely overturning the specific subject-object diffusion triggered by puppetry is the myth of Sisyphus. On first impression, the Sisyphus myth seems to have nothing to do with puppetry. Sisyphus and the rock both participate in an endless and futile process. One can imagine that after such a long time, a relationship forms between the two: Sisyphus must know every crack and knobby bump in his rock. His hands have been everywhere on it. He must talk to the rock on occasion, curse it, might even imagine that it is talking back to him. But this interaction with an object is still not puppetry. If anything, part of Sisyphus's punishment relates to his loneliness in the midst of an indifferent reality, one which will not be animated, one which enforces upon him not only the meaninglessness of his actions, but intensifies his suffering by dissociating him from any solace that another's presence could bring.

But now let us advance beyond these familiar impressions, focusing (as urged by Michel Serres) on the rock rather than on the human being punished. The rock is singled out by the myth: unlike all other rocks, it is the one Sisyphus pushes. Perhaps it is the only object that has been placed in an *eternal* relationship with a specific thinking entity. The rock forms part of the punishment. But it is also that which is most intimately close to Sisyphus: it is that which is pushed, handled, sweated, and breathed upon as Sisyphus pants his way up the hill. But it experiences none of these. At one point in his rounds, Sisyphus must access this essential truth regarding his part-scourge part-companion: the rock is that which cannot suffer. The proximity yet unbridgeable distance between his own torment and the rock exacerbates his pain: the entity closest to him does not partake of the strain and futility of the unending task. It is not even indifferent. The rock now becomes a source of envy too. In his craving to become an object like the rock, Sisyphus now embodies a reversal of Pinocchio's wish to be animated into a "real boy."

Here, it seems, lies a further facet of the punishment: the chasm between subject and object becoming a throbbing source of pain. If the subject-object border collapsed, if Sisyphus could become an object—say, a moving doll pushing a bolder—the spectacle would immediately cease to be a punishment, and would demote into a harmless mechanical show. This is why Camus is misreading the story when he says: "A face that toils so close to stones is already stone itself!" It is his *difference* from the rock that Sisyphus is made to be painfully and eternally conscious of. The punishment is centrally about the maximal reduction of the human to the world of senseless motions while forcing him to survive as an unerasable subject. Camus is interested in Sisyphus's return to the rock for another go: "It is during that return, that pause, that Sisyphus interests me."[22] Camus's disinterest in the ascent follows from his graver misreading of the myth: his seeing in the climb with the rock nothing more than a repetitive, futile action. But if we decline Camus's invitation and interest ourselves in the unending pushing of the bolder, we access the remarkable depth of this image and also the source of Camus's precise misreading.

Instilling into Sisyphus the desire to become an object so that the pain would vanish is a diabolically profound dimension of the punishment for his unique transgression: Sisyphus was not merely an informant against Zeus, but has also duped Death into shackling himself, thereby momentarily freeing fellow humans from dying. The man who tried to deceive death—the process by which subjects turn into objects—the man who presumed that he would never become an object, will crave becoming one. A punishment calculated to instill the advantage of being a non-experiencing object would ram down Sisyphus's throat an object's superiority over a subject. Here is one (still oblique) way in which the punishment is a form of reversed puppetry: celebrating the object's triumph over its user.

Sisyphus could have been forced to repeat some other action indefinitely—say, humming a particular tune eternally. But his punishment highlights *effort* and apparent *usage*. Note the difference between an eternity of hard labor and this, Sisyphus's particular punishment, in which a structural permutation of his experience as human is being effected. Use is the default relationship of humans with the nonhuman world. It is also a self-distinguishing feature: I use, therefore I am. A Kantian would summon an alternative phrasing: I am because I am not that which is merely used (not merely a means). Sisyphus's unique punishment is designed to dissociate industrious usage of the nonhuman from objectives. Sisyphus's action possesses a goal (carrying the stone to the top of the hill), but lacks a purpose, an object*ive*. But then: In what sense is the rock *used* when its user lacks an objective? What could the intention that underlies this particular usage be?

Here is what is at stake in responding to this last question: if the intention disappears, if it cannot be clearly articulated, the action no longer counts as usage; it is no more than a cluster of goal-oriented motions. A sharp Sisyphus—and Homer describes him as the craftiest of all men (*Iliad*, bk. 6)—will recognize that his usage of the rock differs from how fellow humans employ objects. *No human being pushes a rock the way he does.* Whereas for fellow humans use is woven into a fabric of intentions and a reorganization of reality, Sisyphus acts *like* a man handling an object. His effort is all too real, but his actions become quasi-actions. The dissociation from an objective has not merely rendered his actions meaningless—as Camus sees—but has turned his life into an eternal theater.

Acknowledging the theatrical dimension of Sisyphus's toil sharpens our sense of his particular sentence. Many punishments involve insulating the condemned. Yet his own sentence secludes Sisyphus from the imaginative pity of fellow humans. What they respond to in horror and dread—futile action—is *not* what he is undergoing. Futility is merely a condition, a first step after which other thoughts materialize and govern his experience. What Sisyphus is subjected to is an entire overhaul of his experience of using the world. Those who hear of his fate—compassionate readers like Camus—will be thinking of meaninglessness. But this is to misread him because futility is a predicate of actions, whereas Sisyphus is—for an eternity now—*no longer acting*. He merely moves in relation to objects. Aping action, he occasions the wrong kind of sympathy. He is not merely doomed to eternally push the rock but to be eternally pitied in the wrong way. Which leaves him alone. Truly alone.

Puppetry invites human beings to ponder over humanized objects. The puppeteer breathes life into inanimate material, rendering objects momentarily available to a rapport that ordinary life suppresses. Sisyphus, by contrast, is metamorphosed from an agent into an operator. He does not become an object any more than the puppet becomes human. But like the puppet, he is suspended midway between the animate and the inanimate. In puppetry, the puppeteer retains control over the puppet (the inversion of such relations mentioned earlier often underlies the wit characteristic of puppetry). Similarly, Sisyphus seems to maintain control over his rock. But because his volition has been preempted and because he no longer acts, his control boils down to nothing. He has no choice in the matter; his rock will be rolled by him. The rock thus becomes the closest object analogue to a puppeteer-object handling a human puppet.

Pygmalion provokes his author to impose a pacifying plot (Pygmalion wants a fellow subject) on a truly disturbing desire (Pygmalion pines for normative acceptance of his love for an object). Puppetry harmonizes with this tacit ideology: by celebrating objects but also jovially anthropomorphizing them, the animated object is still positioned at a point of inferiority in a human-centered continuum—objects would be human, if only they could. Sisyphus is situated at the opposite, less soothing, mythical pole: the reshuffling of the self when one's relationship with objects is reorganized. In puppetry the human being remains unchanged, whereas objects are reconstructed into pseudo-humans. Sisyphus, on the contrary, shows how leaving the object as is may augment the human. If objects could enjoy puppetry, *The Myth of Sisyphus* is the puppet show they would choose.

Puppetry and Acting

"What would you say is unique about the expressive range of puppets as distinct from actors?" I ask puppeteer Neville Tranter in a master-class.[23] "I will show you," he says, demonstrating a short scene in which he is withholding something from his puppet. The puppet's response takes a good twenty seconds: it slowly shifts from looking in amazement at Tranter, to a moving silent plea, to dropping its head in profound sadness. "You cannot do this as a human actor" he says, "it would seem contrived. Puppets enable slowing down emotion."

Slowing down emotion, breaking down emotional expression into discrete units, enables puppets to represent by capturing a fragment of a larger whole. Pygmalion, recall, does not relate to the statue as if it were human, but forms a relationship that mobilizes merely partial attributes of a living beloved. And it is precisely this partiality that he has to relinquish in the seemingly happy ending of the story. Such need for a fraction-attuned relationship accounts for our fascination with puppets and the incomplete characterization that they allow. The puppet's resistance to absorbing realistic projections, its dissimilarity from actors and the inner processes that the latter appear to disclose, transports it into the sphere of incomplete similitude. Here our predilection to favor mimetic acting—the kind of acting that would enable us to perceive characters as people—may obstruct our capacity to understand the specific language of fractional characterization captured by puppetry.

Puppets are by no means the only members of the community of fragments that populates art, literature, and theater (particularly stylized theater). Caricatures, allegorical figures, secondary characters, types, clowns, fools, nameless Vices and Everymans—a host of theatrical creations cannot be processed as fully rounded creations. Instead of humanizing them in performance and thereby resisting their originating context, one should, rather, embrace the invitation that they constitute on its own terms, making room for the need for partiality that they communicate with. "Art is subtraction," says H. C. Heffner in his introduction to a book that applies this proposition to puppetry, aligning puppets with a form of minimalist expression that avoids the richer mimesis that we have come to expect from theater.[24] That "caricature"—an entire language of art—is used as a derogatory term in criticizing faulty art, points to our current limitations in responding to modes of artistic creation which intentionally avoid holding up to nature a too accurate mirror.

But the puppet is not merely incomplete. Nor is it merely limited to a narrow range of gestures. Like Pygmalion's stony beloved, it announces vocally its own lack of an inner world. The debate surrounding conflicting schools of theatrical acting, contesting whether acting should express interiority or merely convincingly convey it, is hushed by the puppet's wooden inner life. The effect of this inner lack on its living spectatorship can be easily missed, even by discriminating enthusiasts:

> I always hold up the wooden actors as instructive object-lessons to our flesh-and-blood players. The wooden ones, though stiff and continually glaring at you with the same overcharged expression, yet move you as only the most experienced living actors can. What really affects us in the theatre is not the muscular activities of the performers, but the feelings they awaken in us by their aspect; for the imagination of the spectator plays a far greater part there than the exertions of the actors.[25]

Bernard Shaw's panegyric of puppets is distinct from others who have preferred puppets over actors—like Kleist or Craig—by associating the puppet's aesthetic effect with the stimulation of the spectator's imagination: the audience is compelled to fill in the details that turn the puppet into a character. Vivid examples of what Shaw describes do exist: a piece by Hugo Suarez ("Teatro Hugo and Ines") in which a performer turns his knee (embellished with a plastic red nose) into a highly expressive guitar player; Chaplin's metamorphosing of bread rolls and forks into a supercilious dancer in *The Gold Rush*—both exemplify Shaw's claims regarding the audience's "completion" of an entity's biography out of minute pieces. But what Shaw overlooks is the *particular* operation of the imagination in attributing expressivity to that which has nothing to express.

In contrast to Shaw's appraisal of actors as merely quantitatively inferior in expression vis-à-vis puppets, we can pinpoint a qualitative difference in the operations of thought and imagination that puppets release: the actor discloses an inner life which may or may not cohere with what is being projected; the puppet, by contrast, is internally empty and externally alive. The imagination, in this instance, does not merely fill out a missing picture (which is what Shaw sees), but orbits a recognition of a void shrouded by expression. To state the point differently, puppetry does not follow the logic of synecdoche: the action fragments being exhibited are unrelated to some "whole" that needs to be reconstructed. They move us powerfully, but not because our imagination turns them into full human beings but because they allow internal nothingness to peek through a piece of fervent life. My point in saying this is not to link puppetry with various rejections of the subject or deconstructions of a metaphysics of presence and siding with some metaphysics of playful signs.[26] It is, rather, to highlight puppetry's exhibition of the freedom of *partial* manifestation and what this means, its capacity to dissociate itself from an internal author, touching in us the unease that accompanies the perception of the growing autonomy of one's roles, their capacity to become self-sufficient, and to even usurp the self by determining its "identity" as "this or that."

What, finally, does puppetry tell us about the process of animation that all acting involves? Acting, I argued, is a form of existential growth, a route which enables increasing the possible manifestations that jointly constitute the self. Puppets, by contrast, do not formulate make-believe possibilities of self-amplification, but touch a facet of experience that is altogether disengaged from actual and potential agency. The animation they present involves a more evasive dimension of personal experience: the oscillation between object and subject; the animation involved in realizing any possibility as a subject; the manner whereby the seemingly genuine personal experience that acting is supposed to mimetically capture, itself involves a summoning into being of a subject. To animate, whether one animates a puppet or a role, thereby touches and reflects a dimension of identifying oneself with a subject. Acting is a gateway to living more, but overlaps with puppetry in also being a reified presentment of such identification.

Puppets display an activity that emanates from a nothing—the nothingness of an object—relentlessly surfacing in a puppet's performance, peeping from the cracks within its frantic doings. Yet, perhaps because they visibly reenact the process of animation through the imaginative partnership between the performer and the audience, perhaps, that is, because they are related to a collectively attained achievement orchestrated by the puppeteer, there is nothing lugubrious about watching puppets. They partake of comedy's ability to both touch and acknowledge a potentially anxiety-ridden dimension of subjective experience. Providing an external shape to the act of self-animation, the process whereby acts of "selfing" are repeatedly performed outside the theater, puppets are an offering of a truce—if not of compassion or even friendship—with the object within.

PART III

BETWEEN LIFE AND STAGE

We have so far explored processes in which "being in another way" through acting facilitates transcending the boundaries of one's identity in various ways. But there is an altogether different manner of becoming other through acting, in which identity is not momentarily abandoned, but is actually recreated through the acting process. Like stage-acting, one becomes other through a particular kind of performance. The difference is that instead of effecting a clear-cut transition into experiencing a fictional possibility as if it were one's own, this kind of performance shapes one's non-fictional identity. Such self-redefining existential amplification does not involve an entry into a *fictional* space upheld by the shared imaginative effort of a performer and a spectator, but genuinely becoming another through being in another way. Such reconfiguring of identity through acting comes in two forms. The first concerns performers: some acting genuinely augments one's own identity. The second relates to forms of self-theatricalization that are not conducted by performers, but nevertheless manifest a committed deployment of acting technique in a self-shaping process. This part of the book discusses the former; its next part explores the latter.

To consider the ways whereby acting may modify an actor's identity brings out the interface between acting and ethics. The long, now discredited, tradition in which such a linkage was insisted upon will be revealed as not utterly irrational. Ethics, a virtually non-existing feature of contemporary writing on acting, will be re-introduced into acting theory and the conceptual underpinnings through which an ethics of performance can be usefully understood will be proposed. The first chapter in this section presents such an attempt in relation to situations that give rise to ethical reservations in acting. The second chapter discusses self-determination through performance as part of pornography. Common to both chapters are the ways whereby roles enacted as part of an allegedly fictionalized performance cannot be insulated from who one believes one is.

UNETHICAL ACTS

> In a fundamental way theatre and prostitution are public and private versions of each other . . . if either profession were absolutely perfected, the other would vanish.
>
> RICHARD SCHECHNER[1]

> The extraordinary thing about acting is that life itself is actually used to create artistic results.
>
> LEE STRASBERG[2]

Jonas Barish's *The Antitheatrical Prejudice* is rightly considered a classic of modern scholarship. Carefully compiling the various strands of antitheatrical thought, Barish exposes and analyses its vicissitudes and implications. Caustic wit animates his evaluation of the literature produced by the "legions of hard-shelled, mole-eyed fanatics" who could find nothing of value and yet much danger in the theater: "an unmistakable crackpot streak runs through much of it," he observes—a remark that is exemplary of virtually all that is said about this grim literature.[3] But the consensual dismissal of anti-theatricality to which Barish's sense of humour appeals, also leads to an important crippling consequence; one that affects both contemporary acting and its theorization: due to the repetitious and religiously flat worldview underlying past denouncements on theater, an unappealing shadow threatens to swallow up anyone who wishes to subject contemporary acting to moral scrutiny. No one wants to be a Malvolio. Yet the introduction of moral dimensions and prescriptions into acting threatens to push the critic precisely into such a preachy stance.

Theater and acting no longer require an apologetics, and can now afford a less defensive reappraisal of past attacks. The repeated uneasiness with the theater—sometimes by minds whose sharpness in other matters cannot be ignored—contains a grain of truth that is still applicable today. Antitheatricalists have hoped that their moral critique would banish theater. Yet such is not the only option. I will argue that clarifying the moral undercurrents implicit in some performed acts provides the vocabulary needed for articulating an undertheorized source of personal complexity that acting sometimes involves. Such understanding need not demote acting's dignity, as enemies of the theater have argued. Paradoxically, it may even promote it. But for this to take place, acting as a practice must open itself to an evaluative prism that, up to now, it has largely ignored.

An Actor's Dilemma

Jim is an actor participating in a production of *Julius Caesar*. He plays Mark Antony. The scene he is presently rehearsing is Antony's discovery of the assassins standing over dead Caesar. Upon reaching the lines in which he expresses Antony's attachment to Caesar ("He was my friend, faithful and just to me . . .") Jim repeatedly experiences an inner deadness. He intuits implicit criticism from his colleagues, and his frustration is aggravated, since other actors he had watched before have performed this episode movingly. His frustration with the quality of his performance leads him to experiment with an acting technique called "emotional recall": he draws on an actual biographical memory that resembles the enacted episode—his witnessing the drowning of Steve, one of his best friends for many years. During rehearsal, Jim tries this out: as he looks at Caesar's body, he envisions the tragic moments in which Steve was dragged out of the water. He had planned to do this, so before the rehearsal he recalls the episode more leisurely: the time of the year, the clothes he was wearing when Steve died, the sights he saw just before the drowning, the smell of the air. Surely enough, as he talks about Caesar, Jim experiences authentic feelings of gnawing loss. His acting becomes mesmerizing, and he is enthusiastically applauded by his colleagues.

Jim is elated—but also disturbed. He feels that he has prostituted the memory of his friend for professional ends. The prospect of having to repeatedly draw on this memory in the numerous performances ahead dismays him. He worries that his pain over losing Steve would be blunted. His past anxiety over mechanical acting is superseded by a present fear of assuming a mechanical sense of self. "Would my cherished memories become reduced into items in a professional toolbox, to be picked, used and returned as the need arises?" he wonders. He is now convinced that, although no one noticed or was harmed by it, what he did during rehearsal was unethical.

Jim browses through his books on acting. He is familiar with the debate between acting as "presenting" as opposed to acting as "re-presenting"; between those who follow Diderot by stressing projection techniques, and those who demand that an inner state, approximating the one performed, be genuinely experienced; between defenders of "Method" and those who regard experience-based acting, even if momentarily successful, as unreliable. Jim is experienced enough to know that acting—even when considered by the staunchest defenders of inner-state arousal—is never reducible to a mere regurgitation of personal memories. Nevertheless, his dilemma strikes him as unrelated to the abstract debates within acting theory. He senses that after all is said and done, an effective performance of that particular scene requires more than his technique is able to deliver. Convinced that using the memory of Steve's death can make the difference between a merely successful professional performance and a profoundly touching one, Jim feels torn between the demands of his calling—the ethics implicit in his art—and his acute sense of debasing Steve's memory.

Acting and Being

The use of the term *prostitution* above is not accidental. Prostitution and acting have long been perceived as overlapping vocations by enemies of the theater.[4] Blatant versions of this claim have held that acting provokes licentiousness, or that brothels and theaters maintain implicit institutional connections.[5] At its more interesting moments, though, the interface between acting and prostitution drew on a psychology of acting: actors corrupt themselves by incarnating dubious identities. To act is to create a dangerous imaginative space in which actors and their audience are licensed to suspend expected moral responses. Actors practice and present an undesirable flexibility between identity and embodiment. They even intentionally select roles that enable them to realize secretly nurtured immoral inclinations that they cannot manifest in life.[6]

If one strips it off from the allusions to the devil through which the rhetoric of such accusations was often delivered, the argument is not insubstantial. Overestimating their capacity to dissociate their role-playing from their being—a contemporary version of the antitheatrical argument would read—actors traffic in elements of their own biographies for the sake of performance. Marlon Brando's description of being coerced into passionate kissing by an older actress exemplifies this morally dubious process:

> The play opened in New England with me playing Tallulah [Bankhead's] young lover . . . whenever I was onstage with her and the moment approached when I was supposed to kiss her, I couldn't bear it. For some reason, she had a cool mouth and her tongue was especially cold. Onstage, she was forever plunging it into my mouth without so much as a how-do-you-do. It was like an eel trying to slide backward into a hole. At first I was as casual as I could be under the circumstances and tried to avoid her tongue without offending her, thinking, How am I going to keep the part? Her tongue would explore every cranny in my mouth before forcing itself down my throat. I tried to back away coyly, pretending my character was bashful; then I began kissing her on the neck, trying to look appropriately romantic as the male ingénue. But she didn't like neck kisses and lowered her head and pursued my mouth with her lips. I tried eating a lot of garlic, but that didn't stop her, so I asked a stagehand to buy me a bottle of mouthwash, and after each time I had to kiss her I went offstage and took a swig . . . unfortunately, a spy informed her that I was gargling after kissing her . . . she told the producers I wasn't right for the part, and after about six weeks of out-of-town tryouts I was fired. . . .[7]

Behind the humorous language, Brando's anxiety over losing his job should he express his discomfort over being kissed in this manner (and the fact that this particular worry materialized) exemplifies how fictional role-playing may metamorphose into an excuse for sexual harassment. But the more interesting question relates to Brando's inability to perform kissing. Erotic acting is shown to bring out a genuine problem: what happens to kissing and embracing—a contemporary antitheatricalist would ask—once the usual meanings with which they are invested are withheld? Is such suspension always possible? Moreover, since Tallulah Bankhead was obviously genuinely kissing Brando, then, regardless of his own ability to infuse the kissing with meaning, to cooperate with her while aware of her own intentions, would, in itself, constitute willingness to be truly kissed. The performer, it seems, does not fully control the interpersonal meaning of his act.

A specific paradigm of embodiment is responsible for this clash between moral unease and artistic objectives in relation to erotic gestures in acting. The paradigm—introduced throughout modernity and rendered explicit by Julien Offray de la Mettrie—holds that the body is merely an elaborate machine, an organic robot that can be driven according to one's intentions. Contemporary actors have either inherited this paradigm or, when trained in more physically-oriented systems, limited the self-determining capacity of the body to a release of creative energy through somatic modifications.[8] Either way, identity-related implications of embodied acts are left unmentioned, so in practice the result is the same: actors are urged to deflate value-laden acts—kissing, embracing—into value-neutral bodily operations. The error entailed in this dismissal has recently become more obvious, given the thoroughgoing rethinking of such mechanization of the body: we are not as free to use our bodies as we thought.[9] Actors who believe that their physical actions are unrelated to their identities underestimate the body's substantial participation in self-shaping.

Besides the abuse of memories or of the interpersonal values touched upon by erotic acting, a performance may also solicit morally dubious uses of the imagination. Consider the following demand by a director:

> Jennifer recounted a rehearsal experience in which the director told her to use the image of her own mother "hanging from a noose in a corner of the theatre" as a means of achieving her character's emotional state. She found the personal image painful: "That image is in my mind forever. I cannot erase it. And [the director] gave it to me because I did not create that image on my own. He gave it to me."

The actress later characterizes this experience as "emotional prostitution" for which the director served as "pimp." She notes that she would now refuse to use such an acting technique. However, "at the time . . . he was the director, and I was young and inexperienced and . . . I did what he told me."[10] "Imaginative substitution" is the name of this particular technique. Unlike emotional recall or coercive passionate kissing, in Jennifer's case the term "prostitution" describes not a real event—the memory of a death, the performing of actual love gestures—but mere imaginings. Surprisingly, the summoning of unreal events nevertheless leads to a sense of remorse and injury. As in the previous two examples, the use of memories, gestures, or imaginings is *supposed* to be benign—it appears to have nothing to do with the performers' genuine relations to her mother or to who she herself is. Yet in all three examples, performers discover that such dissociation is either awkward or impossible to achieve.

Effect-Related Abuse and Essential Abuse

Character-identity percolation in the examples above gives rise to two questions that are broader than acting. The first is whether there are moral limits to professionalizing aspects of one's identity. The second concerns the meaning of "cheapening." The first question is not restricted to acting: many professions involve some flow between identity and professional persona. Even professions that do not ostensibly involve such permeation may, nevertheless, include the use of one's identity in potentially dubious ways. Consider the example of a factory worker who has tragically lost a child, and who, upon realizing that a cutback is looming, mentions his recent loss to his employer, hoping to be spared due to the sympathy he inevitably arouses. Or a salesman who takes a genuine interest in the welfare of his client's sick wife, deeply empathizing with the latter's plight—while also realizing that the expression of such concern strengthens their professional bond. Or the example of an attractive lawyer who consciously dresses differently when appearing in court, according to the gender of the judge. In all, the idea of a clearly circumscribed "professional" identity is a mirage. Such examples suggest that the significant question is not how to distinguish between professional and nonprofessional aspects of identity, but between benign and disturbing ways of gaining a professionally desired result when using one's nonprofessional identity.

Two considerations substantiate a distinction between permissible and potentially unethical deployments of identity in the context of professional work: the first relates to potential harm to others by the agent (to colleagues or to the practice as such)—the second, to harm inflicted on the agent through the act. Harming others or "the profession" involves unfairness and an undermining of constitutive values of the practice. It is, therefore, largely unrelated to acting and will not be discussed here.[11] Harm to the self, on the other hand, relates precisely to the issues that are relevant for actors. A vague sense of inappropriateness arises from the examples above. One's tragedy or looks should not be manipulated for professional use. But why not?

It is here that we are faced with the second question, relating to "cheapening." Cheapening—either in relation to memories or to the use of professionally irrelevant aspects of one's identity—can be broken down into *effect-related* abuse and *essential* abuse. *Effect-related* abuse means that the use of one's looks, one's personal grief or one's empathy for another's plight entails the disruption of one's experience in a nonprofessional context: one's grief will be blunted (such was Jim's fear); one's experience of attracting a lover, or one's experience of being found attractive will be marred. *Essential* abuse consists of a sense of undermining values regardless of possible long-term harm. When considering effect-related abuse, virtually everything revolves around subjective sensitivities: if an individual is capable of exploiting his or her tragedy to gain a professional advantage while relating to it deeply in one's personal life, no moral claim can be made against such use. The single exception—which should not be overlooked—is that one cannot always be sure what the actual effect of such acting on one's experience would ultimately be. The implication for acting is that, say, Helen's drawing on her actual experience of being raped to lend verisimilitude to her performance of Lavinia, can be benign the first times she performs in *Titus Andronicus*, but may progress into an overwhelming personal crisis later. Actors possess only partial control over long-term psychological effects when opting to recycle charged memories for such purposes.

Essential abuse, by contrast, includes a dimension of evaluation that is determined by more than mere subjective sensitivities. It may be that it is wrong for Jim to use his memory of Steve's death regardless of any erosion of his grief. Here is a proposal regarding why this may be so.

Withdrawal from Care

In his *Ethics of Memory*, Avishai Margalit draws on a familiar distinction between "morality" and "ethics" in order to bring together memory, ethics and care. "Morality" concerns general relations to fellow human beings ("thin relations"), whereas "ethics" encompasses ties to individuals with whom we entertain special ("thick") relations: siblings, colleagues, lovers, parents, friends. Memory failures of a certain class pertain to thick relations; they are ethical rather than moral shortcomings. Margalit then claims that a failure to remember manifests an ethical failure to care.[12]

What Margalit has in mind is not forgetting the person as such, but forgetting something essential about him or her. His main example is an outrage aroused by a colonel who could not recall the name of a soldier who died under his command. To lose possession of such a detail was publicly censured as obtuse indifference—a failure to care.[13] While Margalit does not discuss the kind of abuses of memory that acting involves, the connection he establishes between an ethical failure and a withdrawal from caring can, nevertheless, be extended to include these: Jim's use of Steve's death is not a form of forgetting; it can, however, be perceived as symptomatic of a failure in caring. A similar withdrawal from care holds when actors visualize relatives in degrading, tragic, or horrifying circumstances, such as Jennifer's imagining her mother "hanging from a noose." Thick relations involve care, and some mental or embodied imaginings are unethical because they constitute a withdrawal from care.

Care ethicists provide three different accounts of care: emotional, practice-oriented, and moral. The first emphasizes the affective or psychological state of the carer. The second regards caring as an ongoing activity, much like a work one is obliged to perform. The third attempts to identify care with a virtue.[14] All three share the idea that caring bestows partiality to particular individuals. Depending on the theorist, partiality of this kind may combine a response to needs (rather than merely concern); a non-judgmental acceptance of the individual cared for; a willingness to be changed by the other; an active identification with another's goals—"active" in the sense of attempting to promote these—along with an emotional response to the fulfilment or thwarting of such goals. Empathy (feeling another's pain) and/or sympathy (feeling *for* another's pain, without actually experiencing it) can also be aspects of care. For theorists who regard care as activity or work, caring relationships are not simply emotional givens, but require sustaining and recurrent enactment through multiple performances. As a result of these acts (or *through* such acts) the emotional dimensions of caring relations are established.

Judged from this perspective, an actor's performance may constitute a receding from care (an "essential abuse") in three different ways. Firstly, caring relations involve an awareness of their fragility, and such awareness restricts what may or may not be performed or thought. Embodied imaginative acts can be powerful and unpredictable. Regardless of one's intentions, they may progressively erode caring. The exacerbation of this risk issues from the particular requirement—at least in the theater—to repeat such enactments over and over again. To embody such acts is to take caring for granted: to be *careless* when caution is called for. Even if one's caring will not actually change, by imagining some possibilities one is nevertheless *willing to risk care*, itself a manifestation of uncaring. Genuine attachment—the argument will go—will avoid playing risky imaginative games with one's most significant sentiments. Secondly, the imagined content itself undercuts care because *it involves a mental devaluation or a mental disidentification*: the imagined scenarios either involve an embodied identification with a state that itself manifests uncaring (for instance, embodying a character who is attracted to someone who is not the actor's own lover), or imagining tragic scenarios (Jennifer) or real tragedies (Jim) in order to generate horror or grief for the purpose of art. Caring seems to posit that specific states are of such momentous personal significance that they will either be altogether suppressed (since they are so personally horrifying), or will only be contemplated with genuine terror. Only a withdrawal from care—a momentary devaluation of some states that should not be devalued, a stepping out of identification that should not be suspended in such a way—would enable the metamorphosis of potentially life-defining events into tools. Thirdly, care seems to demand exclusiveness. Consider the following comment in a romantic advice web-page posted by a frustrated husband of an actress:

> It's really hard to be the spouse of an actor/actress, and it's never as easy as clichéd phrases like: "she's going home with you," or "it's just acting." People saying that have never really felt what it's like to be the spouse of an actor/actress. My wife recently took a lead role in a play that requires her to be naked (full frontal nudity) on stage for about 5–7 minutes with another man who is also fully naked. I am completely uncomfortable with this, but she feels that this opportunity is just too important to pass up. It gives her the opportunity to work with the best director in town at the best theatre in a controversial show, so it will get a lot of press and attention. She believes this will be a springboard to her career. I will never stand in her way and hinder her career, but I am so angry, hurt, depressed, etc. Hundreds of people are going to see my wife naked. That is something that I value very highly. It is so special and private to me. Her nudity is something that I alone get to enjoy as her husband. No more. She sees it as just acting and not a big deal. It's just skin she would say. It's not to me. It's intimacy. I feel betrayed, embarrassed, emasculated. I can hardly sleep,

> am struggling with anxiety, etc. I HATE that people I know, actor friends of hers that I have met, etc. are going to see my wife naked. It is a horrible horrible feeling.[15]

Role-identity slippage in stripping has been discussed by theatre theorists before.[16] What has not been emphasized enough is how the implication of the actor in the character's doings may compromise a delicate ethical network that concerns more than the actor's own moral decisions and intuitions. The particular complaint above relates to the husband's sense of his wife's breach of intimacy: something that should remain a private dimension of his marriage is rendered public; his wife's nudity should be reserved for their relationship—not displayed in some indiscriminate way before strangers. Her attempt to trivialize the act ("It's just skin") debases, in his eyes, the complex meaning of such a gesture and its implication for both of them.

In all three ways—manifesting carelessness, devaluation or ignoring implicit assumptions regarding exclusiveness—acting may constitute a withdrawal from care, not merely an emotionally charged demand from individuals to reorganize who they are. Later in this book, we shall pursue the opposite side of this, the manner whereby role-playing can *establish* care precisely through reversing this process: creating intimacy rather than endangering it by singling out a partner for exclusive interaction. But it is the *danger* of such withdrawal from care that we are discussing now, and it is aggravated when directors, acting teachers, and influential instructors present such receding as a benign feature of the artist's professional vocation—a mark of professional dedication. Here is a version of how such a morally loaded process is deflated into a matter of "professionalism" with a pacifying joke thrown in. It features in Michael Caine's book on film acting, in a passage devoted to acting love scenes:

> I find the way to deal with love scenes is to be extremely professional about the whole thing: this is a job, this is what the two of us happen to have been asked to do—lie in bed naked—and it doesn't matter that we have never met before. . . . And then there is the problem for the actress; she has to get herself into a frame of mind where she'd be able to let a strange man stroke her bum. But it's all just part of the job, and none of us can afford to be coy about it. . . .[17]

Caine ends the passage with a joke:

> But what makes me laugh is that the only time a director ever demonstrates things to you is in love scenes! Suddenly he feels the need to show you exactly *how* to hold the actress.

In the context of the discussion above, the joke is less funny. It seems to be part of a vocabulary that professionals learn to depend upon as a means for neutralizing disturbing thoughts. Such thoughts concern not only what they do, but also what they allow others to do. Moreover, like other examples we have considered, such permission is usually granted within the context of asymmetrical power relations.

Ethical Acting?

Three responses to the problem merit discussion. The first (which will be taken up in this section) advocates replacing identity-based acting techniques with other means. The second and third responses (to be addressed in the next section), both accept the unethical nature of some aspects of acting, but then part company: the second holds that potentially unethical acting should, nevertheless, take place because the artistic payoffs for actors are more important than compromising moral values. The third regards the unethical nature of some acting methods as inherent to acting as such, but avoids drawing practical implications from this realization.

The first option—criticizing techniques that rely on autobiographical material and advocating the adoption of other devices instead—is superficial. Even if the problem were limited to experience-based acting it would be substantial: Method-based actor preparation remains the most dominant form of actor training.[18] More importantly, self-implicating acting is not a problem only of schools that emphasize undergoing experiences. Roughly fifty years before Stanislavsky began publishing, François Talma disclosed the following:

> I scarcely know how to confess that, in my own person, in any circumstance of my life in which I experienced deep sorrow, the passion of the theatre was so strong in me that, although oppressed with real sorrow, and disregarding the tears I shed, I made, in spite of myself, a rapid and fugitive observation on the alternation of my voice, and on a certain spasmodic vibration which it contracted as I wept; and, I say it, not without some shame, I even thought

> of making use of this on stage, and, indeed, this experiment on myself has often been of service to me.[19]

Talma describes a form of subordination of self to art: the actor is tempted to relate to his life as material for study, the lessons of which are filed for future deployment. Talma finds shameful some of his own professional inquisitiveness into the externalization of his real emotions. Actors who are keen to merely project may thus discover that their training and vocation modify their lived experience.

We saw that erotic acting—embracing, kissing, sexual caressing, naked intimacy, mimicking intercourse—is another area that challenges the ability to insulate role from identity (regardless of actually experiencing anything). Perceptible in the husband's complaint entry above is not his anxiety over his wife's inner experience, but over the role-identity collapse that evolves from his own interpretation of her actions. If *he* experiences her nakedness as betrayal (he may rationalize that it is not, but nevertheless intuit it as such), then by persisting in exposing herself to the public view, she offends him. On some level she betrays him. Identity can be altered by one's performance, with or without the performer's psychological participation in the performed material (pornography—to be discussed in the next chapter—is obviously the most extreme version of such a collapse of what one performs as character into what one actually does as person, again, regardless of inner experience).

Self-implication through performance independently of inner state can take many other shapes: ingesting foods that violate one's religious or moral convictions, being asked to perform acts that one deems immoral (an actor friend of mine participated in a play in which he had to kill a hen in each performance—to which he did not object, though another might); humiliating or being physically humiliated by another character (for instance, Malcolm McDowell's licking another character's shoe in *Clockwork Orange*)—all exemplify a sense of self-tainting that can arise regardless of inner experience. Suffering from violence is another example. Actress Maya Maoz resigned from a (1998) Haifa Theatre production of *Othello* after repeatedly feeling subjected to genuine violence by Juliano Mer-Khamis, an overly enthusiastic Othello. Long before he was famous, Charlie Chaplin underwent the following ordeal on stage, playing opposite the (then) far more established Harry Weldon:

> Weldon's comedy character was of the cretinous type, a slow-speaking Lancashire boob. That went very well in the north of England, but in the south he was not too well received. . . . [D]uring these weeks he was irritable and performed perfunctorily and took his spleen out on me. In the show he had to slap and knock me about quite a bit. This was called "taking the nap," that is, he would pretend to hit me in the face, but someone would slap his hands in the wings to give it a realistic effect. Sometimes he really slapped me, and unnecessarily hard, provoked, I think, by jealousy. In Belfast the situation came to a head. The critics had given Weldon a dreadful panning but had praised my performance. This was intolerable to Weldon, so that night on the stage he let me have a good one which took all the comedy out of me and made my nose bleed.[20]

Intriguingly, the same performed actions could be construed as accidents—say, if Weldon unintentionally hurt Chaplin—or as genuine interpersonal violence: Chaplin's actual apprehension of Weldon's slap. The point is that regardless of experience, and even if a performer wishes to merely project, he or she may, nevertheless, be unable to circumscribe the potentially hurtful act to the embodied fictional character.

Role-biography percolation without inner identification with the role can also surface when enacting characters that enforce stereotypes the actor finds morally objectionable. Feminist approaches to acting encourage ideological reservations relating to embodying feminine characters in patriarchal literature: enacting these may be perceived or be internally experienced as an implicit cooperation with a scheme one wishes to overthrow—again, regardless of whether the actress undergoes or not the enacted experience.[21] Sometimes such critique has singled out Method technique as a particularly insidious ideological tool through which performers are interpolated, holding that Method techniques coerce actresses into inhabiting an inner experience of oppression and that, by contrast, more subversive acting techniques (such as Brecht's alienation effects) are capable of inserting a wedge between the experience displayed and the actress's politically informed commentary.[22] But the problem runs deeper and does not disappear if an actress shuns experience-based techniques: an actress cast to play a sexy ingénue may feel that an acting choice that projects disidentification with the objectionable role (a choice that she may oppose on aesthetic grounds as well) does not really appease her ideological reservations. She may even feel that such a choice exacerbates her misgivings: instead of acting, her performance is reduced to mimicking and parodying, or to an oversimplified for/against ideological stance.[23] Similar scruples can be formulated in other ideological contexts as well. A Jewish actor may resent playing Shylock, believing that even under the most charitable interpretation the play still enforces anti-Semitic stereotypes. "Being called a nigger in a play is still being called a nigger," writes Afro-American actor David Wiles, describing his difficulties in performing a racially humiliated black character.[24] Required to express shame when his character was addressed as "boy," Wiles found that he resisted expressing shame when performing for a white audience. Again, experiencing (or not) racial shame was not the issue for Wiles—projecting shame of one's race before whites, was: he sensed it as corroborating and reenacting an ideology that he opposed.

Wiles's experience is related not only to ideology, but also to his role triggering a painful *collective* memory. Ideological reservations per se (such as a refusal to kill a hen on stage) need not relate to being choreographed into an edgy brush against one's collective history, and the actor's possible obligations to others. Eric Bentley reports of a Jewish actor "who stripped in *Fortune and Men's Eyes* in London," and told him that "he hated it because it made him think of Auschwitz."[25] Bentley does not analyse the anecdote, but it is revealing. Stripping off his clothes before non-Jews (in *men's eyes*), brought up an association of trauma and humiliation. It did not elicit this because the part required the summoning of such experience, but because the performance—exposing a circumcised penis in front of a non-Jewish audience—placed the performer in a traumatic relationship vis-à-vis his collective past. One wonders whether Juliano Mer-Khamis's excessive violence to Maya Maoz in the *Othello* production described above was somehow related to the experience of an Arab actor performing as a moor attached to a Desdemona played by a Jewish-Israeli actress before a Jewish-Israeli audience. To consciously perform in a way that manifests hyper-conformity to the stereotype associating Arabs with unbridled violence is an implicit means of acting against this stereotype. Such, at least, is one way of understanding Mer-Khamis's choice. If it was not deliberate, but rather a genuine inability to control his violence, such behaviour could arise from his being thrown into such a complex institutional, aesthetic, and autobiographical matrix.

These examples support the contemporary version of the traditional anti-theatricalist hostility to embodying nonbelievers, villains, and other sinners: the belief that acting based on mere projection—rather than on inner experience—can succeed in keeping identity and performance separate, underestimates the potential of bodily acts and their interaction with verbal ones to determine selfhood. As Bruce Wilshire claims, by being related to the world of the audience but by also participating in the staged fictional events, the actor is a citizen of two worlds, standing in for the audience in the fictional domain.[26] Theater is thus able to play upon and comically exploit such dual citizenship (for example, when in *Twelfth Night* Olivia demands to know whether Viola is a comedian, an "accusation" that the latter emphatically denies). But, as the examples above show, twin citizenship may also evolve into an experience of betrayal. Actors are trained (perhaps too well) to avoid the opposite kind of betrayal: being too faithful to their own personality, and thereby being unfaithful to the enacted persona. The cases examined above show that it is possible to gravitate towards the opposite problematic pole: fictionality may draw the performer out of forms of biographical identification that cannot be easily reassumed. Wilshire's metaphor of citizenship is important in this context, since citizenship does not necessarily rely upon a strong inner experience of belonging, and may, nevertheless, be felt to be personally binding.

The moral underpinning of the process noted in the above examples is the following: self-shaping in acting can arise through withdrawal from care. An ideologically-committed actor for whom racial, gendered, or religious discrimination is related to suffering and pain, tightly bonds with a shared community. The examples above show that such bonding may surface involuntarily also in actors who are not self-consciously ideologically committed. To momentarily suspend one's convictions in order to portray the opposite ideology is experienced as a withdrawal from care for fellow blacks, fellow women, fellow Jews. If an actress is willing to enact what she considers to be an ideologically regressive role, she may sense that she reveals a lack of commitment; she introduces inappropriate playfulness into sentiments and beliefs that should not be downplayed. She does not sufficiently care for the cause, or for the fact that others who share her ideological convictions would not allow such playfulness permeate their own embodied acts.[27] To conclude: in too many domains of acting, projecting—with or without inner experience—spills onto identity through the liability of a performed act to constitute a withdrawal from care.

Unethical Acting?

The second option is to accept the unethical nature of some forms of acting, holding that aesthetic values are more important than moral ones. Nietzsche is sometimes interpreted as urging such a categorical subordination of existence to aesthetic ideals; an actor may likewise explain away ethical scruples by subscribing to a higher, more binding fidelity to art.

The problem with this solution is that what appears to be a personal decision is too often a complex intersubjective act that concerns one's audience and its own values as well. In *Rumstick Road*, a Wooster Group production in 1978, Spalding Gray was performing as himself in a play dealing with his mother's suicide. The performance included playing recorded conversations between Gray's mother and her therapist. A member of the audience wrote a complaint letter, claiming that he felt "cheapened" and "brutalized" by becoming part of a violation of a stranger's privacy.[28] The point is not whether or not Gray should have respected his audience's reservations, but that the decision to allow aesthetic values to trump moral ones does not concern only the performer. Precisely because spectatorship is not passive reception but a form of participation and validation of a creative offering, to suspend moral values or to subordinate them to aesthetic ones is to make a decision for the audience. One may accept such aggression on the part of the artist, or argue for the necessity to allow art margins for such aggression—under the view that art is supposed to sometimes undermine complacency rather than cater to it. But the point here is not whether or not such aggression should be accepted, but to recognize it as such: decisions of this kind are invasive.

In *Rumstick Road*, the audience is conscious of the living content it is invited to enjoy. But the aggressive nature of such choices by a performer does not depend upon the audience's awareness. The following example suggests that when it is clandestine, such aggression may even be aggravated:

> The actress Vera Vasilyeva could not bring herself to cry on stage. She accordingly began recalling the death of her mother when she was supposed to cry, and the tears dropped naturally.[29]

By concealing from her audience the psychological mechanisms that enable her successful performance, Vasilyeva makes them consume a spectacle which, if fully understood, might have been avoided by them. The hypothetical nature of the audience's reservation does not annul the dubious status of the act; if anything, an added dimension of dishonesty—missing from the blatant aggression involved in *Rumstick Road*—infuses this example. Once again, the important point is that the decision of an actress to prioritize aesthetic over ethical values is not always hers to make, since it does not concern her alone.

The same holds for ideologically problematic acting, such as the cases mentioned above. Incarnating Jewish characters in plays that are deeply anti-Semitic can offend a Jewish audience. By attending the play, such an audience is implicitly required to suspend or subordinate ethical values to aesthetic ones (the heated public debates over performing Wagner in Israel exemplify this issue in a parallel context; the disappearance of *The Merchant of Venice* from the postwar German stage constitutes another example that may relate to sensitivity regarding the ethics of spectatorship). Audience members who did not fully take in a play's anti-Semitism and discover it during the performance may feel coerced into choosing between leaving the performance they have paid to watch, or staying and thus implicitly accepting, by their mere attendance, the packaging of such material as art. The Wagner debate in Israel shows even more: how people can be offended by merely allowing a particular work of art to be presented as such, without even being its direct audience.

A performer can obviously decide to ignore the values of her audience. But such a choice differs from simplistically thinking that her choices concern only her own values, or even only the values of those who are watching her. Aesthetic consumption is not value-neutral, and acknowledging this should inform the ethics of aesthetic production.

Acting as Prostitution

A third option is not to focus on the practical question raised by the above analysis—that is, whether or not using some acting techniques should be discontinued—but rather to perceive the overlapping of acting with the unethical not merely as a problem, but as illuminating the unique nature of acting. The implications resulting from this awareness would relate to perception, understanding, preparation, training and a fuller intake of what some performances demand.

Suppose that one accepts the idea—relentlessly advanced by the opponents of acting—that acting *is* deeply related to prostitution. Such an admission obviously need not be grounded on the reasons given in the past for this identification; it can stem from the willingness—shared by actors and prostitutes alike—to suspend the connection between performed acts and held values for the sake of some other desired end, be it money, or art. Yet rather than occlude this overlap, actors should come to terms with the flow from acting to the unethical as a movement intrinsic to and even solicited by their art. The point, it should be clearly stated, is not to squarely equate acting with prostitution: anyone with some familiarity of field work on prostitutes would be alert to the radically different backgrounds, goals, aspirations, and the nature of the actual work that separates them from actors—a full-fledged identification between them is not only theoretically hyperbolic but is also heartless. At the same time, while the ethical dissonance effected by some contexts of acting is certainly mild when compared with the emotionally deadening violence inherent to many forms of prostitution, to suggest an overlap is not to argue for identity.

The acting/prostitution overlap suggests itself, because, for those who oppose it, prostitution is the giving over of that which should not be given over. It is the act whereby intimate gestures are artificially dissociated from inner meaning and care. Such a process shares the invitation of acting to effect a momentary receding from commitments and values with which the performing body is ordinarily associated. As Lee Strasberg's remark—quoted in the epigraph to this chapter—asserts, the "extraordinary" thing about acting is that life itself is actually used to generate artistic results. Extraordinary, no doubt; but this also suggests that acting implies a willingness to turn one's life and one's structure of caring into creative material. In the manner of the prostitute, the actor disengages this "material" from the values with which it is usually infused, exchanging them for values of a different kind. For the courtesan, such values are economic, for the actor—aesthetic. In both practices, a deep substitution takes place. The unsmooth nature of such substitution may explain why theater visionaries such as Kleist, Craig, or Shaw have repeatedly dreamed of replacing actors with marionettes: advocating an ideal of acting in which the actor's inner attachments pose no resistance at all, they dreamed of a limitlessly pliable actor who would merge in a frictionless way with the role. We are now positioned to sense the aggression implicit in this ideal: gestures devoid of expected inner meanings are precisely what one recoils from in prostitution.

What follows from admitting such overlap between acting and prostitution? For traditional antitheatrical thinking the answer is easy: to perceive similarity between acting and prostitution is tantamount to claiming that acting should be avoided by decent individuals. Yet contemporary defences of sex work invite pausing before committing to this final verdict. Such defences enable the recognition of a similarity between acting and prostitution *without* automatically turning this into a ground for accusation, but into a reason for concern—one that needs to be unpacked into detailed practical proposals. Vindicators of sex work try to dissociate the secondary harms typically involved in prostitution—substance abuse, violence, exploitation, risk, health hazards, social opprobrium, the disempowerment that prostitution creates and relies upon—from the commodification of the body as such.[30] They argue that, when compared with other forms of unappealing, even nauseating, jobs that no one considers criminalizing, it becomes evident that what underlies the singling out of prostitution for special treatment are only retrograde, ultimately indefensible, typically patriarchal assumptions regarding sexuality as some privileged core of the self, and that once sexuality is not granted such sacred status, transacting in sex need not be perceived as involving a profound violation of the person. To use this for our concerns: nothing follows from exposing an overlap between acting and prostitution, since it is unclear whether and how such overlap even constitutes an accusation. Indeed, if the label "prostitution" amounted to an immediate accusation, it would be strange why defenders of the theater, and not just its enemies, have repeatedly invoked the similarity between acting and prostitution.[31]

And yet, to present prostitution as a profession like all others risks adopting the same mechanical picture of embodied experience encountered above, for which the connections between values and embodiment are regarded as fully controllable. The prostitute—the argument suggests—can be a loving wife, leave for a "shift" in which she has merely professional sex with five or six clients, return home to her husband, and enjoy loving sex with him later. To dismiss such a scenario as implausible is to sense that the connection between embodied acts and values such as intimacy or pleasure are not as open to inventive recreation as the defender of prostitution may suppose; links of this kind are less flexible and—rightly or wrongly—are typically associated with exclusivity. What is far more likely is that a person who works as a prostitute will be unable to maintain a loving relationship. Her work is no ordinary labour. It is a practice that inserts a wedge between her body and her values.[32] Likewise in the context of acting, to perceive the actor as someone who is entirely free to recreate the relations between experiences, embodied acts and identity may involve a similar simplification of the meaning of embodied acts—an overestimation of the mind's capacity to determine experiences.

Yet a tough ideal is not an unattainable one. Who is to say that the loosening of connections between performed acts and ideals, even if it presents a formidable challenge, cannot be ultimately achieved through a psychologically attuned, morally-sensitive process? One may well imagine that a committed actor would (or even should) be able to perceive a high degree of disembodiment as an artistic challenge. Such a "total" actor will overcome the limits posed by conventions that place some gestures outside the pale of acting: consider scenes such as Paul Dawson ejaculating into his own mouth in the film *Shortbus*, or the performance of unsimulated sex scenes in films such as *Intimité*.[33] Indeed, some highly demanding schools of actor training aspire precisely to fostering such totality; extricating acts from values becomes part of an attempt to undermine the actor's identity. Field work conducted by Sabina Krüger on the Catalan group La Fura dels Baus describes disturbing exercises that appear to be intentionally calculated to break the limits that define the performers' own identities.[34] Books for actors repeatedly express fidelity to the ideal of personal remaking, devising drills that can help the initiate achieve such rebirth.[35]

Regardless of the moral or aesthetic desirability of this ideal, it is doubtful whether it can be fully realized. Disengaging acts from the meanings with which they are usually associated is not always achievable by an act of thought or through prolonged practice. This holds true even for highly trained performers who consciously endorse such far-reaching ideals, and who are willing to experiment in unorthodox ways with their performing bodies. Richard Schechner's *Dionysus in 69* involved scenes in which experienced performers, who were supposed to be psychologically prepared for avant-garde theatrical work, caressed audience members and invited them to caress them in turn. The scenes had to be dropped since, according to Schechner, the touching got "heavy" and the actresses "felt used, prostituted."[36] Krüger describes an improvisation in which performers were treated as dogs. In that particular exercise, the participants ended up in tears.

What follows from such pain? On the most abstract level: nothing. For the enthusiast it merely suggests that a committed and taxing form of self-remaking is occurring. But the existence of such pain and the possibility that victimization rather than liberation is taking place, introduces a range of ethical concerns that should be explicitly addressed by whoever undertakes to subject people to such methods. Who is in charge of performing such identity modifications on others? How is the process controlled? When should it be stopped? How and in what way does the actor fully and knowledgably consent to such self-recreation? Which mechanisms preserve a would-be performer's right to dissent while undergoing a training in which unreserved consent is being upheld as artistically desired? If acting's overlap with prostitution is accepted while, simultaneously, one resists the idea that this overlap amounts to an automatic accusation, such questions need to be addressed (theoretically, institutionally, legally, and individually).

Nothing in the above analysis precludes the possibility that an actor develop total flexibility, one in which bodily and imaginative acts of whichever kind could be freely dissociated from identity and given over to the role. In much the same way, nothing bars the possibility of a non-damaging form of prostitution, in which the body's sexual use is dissociated from inner meanings in a manner that is not personally crippling (sexual surrogates may exemplify such ability). But in both cases, a hypothetical postulation should not be confused with the reality of the psychological makeup of the individuals one is likely to encounter. As long as complete personal recreation is not commonly reached (and I have expressed skepticism regarding this possibility), both performers and their teachers should clarify the moral stakes involved in acting—*not* occlude them. That way, the process of negotiating boundaries and legitimizing them (rather than misconstruing them for uncommitted acting) can be authentically and reflectively undertaken.

Implications

In 2004, the United States Court of Appeals for the Tenth Circuit discussed the case of Christina Axson-Flynn, a Mormon acting student who withdrew from an actor training program at the University of Utah because she would not curse or invoke God's name in vain. A promising actress who had received consistently high grades, Axson-Flynn was, nevertheless, repeatedly pressured to compromise her values. In a meeting initiated by three of her instructors, she was told that she can: "Choose to continue in the program if you modify your values. If you don't, you can leave. That's your choice." She left. She then sued the University of Utah for violating her freedom of speech and free exercise of religion rights under the First Amendment. The district court dismissed both charges. The court of appeals overturned this decision, ruling in her favor.[37]

The case above offers a rare glimpse into the coercive treatment of moral reservations within an acting program, not by a single instructor, and in full support of the program coordinator. The careless way in which Axson-Flynn's reservations were addressed by her teachers also attests to their own simplification of the fraught relations between acting and identity. It evidences their own lack of preparation to handle a rare case of this kind—they probably expected her to grow out of her reservations once her commitment to her art deepened. Axson-Flynn's case also suggests that the acting profession misses gifted talents through self-selection: individuals possessing a stronger sense of moral limits, and who are less optimistic than Axson-Flynn regarding having their values respected, will prudently avoid acting.

Axson-Flynn's awareness that lending one's voice to a script is not always morally benign has been articulated before; but only in the literature which theorists like Barish have taught us to ridicule. In traditional antitheatrical thinking, the danger of committing heresy by appealing to the wrong gods through the words delivered by the actor was highlighted as a genuine threat.[38] This is why dramatic texts involving potential heresy were sometimes written in a way that preserved the actor from damnation. Marlowe's *Dr. Faustus* exemplifies this: many of Faustus's lines are written in the third person; the scripted text thus avoids the very real threat of self-damnation for an Elizabethan actor, who is called upon to invoke Satan or to bargain away his soul.[39]

Marlowe was a very daring author. He did not flinch from touching explosive themes, such as homoeroticism, religious hypocrisy, and class mobility. Marlowe was not a prude. He was, nevertheless, sensitive to the moral and theological dimensions of the identity of those performing his plays, and wrote in a way that respected their limits. Regrettably, such sensitivity seems to have disappeared. Ethical dimensions of acting and actor-training are never—as far as my reading or my own (limited) participation in actor-training programs reveals—explicitly addressed.[40] Pronouncements regarding the need to manage some exercises "carefully" are made; "responsible" directors and acting teachers are advised to help the actor cope with the emotionally overwhelming experience exacted by some techniques, and to maintain "safety" in rehearsal or performance.[41] Yet the analysis in this chapter suggests that the "emotionally overwhelming" issues are sometimes symptomatic of a more fundamental violation which should be patiently understood and articulated through a moral vocabulary that is currently unavailable.

Actors are rarely candidly presented with the ethical issues of performance—the manner whereby some forms of acting, training, or rehearsing may relax connections between their values and their performance. Would-be actors are therefore unable to reflect, consent, and absorb this significant dimension of their profession and training as they undergo it. They are not urged to specify their own limits, or to understand, *before* the event, what maintaining or forgoing these limits entails. Worse, the ethical tensions that acting involves may be mischaracterized as the voice of uncommitted acting; and such can surface not necessarily as an explicit reproach by a teacher or a director, but by an inner monitoring that the actor cultivates as part of the initiation into acting. Would-be actors may even be presented with the opposite argument—Susan Verducci's—according to which actortraining (specifically Method training) is able to turn them into morally better human beings by cultivating empathy.[42] The idea that throughout this process of amelioration (which no doubt may transpire) something of importance *may also be taken away* is left for them to discover on their own, cope with it as they may.

In previous parts of this book I have suggested that acting is an attempt to embody and explore unrealized possibilities of the self. Acting constitutes a reconfiguration of identity. It offers an alternative way of inhabiting the world that is not merely personally undertaken, but that becomes momentarily validated by fellow actors and audience. We now see that imaginatively reaching out into other possibilities of being may also weaken one's hold over the single possibility that makes up one's actual identity. The actor's willingness to suspend a particular inflexibility, an inflexibility that nonactors take for granted, establishes the interface between acting and unethical experiences: by admitting a dimension of play into one's attachments, feelings and the links between praxis and being, one opens the door to potentially unethical exercises, training, and performance; a process that resembles the inner structure of prostitution. I have further suggested that the brushes with prostitution are not necessarily abusive mischaracterizations of acting: like prostitution, acting involves lending elements of identity to a role; some of these are unproblematic (say, one's moving body or most uses of one's voice), others are difficult and self-implicating (sexual gestures or nakedness). Either way, in acting, the limits of such "lending" become an open question that needs to be repeatedly negotiated, both internally and externally.

The aim of this analysis, I reiterate, is not to resuscitate a credible version of antitheatricality. My aim is, rather, to invite actors and instructors to clarify and state the ethical dimension of what acting involves. Informed ethical concerns should genuinely shape the choices one makes as a performer. They ought to guide those who possess power over performers: directors, instructors and writers. In the current context of professional acting, in which art and entertainment are so inextricably bound, in which the overlap between eroticism for its own sake and aesthetic goals is systematically blurred, in which "professionalism" in acting entails unreserved compliance with any manipulation demanded by any acting coach, it may be utterly naïve to attempt to meaningfully introduce ethical concerns. Such pessimism is even more pertinent when one begins factoring in, firstly, the extent to which supply and demand are cruelly tipped against performers—both in relation to the fierce competition over slots in prestigious training programs and, later, over available work—and, secondly, the uncompromising hierarchic structures in which actors operate, not only in relation to directors, but also to fellow performers (note how so many of the examples surveyed above—Brando-Bankhead, Chaplin-Weldon, Maoz-Mer—involve junior performers being subjected to violence by senior partners). And yet, such defeatism should be resisted by anyone who cares for acting.

PORNOGRAPHY AND ACTING

Pornographic performance constitutes a philosophically riddling form of role-playing. Those who merely distinguish between authentic agency and artificial pretense are likely to altogether miss the problem. They would simply identify acting with pretending, and perceive pornographic acting—if it is acting—as no more than another kind of mimicry. From such a perspective, the philosophical questions raised by pornography are mostly moral in nature. They concern the moral desirability of pornography as such, or its desirability given the exploitative conditions underlying most of its production. But when analysed as imaginative embodied role-playing, pornography raises less familiar puzzles relating to performed agency rather than to its moral status. Does participating in a pornographic performance constitute acting? Does it make sense to claim that the performer goes through an entire array of sexual motions: foreplay, penetration, orgasm (surely the case for performing men, though doubtfully so for female performers)—and, still, is merely playing a role? Would, for instance, performing in a pornographic film amount to adultery if the actor were married? A response to such questions demands inquiring after the precise form of role-playing involved in performed sex, whether such performance takes place within a pornographic context, or in a non-pornographic one.

The previous chapter discussed episodes in which genuine self-shaping through acting was rooted in a withdrawal from care. When the body is demechanized, some types of performance are exposed as potentially overestimating the extent to which an actor is free to dissociate performance from constitutive, identity-related values. All of the episodes discussed in the previous chapter concerned actors or acting students who perceive themselves as such. By contrast, pornography is a form of performance in which self-shaping through performed action is so immediate and obvious that the identification of the action as *role-playing* itself becomes questionable.

Pornography is the clearest example of the inability to maintain a distinction between role and identity, between performed act and genuine, self-determining agency, between representation and presentation. This chapter attempts to understand what makes such distinctions collapse. The first sections attempt to disentangle the unobvious relationship between pornographic role-playing and acting. I then proceed to de-automate the ascription of "exploitation" to porn, by bringing out porn's surprising capacity to establish care rather than undermine it. Pornography's self-shaping capacity will then be examined, and several moral implications will be formulated.

Is Pornography (sometimes) a Form of Acting?

Porn is typically produced in a fast and careless industry. For this reason, any sampling of actual acting done as part of porn will probably reveal a hastily created performance that cannot compete in quality even with the most inferior mainstream films. Judging its status as acting by viewing such a sampling, one is likely to say that *if* porn does involve acting, then such oscillates between the merely substandard and the laughably pathetic.

But how about patiently and thoughtfully produced porn? Can carefully rehearsed pornography—if it were produced—constitute acting? To answer this question, porn needs to be related to the definition of acting proposed earlier in this book, in which acting was associated with an intended artistic achievement. Values such authenticity, originality, commitment, inventiveness, attentiveness, depth of embodiment and inquisitiveness were claimed to figure in such achievement. If a well-off porn producer were to commission excellently trained actors, such values could be exemplified in a pornographic film—why shouldn't they? It is, nevertheless, difficult to dismiss the thought that there is something unsound about such a project: imagining good acting in porn is not self-contradictory; it is just bizarre. Quality of acting seems simply irrelevant. Granted, few would relish watching indifferent or bored performers. But this merely shows that the *attitude* of the performers can be important to the spectator. Yet attitude is not the same as acting.

Straitjacketing pornography into an aesthetic frame suggested by the term "acting"—and consequently relegating it into a second-rate art—is not our only (or most fruitful) option when attempting to pinpoint its precise form of embodied role-playing. Instead, we can more plausibly follow others in regarding pornography as a practice in its own right, governed by its own conventions and objectives.[1] What is this practice? I will employ the following definition: Pornography is a graphic (pictorial, cinematic, photographic, acoustic, staged) depiction of bodily display and action that is projected to generate sexual excitement in its beholder.[2] It is mostly commercialized, but it need not be. Erotic art ("erotica") meets this definition too. Yet pornography differs from erotica in two ways. The first has to do with the range of targeted values: unlike the pornographer, producers and beholders of erotic art typically aim for other values besides sexual stimulation.[3] The second relates to two different aspects of pornography's "explicitness" when compared to erotica. The explicitness of pornography relates, first, to the function of the imagination: unlike erotica, which would typically invite the spectator to imaginatively complete a suggestive representation, a pornographic depiction is calculated to restrict, rather than provoke, imaginative participation ("leaving nothing for the imagination"). Secondly, explicitness has to do with fixation and repetition: pornographic "explicitness" involves the repetitive display of images that are calculated to stimulate; erotica, by contrast, is not fixated on an image or a repeated pattern. "One knows it when one sees it," as justice Potter Stewart did, not because pornography possesses some inexplicable mysterious quality, but because these facets of the pornographic image—focus, repetition, and an attempt to limit the engagement of the imagination—are all subordinate to a single intent: stimulation.[4]

By switching organizing paradigms, by regarding pornographic enactment as a practice in its own right, rather than a second-rate art, pornography's genuine relationship to acting is exposed: while pornographic performance draws on the language of acting and the performing arts, they are but its borrowed trappings. Pornography is not a performing art. It merely *utilizes* elements of performing art for its own ends. Pornography *uses* acting, pretense, staging, script, elements of photography, and makeup. Participants in a pornographic work will, perhaps, invoke the vocabulary of acting or undergo acting-like experiences. Their role-playing will also rely on pretense (which, as we saw, is not the same as acting). But they do not act.

The acting/using acting distinction rests on a projected prioritizing of values in cases of a clash between them. When pornographic and aesthetic values conflict (that is, when features that are calculated to stimulate are undercut by those that relate to artistic achievement), a porn producer would sacrifice aesthetic values in order to promote pornographic ones: a producer who must choose between two versions of the same scene—one better acted than the other yet also less sexually exciting—will not hesitate to select the more stimulating take. Such is manifestly *not* the case in an aesthetically oriented undertaking, in which better acting is autonomously desired (meaning that, for example, a scene could be repeated only because its acting can be improved). It is in this sense that porn, whether actual or idealized, *uses* acting rather than intrinsically interested in it.[5]

The distinction between acting and using acting does not imply that the latter is necessarily inferior in quality to the former: a professional actor in a porn film might still be able to "do better" than an amateur acting on stage. The point is that, given the radical difference between their respective governing values, the two processes must be classified into different categories of performance. Nor should this distinction be taken to imply that the quality of the acting being used in porn is altogether negligible. While there is no incontestable positive relationship between aesthetic and pornographic values, there exists a negative relationship between the two: while the acting of the porn performer can be mediocre, if it drops low enough, this can prove detrimental to the attempted objective to stimulate.

Is Acting (sometimes) a Form of Pornography?

In an interview given four years before her death, Maria Schneider commented upon a controversial scene in *Last Tango in Paris*, in which she and Marlon Brando simulated anal sex:

> "Marlon said to me: 'Maria, don't worry, it's just a movie,' but during the scene, even though what Marlon was doing wasn't real, I was crying real tears. . . . I felt humiliated and to be honest, I felt a little raped, both by Marlon and by Bertolucci. After the scene, Marlon didn't console me or apologize. Thankfully, there was just one take."[6]

We are not now considering the milder forms of awkwardness involved in acting erotic gestures that were discussed in the previous chapter. Schneider summons a hard word—rape—to describe her experience. But why would Schneider feel "a little raped" by enacting a feigned sex scene in the context of a film in which she was called upon to seriously act and to achieve many other artistic goals? The answer appears to be simple: she has been manipulated into a specific kind of self-exposure. The manipulation plays on a vagueness that is intrinsic to acting, and that was presented in the previous chapter as the cause of acting's brush with unethical agency: actors are required to turn aspects of their being into the raw materials of their performance. Nudity which is experienced by the performer as dispensable—as being only strenuously related to the various objectives of the film; a means for generating additional sexual stimulation by catering to the projected voyeuristic curiosity of the audience—may elicit the feeling of being exploited. Cast as argument, the complaint would be that while stimulating the audience does not turn acting into porn (but rather into erotica), once stimulation becomes an overarching objective, a significant overlap between the two practices is established: if porn combines an attempt to arouse coupled with a use of acting, actors in a non-pornographic film may feel that their acting is similarly used, since the objective to stimulate becomes overriding, or that this objective is being pursued in what they regard as a needlessly explicit way relative to the work's other objectives. Could the fact that there was, as Schneider says, "only one take," indicate that another take was unnecessary partly because the acting value of the scene was—as in porn—largely irrelevant?

Why was it hurtful to participate in *that* particular scene? The scene involved Brando smearing butter on Schneider's nether parts and simulating penetration. The scene is memorable. Intriguingly, it is the butter that people seem to remember. When one tries to account for this, a pattern discussed by Elaine Scarry in the context of torture comes to mind. Scarry points out that, when geared for torture, benign household utensils—a refrigerator's door, an iron, gardening equipment, dentist's tools—acquire a new sinister meaning. One of the psychological effects of torture, she writes, depends on overturning predictable meanings routinely attached to objects. They are defamiliarized. In Bertolucci's scene, butter is similarly defamiliarized: it turns from a mundane feature in every kitchen to a sexually loaded object.

It is the inventive use of butter that makes this scene memorable. But the centrality of butter also marginalizes the characters played by Brando and Schneider: any two bodies performing the scene would have sufficed to get *this* meaning across. The tool-like experience of participating in such a scene—apparently Brando, too, felt raped and manipulated by the film[7]—is exacerbated by the implication that a particular body, Schneider's, is being penetrated in public in a specific manner. It is this latter process, the rendering public of something one deems essentially private, that forms a further distinguishing feature of pornographic role-playing: the performer, not the character, is directly perceived by strangers (spectators) as doing something that he or she would usually keep private. Porn shows this explicitly, while in *Last Tango in Paris* it is more implicit. But the implication itself can be hurtful to a performer who has not consented—or has not taken in the significance of agreeing—to be perceived or imagined in this particular way. Significant too, is the suggestion that anal rather than some other form of penetration is taking place: an actress may be prepared to be imagined by a spectator in one way but not in another. Indeed, in all testimonials by porn performers footnoted later in this chapter, the decision to enter porn has not been taken lightly. Extensive soul-searching is typically involved, precisely because of the implications not just to the performer, but also to his or her acquaintances and relatives. Porn performers are also usually required by casting agencies to specify in advance what they are willing and unwilling to do.[8] Unlike them, Schneider was evidently unprepared for the type of exposure she was asked to undergo as part of a role-playing that was no longer experienced by her as mere acting.

Empowerment and Disempowerment

One would expect Schneider's testimony to be a mild instance of what women feel like when they participate in full-fledged porn. Andrea Dworkin's or Catherine MacKinnon's well-known writings strongly suggest this—as does the autobiography by Linda "Lovelace" (Marchiano) regarding her experiences in the making of *Deep Throat*.

But there are different voices. Sunset Thomas, Georgina Spelvin, Jenna Jameson, as well as other female sex workers contributing to Carly Milne's *Naked Ambition*, all refuse to perceive themselves as exploited victims.[9] Porn, it seems, offers a candid contract: expose yourself in an alluring way for some unknown viewer's pleasure; by contrast, non-pornographic acting (such as starring in a Bertolucci film) can be far more deceitful—ostensibly appealing to the actress's aspirations as artist, while in effect using her in an altogether different manner. This explains how feigned anal sex may be experienced as rape, while genuine anal intercourse in a porn film can be perceived as part of a job in which one even takes pride. Here is Tristan Taormino describing her experience of anal sex with no less than ten individuals in a film she had directed and participated in (*The Ultimate Guide to Anal Sex*):

> Lots of people ask me why I decided to be in the movie. That's right, the rumours are true: after spending six scenes dishing out tips and techniques, I surrender to my entire cast, who show me what they've learned in an anal orgy where they each get to have their way with me. I was the subject of a ten-person, all-gender, all-anal gang bang. It was important for me to be in the video to show not only that porn stars can enjoy anal sex, but that any woman can.[10]

Some will claim that remarks of this kind describe a socially sanctioned form of rape, in which victims become ideological mouthpieces. Yet such a position is patronizing towards Taormino, and towards many other contributors to Milne's anthology. Taormino describes a film she directed and produced in an attempt to create feminist porn, explaining that: "Feminist porn is porn that empowers women and men: it gives them information and ideas about sex. It teaches. It inspires fantasy and adventure. It validates viewers when they see themselves or a part of their sexuality represented."[11] Exploitative porn exists, she admits, yet such does not warrant a blanket victimization of porn performers.

Schneider was pressed by the weight of a middle-aged Brando, and her behind was slightly soiled by butter. Taormino, on the other hand, was genuinely penetrated by ten individuals. Yet Schneider cried throughout the scene, believing that both her partner actor and her director were raping her, whereas Taormino experienced the scene as an empowering personal liberation. As is so often the case, it is the context, *not* the gesture, that determines whether or not an enactment is exploitative, as does the frank nature of the practice in which one takes part. It is not porn as such that leads to the exploitative experience.

Taormino is not alone. "Mason," a pseudonym of another female porn director, conceives and films potentially degrading scenes. She describes in detail a sequence in which a woman is made to bark like a dog and to "fetch" a dildo on command. In response to the criticism that she renders acceptable the humiliation of women, "Mason" claims that, on the contrary, she presents adult women who embrace their own sexual preferences rather than avoid them. "Porn has been therapy for me." she writes; "[it] has validated my desires and helped me accept them. Porn has allowed me to develop a more complex image of womanhood, one that isn't exclusively defined by but fully embraces the spirit of women who are proud and unashamed of their sex. . . . I can honestly say, I found myself through porn."[12]

Within the context of gay porn, the expressed enthusiasm for the work by performers is far more unapologetic and direct. "I always wanted to get into porno," says Joey Stefano in an interview. "When I was a young kid I used to watch it and would fantasize about being with that person, especially people I liked. . . . I always wanted to do it . . . I love the business, I really do. . . . Because I like sex, and when I'm on the set, I don't care who's there watching—we're going to have a good time." Wakefield Poole reports of a performer who told him after shooting a scene that it constituted "the most erotic sex he had ever experienced." "I can still recall the rush I got from the thought of being [performing] in those videos," writes Rich Merritt, "I would spend hours daydreaming about what the next video would be like and it made me feel almost high." Apart from the performer's pleasure, implied in such remarks is the suggestion that, while porn performance can be disinterested and alienated, the performers who eventually stand out, are those who enjoy the sex; indeed, the second of Michael Lucas's "ten rules" for being a porn star, is that "you must love sex . . . enjoying it in all its forms."[13]

Again, one can dismiss what these men and women say as predictable rationalizations of individuals who participate in their own victimization by adopting the ideology of their oppressors—a form of Stockholm Syndrome. At least some of the above citations may also be read as public relations pronouncements written in character—not genuine personal disclosures. But one may also choose to accept such testimonies as touching unique modes of experience that can genuinely be released through pornography.

The Uniqueness of Porn

Without doubt, the defenders of porn quoted above are not representative of this industry: most transactions in porn are unsupervised, involving the hiring of disempowered individuals; ideal conditions for a systematically exploitative industry. Even the pro-porn performers cited above do not speak in a unified voice: pseudonyms abound in this literature; its sources, funding and interests are murky; a sense of anger may be detected in it even when it defends porn. Nevertheless, the testimonials regarding porn as inner validation need not be exemplary of the industry to shed light on the potential that pornographic role-playing may fulfil. Our previous analysis of role-playing and its relationship with care assists in exposing why this may be so: while role-playing can constitute a withdrawal from care, it may also be a means of establishing it.

To begin with, pornography can be a detailed embodiment of a sexual fantasy. The actualization may be of the performer's own fantasy—Joey Stefano explicitly describes porn as "one of my fantasies that I'm acting out."[14] But the director, rather than the performer, is typically the one whose fantasy is being realized. Porn is thus (ideally) a co-operation: a fantasy is rendered public by a group of individuals who jointly expose part of someone's hidden self. The logic resembles psychodrama: a collective enacts a submerged aspect of a participant's life, thus enabling it to exist outside the dream-life of the self. The acknowledgment that this constitutes, the therapeutic value attributed to porn by "Mason," is rooted in the interpersonal statement made by the very incarnation: the willingness to play out an inner scene, allowing it to be embodied through one's own flesh. To do this for another, to enable another's inner desires to be externalized and actualized, can be experienced as a form of care, an establishing of erotic intimacy. Beyond the willingness to embody a private fantasy, by playing out the director's fantasy, the participators in a porn film are not only having sex with each other, but also with the director—"having sex" in the sense of satisfying another's desire in the precise manner conceived by that person. Wakefield Poole describes how his difficulties over directing his lover gave way to a feeling of being remade by his camera:

> . . . filming the sex fascinated me. I told them to experiment with each other as if it were the first time (and it was). I wanted them to do everything. No top, no bottom, just two men discovering each other. I had always been observant, but now I was able, with the help of the zoom lens, to actually see things I could never see with the naked eye. It was almost hypnotic, and at times the camera seemed to have a mind of its own. In that viewfinder I found a whole new private world. I was now an official voyeur and felt comfortable in my new role. I almost became invisible to the actors, and surprisingly, I was never tempted to enter into the action. The filming was my participation. I created my reality by selecting what would fill the small frame through which I looked.[15]

From a mere orchestrating overseer of the action, the porn director becomes the target of gratification; he metamorphoses into a participator. The camera becomes more than a recording tool—no longer merely some silent participant which strong performers are in dialogue with. It turns into a mechanism through which the director can choreograph what his sexual imagination dictates. Willing to be directed in such a way can constitute an embracing of another's desire.

Interpersonal validation of this kind is also rooted in the connection between sex and shame. Sex is inextricably bound up with varying degrees of embarrassment and loneliness, even when one's tastes are considered mainstream. If one's wishes are less orthodox—Mason's staging of a desire to become another's pet—the degrading potential of this is momentarily lifted when other individuals are willing to enact the script. This is how porn can become personally empowering and liberating for the director or spectator. Performers, too, may experience such freedom, due to the rendering public of that which is supposedly debasing. Rich Merritt writes of the liberating experience of participating in gay porn as a Marine:

> My country was telling my friends and me that we didn't belong where we were and that we had no right to be who we were. To hell with all of them, I thought. . . . The videos provided me with a powerful outlet for my emotions. I would show them! I resolved to be the best Marine I could possibly be. But I was also going to be as gay as I could possibly be, and I was going to do it where the whole world could see.[16]

"Mason" is not rambling or mindlessly verbalizing a coercive ideology. She is, rather, touching on an ideal that porn can realize. The therapeutic potential of porn lies in its power to show individuals that they are not alone. It can achieve this through the most committed language of the exposed body, submitting itself to another's fantasy and, thereby, establishing a unique form of care. Such care can only be manifested by allowing one's body to act in a particular way. This overcoming of loneliness and shame is not restricted to directing or enacting a specific fantasy, but extends to the spectator as well: pornography can allow its spectators "to explore and even come to grips with [their] sexual desire in all its quirks and moral instability," writes Nancy Bauer; it "enables discovery that the twists and turns of one's erotic longing are not sui generic, that no one is a true sexual freak."[17] The implication is that the more extreme shape it takes, the greater is porn's therapeutic potential, since it becomes more reassuring for those entertaining milder desires: if the woman onscreen is willing to be a fetching dog, perhaps one's far more pedestrian preferences are not as unacceptable as one had always thought them to be.

The manner whereby porn is able to momentarily lift the oppressive weight of norms does not only relieve loneliness. Deeper ties between porn's hetero-normativity and sexual pleasure are suggested by the existence of pornographic subgenres that give voice to culturally repressed desires—think of fat fetishism or desire directed at elderly women. Given a cultural context that revels on thinness and youth, such porn articulates a resistance to ubiquitous social norms; it is counter-power, articulated through the language of sexual arousal.[18] Consider in this context, the puzzling phenomenon within the gay porn of the eighties: porn stars who are known to be straight, yet participate in gay porn.[19] One of the more interesting explanations for a gay audience's preference to watch nongay performers is that porn scenes with known straight men establish a utopian eroticism: all-important, self-defining divisions and classifications collapse in this kind of pornography.

Counter to the view that porn presents mechanized sex, it might be argued that something far more radical than the physical sexual gestures is being consumed by porn's target audience. Such a view contests the strand of feminism for which porn is merely an assertion of patriarchy. It holds that, in addition to ideological reinstatement, porn can sometimes become a shared language of subversion: a resistance to accepted norms; a form of embodied release in which one's counter-voice finds expression. The pornographer empowers marginalized voices, establishing an external anchoring for spectators. When spectators discover in porn a new "perverse" pleasure to which they are unexpectedly attracted—the contagious nature of porn, presented as one of its more sinister dangers by its opponents—they are in fact drawn to ways of being other in sex, sometimes in ways that undercut their previous fantasies. Diminishing loneliness and relaxing the social regimentation of sexual imagination thereby combine in porn's capacity to touch and connect with an unknown spectator.

Factor in the money, and the suspicion that there is something far too rosy in such a glorification of porn will be substantiated. Porn could be a means of self-validation were it enacted by a group of caring individuals: altruistic surrogates who are genuinely motivated by the need to reach out and assuage the loneliness of the director or the spectator. But (amateur porn notwithstanding), commercial porn is mostly a cynical transaction driven by pecuniary motives. As such, the acknowledgment of the financial interest can aggravate—not relieve—the sense of loneliness: only paid individuals are willing to enact one's fantasies. This potential of alienating rather than validating the producer/consumer of the fantasy, holds even when the porn is nonexploitative and involves consenting adults. But when it relies upon implicit or explicit coercion, porn turns from a vehicle for potential recognition and validation into an instrument for degradation and insulation. Indeed, in some of the filmed sequences described by Linda "Lovelace" (Marchiano), the director's creative choices—unlike Mason's—do not even relate to his own fantasies, but cater to some unspecified curiosity.

So why does "Mason" experience therapy and acceptance rather than a further plunge into loneliness? The answer relates not to the filmed content, but to a particular quality emitted by the performers, and by the manner whereby that particular performance succeeded in establishing care. Commodification does not, on its own, annul interpersonal recognition and empathy: one can, for example, sense that although being paid, a therapist truly empathizes with one's plight. Commodified sex, too, possesses this potential—no reason to deny that some clients may find deep intimacy and acceptance with some prostitutes. Nor is it necessary to rule out that sex workers may (rarely) reach a fuller experience of self-acceptance and personal empowerment through their work.[20] The performer that "Mason" interacted with was, for example, apparently going beyond the paid role, and communicated something to her director—"Mason" says that she stopped the scene to ensure that the performer was not unnerved by what she was asked to perform, resuming the shoot upon being reassured; one guesses that such gestures by her director induced the performer to not merely play along with a script, but to also respond to and comply with a submission fantasy of her director.

Porn seems to possess this potential since, as suggested above, the willingness to be orchestrated according to the script that animates the director's own actual desires can be a form of lovemaking. The performer presents a voluntary bodily response to another's secretive and private wishes—a meaningful interpersonal gesture, an act manifesting care.

Porn, Sex, and Pleasure

It might seem obvious that porn involves a presentment of sex. Indeed, porn performer "Sunset Thomas" writes the following:

> An adult film star has to lie on a bed (or couch or floor or pool deck chair or copier machine) and have sex in front of a camera with one or more boys and/or girls. If the performance is going to be credible, the girl either has to enjoy the sex or be a talented actress. Most of the girls like sex.[21]

Likewise, the feminist critique according to which porn involves a collapse of the representation into the represented, also assumes that the "represented" is actual sex.[22] All of the sources on gay porn cited earlier present the desire for sex as a motivation for becoming a porn performer. But there is substantial reason to pause before accepting the idea that porn presents sex. Unlike simply having sex, participants in porn do not fully determine what they are about to do. Unlike simply having sex, close-ups, and repeated shots, as well as withholding ejaculation (or maintaining an erection between shots), can be mandatory. Finally, unlike sex, in porn, the sexual gestures themselves are manufactured or sometimes pretended—catering, for example, to the time-honoured tradition of showing that an ejaculation has taken place, or projecting taking orgasmic pleasure in acts that are not as pleasuring (such as vaginal penetration). Porn often diverges from sex by configuring an imagined utopia in which the precise source of one's desire magically becomes another's pleasure (such as the *Deep Throat* theme of a clitoris in a woman's throat).[23] Refusing to squarely identify porn with sex is also supported by some testimonials. An anonymous male performer interviewed by Jenna Jameson categorically denies that a pornographic performance amounts to having sex: "[P]eople think [that] when you get on set, you are actually having sex, but you aren't. You are performing for the camera." He goes on to describe the difficulties of obtaining and maintaining an erection in a room full of strangers. He says that most male performers rely on Viagra, humorously advising would-be porn male performers to practice by masturbating in front of their parents or being "on the phone with the gas company, trying to get a hard-on."[24]

The sex is orchestrated. This does not, however, entail that it is "role-playing" as opposed to "sex" due to the artificial nature of this latter distinction. "Simply having sex" is itself a simplification: from "talking dirty" to the fully dramatized sadomasochistic fantasies that will be discussed in the next chapter, "having sex" includes its own repertoire of orchestrated behaviour and forms of self/other scripting. Indeed, if not altogether socially constructed, "passion-performance" is itself a role which is, at the very least, significantly learnt. Yet, while sex in general is not insulated from performing, pornographic role-playing is nevertheless distinct: role-playing in sex is a means of generating pleasure for the players whereas role-playing in porn is meant to gratify a projected *spectator*. Genuine pleasure for the players is essentially dispensable; if it exists, it is an added bonus which may add stimulation to the viewer. Group sex, the use of mirrors, the role of public humiliation in masochistic fantasy, all exemplify how nonpornographic sex can also address real or imagined spectators. But here too, the audience is a means for the pleasure of the players—not an entity that one aims to gratify.

The relationships between pornographic performance and sex are accordingly complex. Denying that porn involves having sex is strenuous: performing some sexual gestures constitutes a sufficient condition for the occurrence of sex—most would regard vaginal, anal, and oral penetration, for example, as obvious sufficient conditions for a gesture constituting sex (though an American president has been known to deny the latter). When performers doubt that they are really having sex on set, they are in fact implicitly distinguishing between the role-playing they are engaging in and the kind of pleasurable action they associate with "real" sex. But the logic is unsound: unpleasant sex is still sex. Porn calls for a particular form of other-attuned role-playing, involving the performance of sexual gestures. Such (usually) constitutes sex.[25]

The relationship between this kind of performance and sexual pleasure is varied. To begin with, because porn involves other-oriented role-playing, the performer's pleasure is beside the point. As for its actual existence, testimonials point both ways: the male performer cited earlier denies experiencing pleasure; performers such as Jenna Jameson, Sunset Thomas, Tracy Lords, and many gay performers say the opposite.[26] A more interesting ambivalence concerns contradictory evidence regarding the relationship between pleasure and other-oriented performance. On the one hand, perhaps precisely because it is other-oriented, such performance may be experienced as positively hurtful and instrumental: Linda "Lovelace" (Marchiano) categorically denies ever having experienced pleasure as part of such films: "Did I enjoy any of it? Did I ever have a moment's pleasure? I want to state this as clearly as I can. There was no pleasure. . . . I did not have a single orgasm for six or seven years. I never had any enjoyment from any of it at all."[27] In the opposite direction, the other-oriented nature of the performance may increase rather than stifle sexual pleasure: Jenna Jameson describes her participation in a very passionate and enjoyable scene with another performer, which led them to have sex off camera. Interestingly, the stimulation experienced onscreen vanished with the cameras: "[I]t just felt weird having sex together in real life. The chemistry on screen was not that of attraction but a different kind of partnership, the bond of two actors emotionally invested in creating a perfect scene together."[28] This episode reveals the power of the camera to ignite, rather than quench, pleasure.

Again, some might be quick to diagnose this latter possibility as indicative of the depth of psychological trauma that porn performers allegedly suffer from (Jameson tells readers of her autobiography that she was a victim of rape and of gang-rape). Authentic sexual pleasure, it will be maintained, cannot be directly experienced by these victims. Oblique pleasure is the result: sex enjoyed solely when produced for the sake of some abstract viewer for which the camera stands. But porn performers, Jameson included, resent being victimized—and certainly do not report sexual impotence. While some of them have been the subject of sexual violence, the camera's function may be understood not as facilitating the avoidance of the traumatized self, but as establishing other-oriented performance—enabling body-identity dissociation in the manner described earlier in this book. Existential amplification thereby allows role-playing to unleash new kinds of pleasure. In fact, when porn is assessed in relation to its aphrodisiacal function for couples that watch it, its capacity to invigorate sex may be related precisely to putting such dissociation on display: beholding a performer's willingness to dissociate identity from body to this degree, catalyzes one's own release from the grip of familiar body-identity restrictions. Unpredictable sex with a familiar partner is the result.

Pretense, Enacted Role-Playing, and Agent-Determining Role-Playing

To understand the collapse between representation and presentation in pornography, I propose a distinction between pretense, enacted role-playing, and agent-determining role-playing. *Pretense*, as previously characterized in this book, is a withdrawal from experience. When pretending, one does not undergo the performed condition; the distinction between appearance and reality is non-problematically maintained. *Enacted role-playing* occurs when the performed act or experience is—unlike pretense—genuinely undergone or enacted, but is containable by the role-playing: it is fully attributable to the character. When, for example, an actress slaps another in character, she is genuinely slapping; she can play around with the strength of the slap, pretending that it is stronger or weaker than it actually is—but the slapping is real. Yet, while the gesture is genuine, and while, as we saw, performers may infuse it with real violence, it is usually divested of interpersonal significance. The same holds for acts that involve no one else, such as swimming or dressing: the actor really performs such acts, but they are easily assigned to the character, not to the actor.

By contrast, in *agent-determining role-playing*, the performed act is (like enacted role-playing) really performed. Yet it also carries interpersonal or value-related accountability that cannot be contained by the character. If a sworn vegetarian consumes meat on stage as part of a role, or if a religious Jew, or a Muslim, eats pork, or if an actor is filmed urinating on someone else's holy text, he or she cannot absolve their betrayal of their beliefs or the offensiveness of their performance by claiming that the acts were merely a form of role-playing: one did not just pretend to eat (nonkosher) meat, one *actually* did so; one did not merely pretend to degrade another's prized symbol, one really did so.[29]

By virtue of what do such acts transcend the role and "determine" the agent? The examples above suggest that performing specific acts places the agent in a relationship with a value (violating/ confirming/ instantiating): eating meat for vegetarians, or eating *haraam* meat for an observant Muslim constitutes an obvious violation of an upheld value; spitting on holy books is disrespectful to what another person values.[30] But since role-playing is able to touch values *without* determining the agent—when an actor playing Iago lies to Othello, such does not entail a violation of values by the actor—saying this much (or merely alluding to a "withdrawal" from care, which seemed sufficient for the cases discussed in the previous chapter), is, here, not enough. What sets the difference between the violation involved in acts such as demeaning a prized symbol and the performing of other immoral acts that do not determine the role-player? Why are the former uncontained by the role, whereas the latter are? The answer seems simple, relating to the distinction between presented and represented acts: the actor playing Iago merely *represents* an immoral act, not genuinely swindling the Othello actor, whereas when an actor ingests something that ought not to be eaten, the act actually takes place—hence it is *presented*. But this answer will not do, since it begs the question which would be reformulated thus: by virtue of what do value-related acts become presentations (or "genuinely performed") rather than mere representations?

A philosophically substantive answer will begin with the relationship between values and the *undesirable states* that are being singled out. Suffering is an example of such a state in relation to moral values. Lying and robbing someone produces suffering, but not when lying is part of dramatic role-playing. This is why, while an actor playing a liar genuinely touches a value, the act is, nevertheless, fully containable within the role: the *state* to which the value refers never occurs. By contrast, if a moral vegetarian holds that animals should not be eaten because eating meat involves needless suffering, the suffering he objects to has genuinely taken place; it is causally related to the meat he is asked to consume on stage. When it comes to religious values, the state singled out is the failure to observe an aspect of the religious life, the state of transgressing God's commands, and since dietary religious laws do not include exemptions for violations performed as part of role-playing, when a religious actor ignores such edicts, the state of breaking God's commands genuinely occurs. Symbolic values, likewise, single out particular objects for special respect. Since it is unknown whether those who prize the object would be willing to suspend their veneration were it demeaned on stage (or if they are explicitly known to be unwilling to do so), debasing a symbol in the theater amounts to the state of genuinely disrespecting others. In sum, role-playing becomes agent-determining if the act brings into being, or constitutes acceptance of, a genuinely existing undesired state related to held values.[31]

Sexual Performance as Agent-Determining Role-Playing

Applying the analysis above to sexual performance, pornographic or not, requires showing that sex is underpinned by specifiable values. Such values (which need not be moral, religious or symbolic) must then be associated with distinct states that are, somehow, brought about or implicitly accepted by performing sexual gestures. A specification of these values and states will explain the manner whereby sexual performance can become agent-determining. The implicit mechanism being intuited when "representation collapses into presentation" will thereby be revealed.

Sex does not involve endorsing or violating moral values (aside from, when applicable, fidelity). Nevertheless, it is linked with nonmoral values—by a "nonmoral value" I mean desired goods sought and prized as ends—in four distinct ways. To begin with, by having fulfilling sex, one experiences a range of nonmoral values afforded by sexual pleasure: the distinct pleasures involved in sensing, looking, touching, hearing, and smelling; the enjoyable sensations involved in acting and being acted upon; the pleasure of enacting a fantasy. Secondly, sex can also be understood and experienced as expressive of love. Valued for what it communicates, sex is thereby being yoked to the value of love, and to the value of a specifically bodily expression of such love. Exclusiveness constitutes a third source for perceiving value in sex: the willingness to enjoy sexual intercourse with a particular individual is an experience in which one is being singled out. Fourthly, sex can also involve the value of trust—a value that surfaces when one is willing to expose one's nakedness and sexuality to another. Here, the value relates to establishing intimacy, to the interpersonal meaning attached to exposure, and to the choice to be repeatedly revealed to a particular partner.

Such values can overlap or exist independently: pleasurable sex need not involve love or exclusiveness; loving sex need not be pleasurable; exclusivity can exist without the other two values—as when someone has sex with powerful individuals, thus singling them out without necessarily experiencing either love or pleasure. Sex may be pleasurable without privacy or trust. Alternatively, it can constitute an expression of trust without being accompanied by pleasure or love.

The values, then, are clear enough. The states related to these values are also not difficult to specify: the hedonistic value of sex is linked to the state of being pleasured and giving pleasure; the expressive value of sex concerns a prized emotional state—love—and its communication through the body; exclusiveness involves the potentially flattering state of choosing and being chosen by another for sex; trust issues from the state of sharing something with another that is unavailable to the world at large, be this one's nakedness or one's sexual predilections.

Returning to sexual performance, we can now discern two ways whereby the states established through sexual role-playing differ from the ones that figured in relation to actors consuming non-kosher meat, or tearing up a holy text as part of a role. In these examples of agent-determining role-playing, the actor brings about or accepts a state that firstly, genuinely exists—suffering, departing from God's ways, demeaning others—and, secondly, is deemed undesirable. Because the role-playing is either causally related to the creating of such a genuinely existing undesirable state, or because it constitutes implicit acceptance of it, such performance becomes agent-determining. By contrast, in performed sex, the states brought about—arousing pleasure, being loved or expressing love, singling out and being singled out for reciprocal sexual pleasure, inviting another into one's private space—appear to be, firstly, desirable and, secondly, usually do not genuinely exist: a porn performer neither expresses love nor communicates exclusiveness to her partner in a sex scene; nor does the performer genuinely expose her body or erotic mind for her partner's acknowledgment as part of intimate trust—her exposure is generalized, targeting the camera and the anonymous viewers of the film. As for pleasure, the evidence cited earlier is inconclusive: while it may exist, we saw that even male porn performers who are shown to sexually climax may deny that pleasure is actually experienced.

It would now appear that porn is not agent-determining role-playing: the states such role-playing elicits through the values it touches upon do not genuinely exist. Even the pleasure aspect may not exist. Such a conclusion is, however, premature: porn can determine the agent, not because the role-player brings into being an independently valued state, but because the performer brings into being a condition in which links that *ought* to exist between acts and desirable states *are being suspended.* The process of withdrawal from care that preoccupied us in the previous chapter is seen at work here, too. Yet in the context of porn, the argument is familiar, and versions of it appear in conservative and feminist literature on porn. The gist of it is that, in porn, acts typically associated with exclusiveness, expressiveness, trust, privacy, and particular pleasures given and received are being artificially divorced from these values. Profound agent-determination is being mobilized. A false, mechanomorphic view of sexuality and embodiment, according to which values associated with sexual gestures can be withheld and attached simply by an act of will, is being simultaneously assumed and imposed.[32] Porn compels performers to disentangle embodied acts from the meanings and values with which they are conventionally (and, usually, personally for the performers themselves) associated. The point is not that the inner experience of the performer is such that the gesture is necessarily experienced as meaningful. It is, rather, that in porn (and significantly in prostitution too) the performer's experience of sex and of her body-in-sex is being recreated: to ask a performer to enact a sexual gesture is *to do this* to him or her.

The counterargument is also familiar: to perceive sex as inherently linked with love, or with expression, or with some prized acknowledgment bearing deep interpersonal meaning, and to then assume that porn performers "withdraw" from such embodiment, is to fallaciously naturalize what is, in fact, a dubious arbitrary norm. Sex can be, and often is, an ends in its own right. Accordingly, no significant form of self-fragmentation need be involved in pursuing it as such. It can even be superior as sex when dissociated from a view that instrumentalizes sexuality by burdening it with other meanings.[33] Yet this counterargument is more plausible when applied to the general relations between sex and love than as a basis for defending practices such as pornography or prostitution: unlike intercourse for personal pleasure, when sex is disengaged not only from expressive values but from pleasure as well, it can create or heighten forms of alienation from one's own body. Linda Marciano's experience of being filmed for the first time, exemplifies such alienation:

> As that was happening, I made myself go numb. I thought of myself as a metal robot, no human feelings at all, and that worked for a while. I was feeling nothing. A skinny naked girl was kissing me on the mouth and I felt nothing at all. She tried to put her tongue in my mouth but she learned that you can't pry open a robot's lips.[34]

Similar embodied dissociation is also evidenced by field work on the experience of prostitution.[35] To hold that sexual gestures can be flexibly attached or detached from values is a dangerous overestimation of one's ability to determine the meaning of embodied acts.

Moral Implications

What is missing in feminist criticism of the kind that merely stresses victimization, self-harm, objectification, and exploitation, is the potential for acknowledgment and recreation of the embodied sexual self that pornography may achieve. Docile conformity to sexual norms should be undermined. Porn is sometimes able to mobilize this intervention, as is implied by the experience of performers such as "Mason," Taormino, and Rich Babbitt. Porn achieves this by dissociating the body's ties from identity, from accepted forms of experiencing sexual pleasure, unapologetically projecting new ways of being in sex to the world through the power of a camera. Wakefield Poole describes "a sort of freedom" that comes from being filmed for the first time, an experience of getting rid of fear.[36] As suggested earlier, porn's spectators may respond to this self-liberation of a performer, a perception that may be constitutive of their own sexual response. Sexual arousal is, thus, implicitly infused with moral and political values—and can be related to watching someone being accepted on one's own terms.

A courageous self-disclosure through some forms of porn is possible. But the same depth-structure that shows how this may be so, also conveys more keenly the harm perceived in most actual porn, in which, instead of attaining an enviable level of self-acceptance triggered by the freedom to explore their boundaries, porn performers are diminished by what they are asked to do. An abandonment of one's gestures, limbs, and sensual experience—not some authentic reincarnation—is more likely to be the result. If in self-validating porn, role-playing becomes existential amplification (the process whereby the usually unavailable possibilities of the self are fictionally actualized and can, thus, genuinely empower), when the performer is not living more through the enactment, but is being fragmented by it, porn becomes a form of *existential diminution*. Individuals do not access new experiences through such performance. Rather, they lose touch with the experiences they are already meant to have. This is, perhaps, why porn performer Tera Patrick writes: "Every time you have sex on camera you give a little piece of your soul away."[37]

My initial question was whether actual or idealized porn constitutes acting. My answer is negative: participating in a pornographic work is not a form of acting but constitutes a use of acting, which is why successful pornography does not require good acting. Porn is a form of other-oriented role-playing, involving actual sexual acts. It is a form of agent-determining role-playing. Porn shapes the identity behind the performed role because sexual gestures touch on values that operate beyond the limits prescribed by roles, due to their links with genuinely existing states. Once we recognize that these values are accountable for the agent-determining dimension of porn, we can also perceive how they are often at work in non-pornographic sexual acting. I have discussed the manner by which an overlap between acting and pornography occurs, not through a convergence of pornography with acting, but through the opposite route: an approximation of acting to porn. This observation revealed some counterintuitive implications regarding the exploitative dimension of non-pornographic sexual acting, as opposed to the nonexploitative possibilities opened up by some forms of porn. I have also attempted to pinpoint a dimension of interpersonal morally valuable acknowledgment that porn is able to establish, while showing why, in most actual porn, it is highly unlikely that such an acknowledgment takes place.

PART IV

LIFE AS STAGE

The previous part of the book discussed self-shaping role-playing by performers who regard themselves as such. In this part, I turn to self-determination through kinds of acting conducted outside the formal boundaries of the theater. Goffmanesque personality theories or the *Theatrum mundi* tradition are the more familiar ways in which such self-creation is typically articulated. Such approaches stress role-playing selves who, juggling among several roles, believe—sometimes more, sometimes less—in their own acts. Post-humanism offers a more contemporary variation: vocabularies of subjectivity are rejected; agency is no longer some authentic core of being, but the accumulated effect of re-enacted performances; discrete episodes of subject positioning are stabilized, reproduced, and then woven into loosely coherent narrative. For either contemporary or older versions of this view, the opposition between self-amplification and what I have repeatedly labeled "identity" is naïve: the latter is nothing more than a set of roles that one identifies with, a repeated enactment of a particular performance. "Identity," according to such views, is actually a selection out of a restricted repertoire of accepted roles on offer. This choice, some post-humanists would add, is what we have been socialized into calling "freedom."

Possibilities for self-shaping through role-playing are not exhausted by these influential paradigms. Unlike many forms of Goffman-like social role-playing or performative agency, in the two processes of self-creating performance explored in this part of the book—masochism and anorexia—the players do not need to be reminded of their own role-playing. They are perfectly aware of abandoning conventional forms of selfhood. Nor do they experience inauthentic hypocrisy in their self-theatricality, or sense vacuous repetitive performance. On the contrary, such acting is often felt to be a realization of a private logic, an experience which is more genuine and self-fulfilling than the identities being left behind. Daring rather than docile forms of self-scripting are attempted in such prolonged "acts," thereby questioning the post-humanist's pessimism regarding an all-embracing interpolation.

In these forms of self-theatricalization, self-world relationships become explicitly or implicitly modeled on theatrical practice, borrowing heavily and inventively from theatrical resources. But, in contrast to kinds of role-playing discussed in the previous parts of this book, this time the direction is not from "life" to "art," but the other way round. A partial list of the theatrical devices that contribute to an involved and self-shaping role-playing in these enactments includes mechanisms such as self/other scripting, implicitly designed dramatic episodes, a choreography of motion and emotion, maskwork, establishing suspense, consolidating an audience, orchestrating embodied icons, tightening one's appropriation of a role through mock-rehearsal and progressively intensifying playing, subtlety in soliciting audience participation, costume work, and Brechtian *Verfremdung*. As for external observers, in these processes the audience is often a self-attuned form of self-spectatorship mobilized by the actor, who is at once consumer and producer, director and, sometimes, even playwright of the theatrical offering.

"Being in another way" is, in such performances, not a playful broadening of subjective experience through the realization of more possibilities. It is, rather, a narrowing down of the self in which relentless, highly demanding forms of performance suppress, sometimes ruthlessly, counter-voices within one's identity. By contrast to acting's subversion of the limitations imposed by identities, in the self-theatricalization of the masochist or the anorectic, acting progressively restricts identity, permitting it to participate in a single play. Role-playing thus attempts to altogether replace who one is, while dramatizing an implicit complex dialogue with the suppressed identity. The liberation and pleasure of performance is, in both, linked with self-violence: an attempt to altogether erase one's previous sense of self. The impossibility of achieving this erasure is the source of the frustration built into such acts: the role-playing cannot become as total as the performer would wish it to be.

The extensive secondary literature that explores masochism and anorexia (rightly) attempts to historicize, politicize, or psychoanalyze them. The most frequently asked questions include why such practices exist, why they arise in a particular cultural matrix, how to understand their ideological significance in relation to existing hegemonic givens, as well as which psychological or psychocultural causality best explains the particular stylization of their enactments. And yet, the following chapters will avoid history, ideology, or etiology, invoking such literature only when it illuminates the dramatic undercurrents of these acts. Anorexia and masochism will be examined as forms of self-staging in which a unique kind of intensity is being experienced and released, and a specific form of theatrical display is being sought. Issues such as work on role, characterization, mask choice, and scene creation will be discussed as constitutive of a potentially empowering recreation of the relationship between identity and embodied performance.

What, then, is the degree of fluidity we need to postulate between staged and non-staged forms of role-playing? It is here that a distinction between acting and other forms of role-playing is (finally) needed. "Acting" was previously defined in this book as an aesthetically-controlled embodied imaginative transformation. Social role-playing—or substitute terms such as "theatricality" or "performativity"—share many traits with acting: the former can involve a progressive realization of a possibility; it benefits from curiosity and identification (either experiential or projected) with the realized state; it demands audience-formation, as well as a gradually internalized self-monitoring guided by audience response; it necessitates repetition; it calls for self-narrativizing according to digestible plot structures; it invites self-discovery and personal growth through the performance; it requires partial subordination of self to aesthetic norms; it includes costume and mask work (in the sense of attaining inner definition through external accessories). Yet extensive as the acting/role-playing overlap is, it should not invite a simplistic collapse of distinctions into some generalized world-as-stage outlook: performance may be ubiquitous, but it comes in different modalities that should be carefully set apart.

The first central difference between lived role-playing and acting relates to the function of the imagination. Acting is an *imagined* metamorphosis that simultaneously commissions an act of imagination from the audience, which is in turn invited to play along with the actor's leap into being other. By contrast, in social role-playing of the kind discussed by Goffman, or in the forms of performative agency discussed by post-humanists, the performance and the response that it elicits lack this dimension: in social performance, the self is presented *as that* which is being performed. Two interrelated claims should here be distinguished. The first concerns the general function played by imagination in acting but not in role-playing (the fictional beliefs the actor aims to establish in an audience as opposed to the genuine beliefs that social role-playing attempts to instill). The second is *the deviation from identity* that one associates with acting but not with social role-playing: in theatrical role-playing we are supposed to be fully aware of the actor's dissimilarity from the character; social role-playing is, by contrast, an attempt to prompt us to identify between agent and performance. Finally, apart from an imagination versus a non-imagination-based activity, and aside from the deviation from identity in acting versus its shaping by social role-playing, a third difference between acting and role-playing is the subordination to an overarching aesthetic offering in acting—a subordination missing from quotidian role-playing. True, social role-playing often involves *importing* aesthetic components from art; and models of self-authorship that relate to the self as a work of art go further, attempting to explicitly turn such borrowing into an intended act. Yet, unless one keenly follows this Nietzschean ideal, aesthetic borrowings into life do not metamorphose into a full-fledged aesthetic invitation extended to another: acting is an aesthetic offering, an attempt to realize aesthetic values; living a life is not.

Life is not a stage. That being said, the three distinctive features of acting—imagination, diversion from identity, and the subordination to an aesthetic offering—help explain why the particular forms of self-theatricalization I am about to discuss overlap with acting in a much more interesting way than routine forms of social role-playing. Consider a victim of child abuse, encouraged to dramatize a conversation with his assailant as part of a drama therapy session. The exercise involves imaginative metamorphosis. It also requires, at least in one sense, a deviation from actual identity, since it digresses from the victim's biographical context (suppose, for example, that the assailant is long dead). Such self-dramatization accordingly meets two of the conditions specified above for acting, while lacking the third—being part of an aesthetic offering. The overlap is comprehensive, but the lack of an attempt to realize aesthetic values explains why the exercise does not amount to acting per se.

The interesting point though, is not how to categorize such an act—Is it acting? Is it role-playing?—but to understand the play on identity achieved through role-playing. Confronting the assailant as an imagined act is meant to enable the victim to register a response that was stifled when the assault took place. While the act requires imaginatively shifting into a different biographical context, it is not a move against one's genuine identity, but involves *accessing* it: *through* an imaginative act that seemingly moves away from one's sense of self, an attempt is being made to overcome a split, a diminishing of self that had decisively shaped the original context. The discussion of masochism in the next chapter exemplifies this process in a nontherapeutic context: when a masochist acts as the slave of another woman that he casts as his mistress, the imaginative transformation is obvious and can be highly stylized. Here too though, the sense is of a movement *into* identity rather than out of it. One is not merely enjoying the release of a suppressed wish by such acting, but is somehow sometimes becoming who one is through it. Existential amplification is not now the actor's leap into alternative unrealized possibilities that thereby enable living more. It is, rather, a realization of who one is. It is here that the life-as-stage metaphor becomes striking: some lives (or some portions of some lives) can only be fully lived when "staged," when they involve an imaginative embodied metamorphosis.

A different manner in which the life-as-stage metaphor becomes unpredictably illuminating surfaces when self-staging is experienced as a problem. This occurs when one grasps the extent to which one has been determined by crisscrossing forms of performance to which one has been socialized. Two abstract options then become available: the first is to be reconciled to the gap between being and performing. The second is to attempt to—in Michael Fried's terms—overcome theatricality. The first option is implied by genres such as comedy or tragedy, which often collapse the difference between what characters try to project and who they actually are—characters are either humbled by this process (comedy), or destroyed by it (tragedy). Playing up the gap between performance and identity, such genres (potentially) offer a view of life in which the difference between being and performing is embraced and regarded as ineliminable.

The second option, overcoming theatricality, comes in two versions. Each of these aims to eliminate a different aspect of the performance-identity dualism: the first involves a refusal to perform. The second endeavors to gradually dispense with one's identity by attempting to fully merge with one's performance. The first option is exemplified by some versions of existentialist philosophy that endorse the ideal of authentic existence: one is urged to distinguish between external and internal constituents of self-shaping, and to progressively choose who one is; success in such an odyssey is taken to imply that one is no longer scripted, agency ceases being a performance. Problems regarding the distinction between "internal" and "external" as well as the dubiousness of "choice" in the above, render this option extremely doubtful: while one can surely see how it operates in more limited therapeutic contexts in which one progressively acquires the status of co-author of one's story, therapeutic success does not indicate a genuine overcoming of theatricality, but the acquiring of greater efficacy in determining its content. I take this pattern, its promise, as well as its flaws, to be familiar, and will not attempt to contribute to it in this book.

A second way through which theatricality may be overcome is to proceed in the opposite route: instead of seeking to eliminate one's performance, one aims to gradually forego one's identity. The vexing discrepancy between being and agency would thus no longer be felt. Again, such performances are not acting. Unlike masochism, they do not share any of the three conditions specified above: imagination is not used at all; a deviation from identity is not experienced or projected; the performance is not explicitly intended to be an aesthetic offering. No attempt is being made to be in another way. Nevertheless, one is progressively and completely turning one's life into a prolonged performance: consolidating and addressing an audience, organizing one's display through plots, establishing interest, conveying a message, choreographing loaded spectacles, and creating and projecting a relationship with a role. "Social role-playing" is too weak a label to characterize such performances, since they are implicitly perceived as attempting to obliterate the identity-role difference by endangering some other source of identity. The chapter on anorexia traces such a process. "Life as stage" is here attributed to organizing a life according to a taxing performance that seeks to *remove* all traces of its own theatricality. Once performance ceases to be a move away from something other, one's life is no longer experienced as a form of self-theatricalization: seeming and being are finally one.

THE THEATRICALIZATION OF LOVE

Masochism is theatricalized love. To access what this statement may mean requires casting a patient glance at a sensitive portrayal of embodied erotic submission. A rich and potent description of this kind is offered in a novel written by the person who gave masochism its name: Leopold Sacher-Masoch's *Venus in Furs* (1870). The novel unfolds the relationship between Severin von Kusiemski—a self-proclaimed dilettante listlessly flirting with the fine arts—and Wanda von Dunajew, a rich, young widow. Severin introduces Wanda to his fantasies of subordination to women in general—and to her in particular. The novel presents the progressive enactment of these gradually intensifying scenarios of humiliation.

The literary merit of the novel is unrelated to imagery, plot, descriptive insight, or quality of dialogue. Its import resides, rather, in its constituting an outstandingly candid psycho-literary exploration into a usually hidden sphere of thought, feeling and desire. Masoch is not interested in explaining his characters. He leaves his readers unguided, inviting them to make (or not) their own sense of the bewildering world they are entering. His focus is, rather, on what his heroes do or say. Given the explicit nature of the events and the obvious way in which they draw on autobiographical material, Masoch's disinterest in shaping or in controlling meaning-making is remarkable. This blend of part autobiography and sustained unapologetic frankness, turns the novel into a rare gateway through which masochistic eroticism may be accessed by a philosophy of lived acting, especially when attempting to take in, rather than pathologize, the evasive phenomenology of such self-dramatization.

Masochism's loving aspect (and in Masoch, it is love), is one of the features that distances it from sadism—as does its theatricality.[1] Unlike pornographic descriptions of male masochism, in Masoch's novel, creating an erotic relationship out of pre-planned role-playing does not take the form of mere sexual encounters, but of prolonged enactments of roles: intimacy is being organized according to a predetermined script, in which self-unmaking and self-objectification can be willed, embraced, and offered as part of an erotic bond. To trace such connections between acting and love forms an alternative to the political or psychoanalytic discourse that has come to monopolize reflections offered in this terrain. Etiological accounts of masochism—the masochist as punishing a father figure by standing in for it; or as being punished by a father/mother substitute—attempt to understand *why* masochism exists. Cultural accounts—the male masochist as subverting or reinforcing patriarchal hegemony—seek to understand the political relationship of masochism to gendered hierarchies. But neither causality nor ideology exhaust the prisms through which masochistic theatricality ought to be understood. To analyze masochism through the vocabulary of a dramatic experience reveals how stylized submission may become a genuine interplay between theater and love.

Apart from offering a detailed scrutiny of masochism as love, by presenting an attempt to totally theatricalize one's life, Masoch's work also becomes a unique meditation on lived role-playing. True, few actors would envy the exclusiveness and devotedness that Masoch's protagonists exhibit in their wholesale transformation of life into theater. On the other hand, such exclusiveness itself creates a qualitatively distinct dramatic experience: unexpected dimensions of the process of animating fictions are revealed, and the limits of self-shaping through performance are explored. Can one intentionally turn one's life into a play? What shape would such existence take? Could it be a blessing? Is there a point at which one's self-shaping performance has gone so far that it may no longer constitute role-playing? Masoch's novel gives rise to such questions;—not in the abstract, but in the context of a living process in which one's happiness depends upon repeated enactments of intimacy.

The Pictorial Basis of Masochism

Understanding the novel's presentment of love as a multi-layered theatrical process, should begin by focusing on its use of icons: the process of turning oneself into a structural component of a carefully choreographed scene. The novel's visual and discursive dialogue with Titian's *Venus with a Mirror* enables a probing of this particularly rich dimension, because the relationship between Severin and Wanda both responds to and transforms Titian's painting.

The painting that the narrator accidentally sees in Severin's study is a "Venus in Furs," a picture of Wanda playfully handling a whip, and resting her foot on a young mesmerized Severin, who devotedly and doggishly gazes at her. The story behind the picture is disclosed much later. We then learn that, as in Titian's painting, the pictured scene between Severin and Wanda had also included a mirror: Wanda steps out of her bath, and rests her foot on Severin; both catch sight of this in the mirror; Wanda's wonder as she looks at the mirror is cast as intimating a moment of discovery; she exclaims ("rief sie aus"): "Ah, yes, it is truly beautiful" ("*Es* ist in der Tat schön").[2] This exclamation suggests that a shared visual structure animating the relationship has been accidentally unveiled; it is one that demands to be recreated and re-projected. Indeed, it is this image that surfaces in different scenes in the novel: it is duplicated when the couple poses for the fictional German painter—an episode in which Wanda will meticulously strive to recreate the precise expression of Severin as a devoted, self-abnegating martyr; it is also conveyed to the real reader of the scene. It gives the novel its name.

The combination of self-perception and participation in masochistic experience emerges from the intertextual relations between Titian's picture and the anonymous "Venus in Furs." In Titian's painting, the mirror is held up by cupids who are trying to increase the delights of an already self-absorbed Venus by embroidering her with one final ornament: a garland of flowers. In Masoch, the "viewer" of the fictional picture inhabits the position of the original mirror. *We* imagine ourselves looking back at Severin and Wanda from the point both had gazed into at a magical moment of erotic connectedness. But in allowing readers to inhabit the very perspective the lovers share, Severin and Wanda do not really merge with their audience: while in gazing at the mirror that we inhabit they appear to look at the very same scene as we do, as *performers*, they create and undergo a significantly different experience involving both being and beholding.

The vision Severin perceives in the mirror is not merely Wanda's beauty (he does not need the mirror for that), but involves his own relation to this beauty. Yet the way he talks at length only about her when he looks at the mirror, as if she were the be-all and end-all of his gaze, performs a self-marginalization that allows him to merge with Titian's cupids. The mirror thereby enables Severin to simultaneously be one of Titian's adoring cupids but, concomitantly, to function as his own spectator;—as if he could somehow become a detached audience. Masochistic theatricality is revealed to be a dance-like dramatic genre revolving around such precisely configured central images. Combining devoted attention and self-marginalization with an attempt to be both an actor and a self-conscious spectator, such images guide the players in their search for additional triggering arch-structures. The repertoire of their particular kind of eroticism is, thereby, progressively established and rehearsed.[3]

An Actor Prepares

In conventional theatrical practice, we previously distinguished between the text ("play"), the cluster of decisions regarding its performance ("interpretation"), and actual, singular enactments that may differ while realizing the same interpretation ("performance"). In masochistic theatricality as presented in Masoch's novel, the "play" corresponds to some general theory of domination and submission—a quasi-philosophical vindication of female supremacy as manifesting an aspect of the war between the sexes. The "interpretation" corresponds to the specific "take" on the theme—in Severin's case, the fascination with furs and cuckoldry, or the particular images Wanda and him try to recreate. The "performance" is the actual, living encounters and the way they are experienced in distinct enactments.

The significance of the "play"—the philosophical organization and rationalization of that which will be interpreted, particularized and enacted—is more complex than what initially meets the eye. On first impression, the characters seem to be rambling—*not* philosophizing—when they present an abstract justification for sadomasochistic practice: men fatuously attempt to formalize love, to institutionalize it into marriage, and to also dissociate sensuality from spirituality; women, by contrast, embody the faithlessly playful pursuit of painless pleasure. The "philosophy" holds that these ideals cannot be reconciled: one will inevitably triumph. Severin's progressive subordination to Wanda, thus partakes of a general triumph of the sensual over any attempt to institutionalize and regulate passion.[4]

If evaluated as a genuine philosophy, one would find very little in this: German Romantics seem to have relished the genre, but few would now sympathize with sweeping descriptions of culture painted through a few confidently eloquent brushstrokes vindicated by some crude metaphysics of gender, race or nation. If such claims are, alternatively, regarded as the outcome of a psychologically motivated process—a rationalization enabling Severin to accept his unorthodox erotic fantasies by relating them to some overarching abstract principles—the philosophical framing becomes more interesting, albeit predictable. If, however, such generalizations are perceived as an aspect of *theatricality*, the novel's pseudo-philosophy becomes fascinating: the function of postulating a war between the sexes is to enable the actors to relate to the characters they are about to embody through a broader framework. Such self-allegorization enables Severin and Wanda to perceive their roles as expressive of a range of meanings that transcend the psychological or the personal. The pseudo-philosophical framing that opens the novel thus becomes an aspect of theatrical *preparation*, performed in order to facilitate and deepen the movement into theatricalized love. Rather than expose their *individual* psyches through a humiliation-play, Severin and Wanda will regard themselves as manifesting something else, particularizing a symbol, some general pattern that need not jeopardize who they are. "Philosophizing" is thereby intriguingly subordinated to the erotic rather than expressive of its avoidance. Such "philosophizing" discloses a perceptive realization of the weighty challenge of maintaining prolonged and awkward role-playing. It assists in overcoming the challenge of turning one's life into theater.

To Be and then Not to Be

An important erotic function is played by the presence of the biographical self within the masochistic role, which both challenges and limits masochistic theatricality. Its incorporation into the play also redefines the meaning of erotic union.

The simplest function of identity is revealed when it appears as unrelated to the role, enabling slavery to be merely a part played, and thus preventing it from being humiliating: "I cannot believe that you would dishonor me," says Severin (p. 196), disclosing how his fantasies of bondage are not experienced by him as debasing: the "role" potentially absorbs all of the demeaning aspects of domination whereas the biographical identity remains unscathed. At the same time, a biographical identity peeping behind the slave is also a precondition for humiliation, itself predicated on an identity being reduced, not obliterated: Severin is renamed by Wanda as

"Gregor" as part of his enslavement; he is made to wear distinct clothing, and to address her only through particular hierarchical titles. Yet this new personality, Gregor, operates as an erotically charged character for both lovers only because Severin is there all along: "Gregor" is an erotically imbued name because it is *not* Severin's own, turning each act of naming into a pretended ignoring. Arguably, it is precisely this merging with a role later in the novel, Gregor's actual transformation into a slave in Wanda's eyes, which bespeaks her genuine—rather than pretended—indifference to him, terminating the relationship. The *play* is by then over.

The complex function of biographical identities in this theatricalized love is also subtly captured in the orchestration of the precise quality of the indifference that should color domination: She asked *lightly* (leichthin), as though it were of no consequence: "Do you want to be my slave?" (p. 163). Similarly, the "casual" (nachlässig) placing of Wanda's foot on Severin in the painting that gives the novel its name is anything but a genuinely indifferent act. On the contrary, it is carefully staged, hovering precisely on the borders between role and identity: while both retain a vivid sense of who they are within the scene, Wanda must be cavalier when she uses Severin as a footstool. The nonchalant nature of the gestures brings out the precise quality sought by the actors, in making the characters *seem* to have utterly forgotten their biographical identities.

Recognition coupled with the desire for carefully structured moments of *misrecognition* of biographical identity also animate the pervasive role played by stone and statues in Severin's world. One thinks here of the garden scene in which Severin genuflects before the statue of Venus, or the multilayered function of the statue in setting off the first communicative exchanges between the lovers, or the role such statues have played in his childhood, or the numerous moments in which he looks at Wanda and perceives a statue. The mirror scene discussed earlier, for example, is suffused with the presence of a statue—*Venus de Medici*—which Severin had seen a while earlier: Wanda's descent into the bath reminds him of the statue. Moments later, in describing the precise image that will be drawn by the painter and ultimately grant the novel its title, Severin perceives Wanda's body as if it were made out of cold marble. The interlacing of the sculptural and the erotic relates to more than the qualitative "coldness" Severin is craving for and attempting to draw out of his mistress. Like Ovid's Pygmalion, the desire to bond with a statue partakes, on some level, of the wish to be unacknowledged.

The hypnotic pull of passing unrecognized by one's love object is the logical extension of the tension between role and identity built into masochistic theatricality. Indifferent as Wanda might be, she will always mar Severin's self-objectification by perceiving a faint echo of Severin in the instrumentalized Gregor. Humiliation-games played with her will, accordingly, always include a vexing reminder of the theatricalization involved. On the other hand, a stony Venus will not see Severin at all. Her marbleized gaze returns nothing to those who worship her. It thus enables a deepening of self-theatricalization by brushing against the point of overcoming theatricality: for a brief moment Severin may believe that he is no longer there. To look at the eyes of a statue establishes a form of theatricality in which the external anchoring of the non-enslaved self is removed, an anchoring provided by the gaze of a despotic flesh-and-blood goddess. Even with a statue, however, the subjectivity that remains is powerful enough to be inerasable. Severin is doomed to remain a subject. An essential frustration inherent in masochism is thereby exposed: progressive self-instrumentalization, however radical and theatrically creative, will never achieve complete self-effacement. The subject-role gap will always remain. The masochist can only hope to narrow it down to an infinitesimal point.

It is in the context of this attempt to be reduced that Masoch's incomplete characterization of his protagonists should be understood. What do Severin and Wanda experience when they are *not* mistress and slave? What are the thoughts that pass through their minds when they are in-between episodes of erotic role-playing? None of this seems to concern Masoch. This omission need not, however, constitute a flaw; it in fact coheres with the attempted theatricality. In practicing and sustaining a partial characterization of himself and of Wanda, Severin sexualizes the way by which he narrativizes reality. By denying the lovers' entire worlds of meaning that are unrelated to their role-playing, the narrative becomes *itself* a kind of masochistic love-play. Circumscribed description is, accordingly, not merely an expression or description of Severin's eroticism (or that which lends the novel its pornographic quality), but a constitutive and performative dimension of such eroticism. We must grasp enough of Severin's personality to experience the sense of an individual being reduced. From then on, however, we can relate to the gaps in the text, the shifts between scenes in which any glimpses of a non-erotic world are systematically omitted, as themselves an aspect of sexualized humiliation through a progressively curtailed self-narrativization.

The Act of Love[5]

Wanda is aware of the instability of the role/identity distinction. She warns Severin that the transition from fantasy to practice can be rough: "Beware, if you do find your ideal you may well be treated more cruelly than you anticipated" (p. 181). She suspects that unleashing the despot within her might undermine Severin's attempts to insulate the fantasy. She is right: once the performance of masochistic theatricality actually begins, the neat dissociation between identity and role crumbles. After the first whipping scene that they share, Wanda retreats into conventional erotic gestures. Severin's own withdrawal from the role that he had so ardently pursued follows shortly. Once Wanda orders him to obtain information regarding a handsome prince, Severin's fantasies of cuckoldry give way to the sobering effect that the mere game of culling information has: "You take my fantasies too seriously" he mawkishly tells Wanda (p. 200). This response elicits her scorn and her insistence that the game be played on a deeper level. Unlike previous incidents—in which we sense that she is being willingly manipulated by Severin into co-orchestrating his domination by her—at this particular moment it is difficult to dismiss a feeling of a genuine retreat on Severin's part. Such a withdrawal from the role is anticipated by the anxious thoughts that beset him whenever he senses that Wanda might seriously take part in the more advanced versions of the play that he is proposing. Contrary to readings that perceive only Severin's manipulative directing of the co-produced scenes, it is the voice of Severin's *resistance* to the role and his unhappy internal submission to it, that are being focalized by Masoch.[6]

Even when she is ushered into the role of a dominatrix, Wanda's own erotic pull to the game is not some mindless playing along with a fantasy to which she is surreptitiously scripted. The more prolonged the role-playing, the more Wanda discovers that she loves the role in the man, Gregor in Severin:

> "Severin, the seriousness with which you are playing your role is very endearing, and I find the constraints we are imposing on ourselves deeply exciting. I can no longer bear it, I am too fond of you, I must have a kiss; come into this house."
>
> "But, madam," I objected.
>
> "Gregor!" She slipped into the nearest entrance, climbed a few steps of

> the dark staircase, threw her arms about me and kissed me ardently. "Ah! Severin, you are very clever; as a slave you are much more dangerous than I expected. I find you irresistible – I am afraid of falling in love with you again." (p. 216)

Alternating between different ways of addressing Severin in this exchange is not just a means, on Wanda's behalf, of getting her way. Masoch discloses an aspect of Wanda's own erotic outlook: Severin's role as Gregor enkindles her love for him *as* Severin. She tells him that, ironically, his submission has spawned her greater admiration for him. His willingness to act out his fantasy is indicative of genuine power (p. 212), and this realization draws from her gestures of warmth and care.

By playing upon his jeopardized masculinity, Wanda's confession that she perceives "power" in Severin's submission may be a way to lure him further into the role, a flattering ploy designed to safeguard the theatricality. But it can also intimate a further dimension of Wanda's own loving gaze: her finding power in slavery voices her attraction to the role Severin plays *with* her. "Power" manifests Severin's capacity to overcome various internal barriers that would intimidate lesser mortals. Her domination of him thereby partakes of an inner dynamics of mastery and submission — what they are sharing, on some level, is Severin's victory over his own resistance to the game; it is the triumph of character over identity, role over actor, Gregor over Severin. This pattern—suppressing identity and allowing it to be mastered by a role—is not limited to Severin. Wanda, too, is compelled to resist the personal closeness, affection, and love that Severin's role-playing triggers in her. The problem with such gestures—the repertoire of normative intimacy—is that they revitalize and foreground the actor rather than the character, forcing the loveable slave to recede. Severin re-emerges while Gregor vanishes like discarded clothes. Wanda is caught up in a Narcissus-like predicament: the attempt to grasp the image in the pond makes it vanish. She can only communicate with Severin's "power"—the source of her love, the space in which they bond—through theatricality.

If we appraise as genuine connection only conventional forms of intimacy, Wanda and Severin enact a tragic love story: moments of misrecognition are carefully orchestrated when the lovers are dangerously nearing intimacy. Masochism would then become for us a variant of Cavell's "avoidance of love": a mode of role-playing designed to shun acknowledgment and mutual perception.[7] And yet, if we relate to *role-playing* as a means of facilitating the uniqueness of Severin and Wanda's bond, we must overturn this evaluation: the repertoire of "vanilla" intimacy—the moments in which Wanda summons Severin back from Gregor, kissing and caressing him—become a fall from the intense intimacy they achieve as mistress and slave. Which is it?

A response to this question involves pausing over the meaning of intimacy, specifically, its association with privacy. "Intimacy" implies that some dimensions of life are only shared with few. Intimacy in love denotes forms of recognition and acceptance of another's body in its nakedness, of another's gestures, actions, history, context, family, profession, sexuality, eating habits, and so forth. It typically involves a desire to understand and to actively promote another's pleasure. Intimacy in love also includes private love-games, private jokes, and private names. It is an exposure and creation of a private space and time in which the less revealed aspects of oneself are acknowledged, not judged. Relevant to us too, are the links between intimacy and the creation of a joint history, in which a particular form of embodied dialogue takes (or has taken) place. *Relinquishing* intimacy accordingly entails a disruption in one of these spheres: a disinclination to participate in love games, a refusal to create a private space or time, appraisal rather than acknowledgment, a withdrawal from shared projects, or a retention of these as little more than a ritualized structuring of shared time.

While Severin and Wanda are clearly intimate in many—perhaps all—these ways, the quality of the thoroughly theatricalized erotic gaze itself may still evoke unease when describing their play as manifesting intimacy. Severin is *seen as* Gregor; Wanda is *seen as* a mistress. Can intimacy truly be associated with a systematic apprehension of one's lover as someone else, a role-playing in which love is turned into an act? The answer depends on whether one identifies such a gaze with disconnection or with a willingness to stretch theatricalized intimacy to its limits, thereby achieving a unique and profound interpersonal connection. The previous part of the book enables to substantiate the latter option: it showed that when role-playing involves a withdrawal from care, it is potentially dangerous and destructive, but that role-playing can also enable caring relations, and, thereby, be experienced as empowering and intimate. In its capacity to establish acknowledgment, mutual pleasure-seeking and the intimacy of erotic privacy, Severin's and Wanda's kind of role-playing instances and creates care in many of its forms. The theatricalization they practice thereby promotes, rather than prevents, love. On a stronger interpretation, their role-playing *is* love.

Private and Public

Theatricality implies an audience. In many of the scenes orchestrated by Severin and Wanda, they situate themselves in relation to a real or an imagined spectator. Aside from the implied audience of readers or the narrator who peruses Severin's memoirs (the writing of which in itself constitutes an audience-invoking practice), or the painting left for some future undesignated spectator, there are less oblique ways by which the lovers create an audience. The casting of Severin as a servant, a message-boy, a driver, a waiter, a gardener-assistant and so forth, all involve situating him in relation to other onlookers. Such an "audience" is basically appropriated by the couple: onlookers are duped into watching a scene that is played out on a seemingly innocent level—a servant carrying his lady's bags—that, in fact, possesses an altogether different hidden sexual meaning. Positioning onlookers in such ways personalizes the look of the other, a look that is only abstractly implied in the more private scenes that the lovers enact (which, incidentally, could also explain why a mirror plays such an important role in these private scenes). That others *accept* Severin's role as a servant confers validity on the theatricality—we meet again the audience's capacity to substantiate the actor's attempt to be in another way. Moreover, by tricking others into co-acting with the couple as role-players, the audience becomes an unwitting participant in the dramatized scenarios:

> I climb up beside the coachman, mopping the sweat from my brow. A few minutes later we draw up in front of a brightly lit doorway.
>
> "Have you any rooms?" She asks the footman.
>
> "Yes, madam."
>
> "Two for me and one for my servant, all with heating."
>
> "Two elegant rooms for you, madam, both with fireplaces, and one without heat for your servant."
>
> "Show me the rooms."
>
> She gives them a cursory look.
>
> "Good, I am satisfied, have the fires lit at once. The servant can sleep in the unheated room." (p. 211)

The footman will be similarly recruited several times in the exchanges that follow. Unaware of the part he actually plays in deepening theatricality for the lovers by providing recognition and social credibility to their roles, he is doubly oblivious of his playing a part in the scenes themselves: "Suddenly the door is flung open and the servant exclaims with a theatrical gesture [!] that could only be Italian: 'Madam demands to see you'" (p. 211). Or: "Early the next morning I stood in readiness before Wanda's door, and when the servant brought up the coffee, I took it from him and served it to my lovely mistress" (p. 215). If intimacy is related to inhabiting, creating and sustaining a private space removed from public identities, such casting of the footman manages to both bring into being an audience and, simultaneously, to establish privacy and intimacy through that very act.

Servitude allows for such playful games with an unwitting audience—slavery does not. When enacting scenes of *slavery* (rather than more benign forms of service), it would prove impossible to withhold truth from the couple's audience. The three "black girls" who would tie Severin up and whip him, the "German painter," or the "Greek lover," will all become a knowing party to the particular nature of the role-playing between Severin and Wanda. Such encounters are tinged with a sense of withdrawal from intimacy. Pleasure remains, even intense pleasure. Yet the *loving* underpinnings of role-playing seem to recede. Deploying a knowing audience intensifies the acting; but it also erodes the intimacy, disrupting the privacy indispensable for its maintenance. The novel is thus able to pinpoint a further limitation of masochistic role-playing: personalizing the implied audience of masochistic theatricality invigorates the histrionics and intensifies the drama. It is thus an expression of intimacy. At the same time, the involvement of others undercuts the very privacy that turns role-playing into love. Notable again, is masochism's reliance upon highly limited characterization: the anonymity of the audience in these scenes—the indistinguishable three black girls, the Greek lover, the German painter—deindividuates them enough to enable their role as audience, yet, simultaneously, leaves them unacknowledged as personalities. An intake of subjects fuller than these nameless background actors, these schematic functions, jeopardizes the role-playing, skewing the erotic distinctiveness of the played-out scenes.

Warm and Cold

The masochist oscillates between two conflicting voices: the desire to tunnel deeper into slavery is one; recoiling from it due to the anxiety that one's identity will be swallowed in the role is the other. It is this dialectical movement that turns cuckoldry into more than another variant of humiliation-play. Cuckoldry is a complex source of fascination and dread for Severin. The introduction of an actual rival lover who may perform as Wanda's worthy partner, rather than as her slave, is a fantasy that Severin repeatedly finds ways of intimating to Wanda. As a sexualized humiliation-game, the desire to be cuckolded implies that, in his craving for further humiliation, his identity as "Severin" under "Gregor" becomes insignificant enough for Wanda to take up a lover. At the same time, the lover not only exacerbates Severin's total reduction into Gregor, but genuinely jeopardizes Severin's and Wanda's relationship as a loving couple. To invite him into their play is to potentially undermine care.

The actual Greek lover chosen by Wanda is described through conflating gendered predicates. We are told that in the past he wore feminine attire and that infatuated men mistook him for a woman. His femininity is not merely an aspect of his history, but transpires in the ultimate scene: he whips Severin, mockingly declaring that Severin's displeasure stems from the Greek being unadorned with furs. The androgynous element renders the cuckoldry scene complex. More than the obvious humiliation—Severin being beaten by the lover of the woman he loves—the androgynous nature of the lover itself reflects the ideal of the defeminized woman, divested of her warmth, embodied in a cold figure that is no longer a woman's. The lover becomes, in a sense, an extended reflection of Wanda. This accounts for the powerful pleasure that intermingles with Severin's genuine, unacted indignation when whipped by the lover.

Male masochism involves a distancing from and a refusal of the beloved's femininity. A woman will be seen as something other than her stereotypic cultural construction, lacking the warmth, compassion and care that are conventionally expected of her. The androgynous lover hypostatizes this emotional refusal: a woman endowed with the body of a man is another version of the ideal of a woman turned into stone, the pattern perceptible in the statues that Severin loves to worship. As for Wanda, we note Severin's craving for her coldness precisely at moments in which the couple lapses into conventional intimacy, when she bestows on him conventionally feminine gestures of closeness and care. As much as he longs for such moments, when these actually transpire, he carefully and persistently ushers her out of them. The abruptness by which he does this, suggests that, for Severin, there is something desired yet unbearable about the experience of feminine caring:

> "Try to forget yesterday's horrible scene," she says, in a trembling voice. "For your sake I satisfied these mad wishes, now let us be reasonable. We shall be happy and love each other, and in a year's time I shall be your wife."
>
> "My mistress," I cry, "and I your slave!" (p.187)

Such a recoiling from warmth on his part—directing her back into the slave/mistress conceptualization when she lapses into conventionality—characterize many of their dialogues. Severin will invoke his need for gestures of intimacy only to invite or even orchestrate her *withholding* of these. He thus turns such expressions of intimacy into a form of punishment. She must possess femininity—hence the resort to items of clothing and footwear codified as ultra-feminine in masochistic scenarios in general. She must also be able to extend such warmth to others—hence the fantasy of cuckoldry. Yet she must also be unwilling to bestow the nurturing and embracing aspects of such femininity *on him*, conveying womanly elegance and vulnerability, yet simultaneously precluding Severin from communicating with these. Her "coldness"—to which, in part, the furs that preoccupy him may relate to—is a physical manifestation of an inner lack in Wanda, one which he projects onto her. The cuckoldry fantasy in Masoch's novel thus bears upon a gendered aspect of masochistic theatricality: in their insistence on withdrawing from warmth—"warmth" being an essential attribute of the cultural fashioning and expectation from women—the cuckoldry scenes and the preoccupation with coldness, with the marble within a woman, seem to disclose an aspect particular to *male* masochism.[8]

Wanda's cruelest withdrawal from warmth (and also a cardinal development in her own relation to her role) occurs after she confesses her sexual fidelity to Severin, when role and identity are abruptly reversed:

> She began to stroke me like a child, to kiss and caress me . . . We spent two heavenly hours together. She was no longer a stern and capricious mistress but an elegant lady, a tender sweetheart. She showed me photographs and books that had just been published and she talked to me with such verve, lucidity and good taste that more than once I carried her hand to my lips, enraptured . . .
>
> "Are you happy now?"
>
> "Not yet."

> She lay back on the cushions and slowly opened her kazabaika. But I promptly drew back the ermine over her half naked bosom.
>
> "You are driving me insane!"
>
> "Come to me."
>
> I fell into her arms; her kisses were like a serpent's.
>
> She whispered once again: "Are you happy?"
>
> "Infinitely," I cried.
>
> She burst out laughing, and her laughter had such an evil ring that it sent a cold shiver down my back.
>
> "You dreamed of being the slave and the plaything of a beautiful woman, and now you imagine you are a free man; you think you are my lover, you insane fellow! I need only make one move and you become a slave again. Down on your knees!" (pp. 231-32)

The significance of this particular scene is that the divide between Wanda and her role is overturned. Until this moment, Severin had perceived Wanda behind the mistress. She could withdraw from the role into her old non-despotic personality. Bondage games were merely scenes played out between them. Yet in this particular episode, the loving gestures and shared intimacy *themselves become a role* that she plays but to torment him further when she drops the caring disguise. The distinction between enacted appearance and reality is no longer upheld.

It is at this precise moment that Masoch adds a subtle touch: the coldness is transferred from Wanda to Severin: her evil and shrill laughter ("ein böses, gellendes Gelächter") triggers cold shivers in him ("es mich Kalt überrieselte"). This is achieved by an initial reinstating of Severin's former identity through conventional intimacy: she caresses and strokes him "like a child"; she swears that she has been faithful to him; they read poetry together; she ardently professes her wish that he be happy. Yet precisely as she invites him to make love with her, leading him to declare his infinite happiness, she drops the caring mask, and mocks his presumed manhood.[9] Now he is no longer the lover with whom she has created a unique intimacy, but is himself rejected. His former identity is no longer sought for through role-playing, but becomes an instrument to further his degradation. Theatricality is exacerbated: rather than play the roles of mistress and slave, they now begin *to play at being lovers*. And it is precisely at this moment that the coldness he imposes on her flows into him. He feels cold all over.

Masochism and Acting

I have argued that masochism involves a prolonged and intense play-acting. But what kind of non-sexualized acting does it approximate? We saw that acting as such could be (and was) construed as expressing and fulfilling "primary masochism," a receding into the Freudian oceanic, the need to—in Cynthia Marshall's phrase—"self-shatter."[10] There is also a subgenre of "masochistic performance" in which the performer's pain itself becomes the currency of an aesthetic offering.[11] Yet masochistic acting is a more self-endangering form of life-acting, relative to the role-playing that is limited by theatrical conventions. It accordingly seeks modalities of performance that succeed in establishing a distance between self and role, drawing on a hyper-artificial visual language that is unrelated to one's "unacted" identity. The hyperbolic nature of masochistic role-playing—the exaggerated gestures, costumes, coldness, haughty rejection and hound-like dependency embedded in this theater's iconography—is fashioned out of visual and symbolic clichés. Particularity is avoided. Like the facial expression of the defeated clown, the attitude of the slave kneeling at his mistress' feet is not unique. He is distinguishable from other such slaves only in the contingency of his physical features. Originality in embodying the role is also played down. Masochistic acting seems to be confined to *types*: being a mistress or a slave means inhabiting a role governed by set expressive conventions.

The masochist as actor does not have to draw on private memories or personal experiences. As actors, slaves and mistresses are closer to the expressive world of the mime artist, the figure of the Vice or the Everyman of the morality play, or the types from the *Commedia dell'Arte*. The enactment of such roles is not modeled after life. It is directed, rather, at capturing and stylizing a distilled core of the staged sentiment, at discovering oneself within the enacted type. Here is Declan Donnellan's perceptive description of acting set types (he calls these "persona") in the *Commedia dell' Arte*:

> A practical example of persona occurs in *Commedia dell' Arte*, where different archetypal characters are available to be adopted, inhabited and played by the performer. The actor need not necessarily have done a wealth of specific research on the character of Pantalone. The actor who recognizes the persona of the foolish old man will be able to adopt the persona of this well-

> known character. Incidentally, the actor adopts a persona; the actor does not adapt a persona. In fact, the more the performer is able to surrender to the persona, the more the persona will adopt and even adapt the actor. It is as if the persona itself has done the background research and lends its findings to the actor.[12]

In a reversal of the power relations between actor and role, the archetypal character overtakes the actor's embodiment. A successful enactment of a type does *not* depend upon filling out the missing details which fully bring the character to life. Becoming a type necessitates a dissipation of the sense of self in the sense that the successful type-actor allows the type to supersede and shape one's identity.

Masochistic role-playing is not an aesthetically-driven form of refined acting. But it overlaps in an illuminating way with the psychological mechanisms underlying stylized acting of types. Masochism is a form of sexualized type-acting, in which resistance and distancing from the role work in tandem with the fascination exerted by it, the willingness and capacity to enter further into it, and permitting it to take over. In masochism the mask is allowed to lead. It occasions discovery. It elicits from the players unforeseen forms of self and self/other scripting. It ultimately leads to either/or conflicts, in which the mask does not merely use identity, but attempts to altogether destroy it. Due to the fact that in this unique performance, to further one's commitment is to intensify one's pleasure, devoted players of this game are likely to reach such disjunctions. And the utmost commitment possible is a complete merging with the role. The dream of altogether eradicating identity develops from this process, which is why, at one point in the novel, Severin manages to sexualize Wanda's indifference to his threat of committing suicide.

I have argued that the theatricality of love in masochism consists, firstly, of love relations that come into fruition through role-playing and which represent an alternative form of intimacy. Such intimacy can be dismissed or pathologized only if one adopts a simplified understanding of disguise, of intimacy, and of the status of communication via roles. Secondly, the scenes involve inviting, while not receiving, normative gestures of love and feminine caring. A withholding of such gestures comprises the expressive to-and-fro vocabulary of the masochistic erotic dialogue, and is interwoven into its fascination with "coldness." Thirdly, masochism is theatrical in the pictorial choreography of the scenes that regulate the erotic play. Fourthly, masochism relies on an imagined or an actual audience which, knowingly or not, becomes co-participant in the scenes. Fifthly, the acting genre of masochistic theatricality is stylized, featuring burlesque hyperbolic types rather than realistic human characters. Such partial characterization accounts for the limited interest bestowed on the other's particular subjectivity, as well as for the constricted self-articulation of the masochist. Sixthly, such theatricality involves fantasized or real attempts to altogether destroy the identity of the role-player, by turning the overlap between role and agent into total identification. Finally, it is the capacity of role-playing to establish care, rather than withdraw from it, which may turn this performance from the kinky sexual perversion with which it tends to be associated into an act of love.

THE THEATRICALIZATION OF DEATH

> As I stepped on the cold scale, the metal parts clanged and I acted surprised as I moved the small arrow down to zero. . . . My dad reached over my shoulder. . . . "Ninety-two pounds, Cherry. Why? Did you know this already? Is that why you didn't want me to weigh you?" . . . I had no answers. Sheepishly I stepped down from the scale's platform—the miniature stage on which I had performed so admirably. It was now being reset for a new drama, with the same cast but with strangers vying for the role of director. This would be the scene of a battle of wills unparalleled in any previous production in the Boone family's Beverly Hills theatre.
>
> CHERRY O'NEILL, *STARVING FOR ATTENTION*[1]

> Like nineteenth-century hunger artists who starved themselves and then displayed themselves as living skeletons, gawped at by people who paid to see these miraculous figures on show, I made my body into a performance.
>
> GRACE BOWMAN, *THIN*[2]

Anorexia is a prolonged unfolding of a theatrical suicidal gesture.[3] Such will be the contention of this chapter. Bewildered relatives, friends, therapists, colleagues, teachers, strangers casually met in the street—all make up the anorectic's audience. The audience also includes the anorectic herself, engaged in complex self-spectating of her acting body's response to her own directing mind.

Theorists have already discussed the external audience-directed dimension of anorexia as performed spectacle and communicative act.[4] But recent attempts within feminist literature to de-emphasize the anorectic body as an image taken in by *others*, as nothing more than a performed duplication of culturally-prized body images, invite a shifting of focus: rather than stress other-oriented communication, dramatic acting theory can illuminate the anorectic's *inner* experience as a performer.[5] More than yet another metaphor for acts of display, theatrical acting is an experience that is both keenly responsive to external perception, but is simultaneously also an absorbing, deeply personal, and self-directed form of attention which has nothing to do with the audience. Acting theory thus provides a potent vocabulary through which some of the enigmas of anorectic experience may be articulated. Given the resistance of anorectics to the very idea of "therapy," of theirs as a "condition" that needs to be "treated," employing non-medical/clinical conceptualizations through which anorectic experience can be internally articulated, externally expressed, and interpersonally discussed, may even ultimately facilitate meaningful help.

Before entering the theatrical specifics of this suicidal gesture, four prior clarifications should be made. Firstly, the emphasis on theatricality as a key constituent in the apprehension of anorexia should not be understood as a denial of the importance of numerous other factors. A cautious attitude—similar to Jean Améry's with regard to well-ordered causal explanations of suicide—should be adopted here too: at some stage, one enters an inexplicable zone—itself an outcome of reasons, but one that can no longer be exhaustively accounted for by them.[6] Secondly, the aesthetic terms that I will impose upon a destructive condition will not, I hope, be perceived as cerebral and cold, or as a capitalization on someone's pain aimed at generating a defensible thesis. The motivation behind the use of the interpretative tools of the humanities stems from a desire to render more intelligible the anorectic's inner world, a process that will hopefully contribute to enabling a more effective intervention mediated through a non-patronizing framework. Thirdly, I assume that some of what follows is applicable to other eating disorders beside anorexia. The distinction between bulimia and anorexia is, for many authorities, a blurry one at best—DSM-IV distinguishes between the two, but explicitly states that their symptoms may overlap—and is, in any case, not overly important to my purposes. My subject matter is an eating disorder that causes a life-threatening condition due to self-induced weightloss and its accompanying symptoms. Fourthly, I will intentionally use the term "anorectic," rather than the morally-sensitive construction "person with anorexia." While in a therapeutic context "anorectic" is sometimes perceived as disempowering, this chapter suggests that the attempt to dissociate anorexia from its subject—in the manner through which one can discuss, say, cancer or depression—is not merely artificial, but is importantly misleading. Boldly stated, once the anorectic progresses into a person-with-anorexia, she is, in many ways, cured.

Anorexia as Performance (A): Plot and Suspense

The literature suggests that the background contextualizing the anorectic "play" is some paradigmatic version of the good life: the protagonist is an intelligent heroine (still typically a white woman, though the situation is changing),[7] from an average to high socioeconomic formative background. Unaware of what they are effecting, "anorectic families"—to borrow Salvador Minuchin's terms—basically condition a would-be performer: "The anorectic family . . . is typically child-oriented. . . . Parental concern is expressed in hypervigilance of the child's movements and intense observation of her psychobiological needs. Since the child experiences family members as focusing on her actions and commenting on them, she develops vigilance over her own actions."[8] The anorectic "plot" then unfolds through the following "five- act" structure. It begins (Act I) with the undertaking of some benign form of dieting, initially encouraged by others. At some stage (Act II) something goes wrong: inexplicably, the happy adolescent persists in a diet that becomes increasingly sinister. In terms of plot organization, we have reached the *peripeteia*, the "turning point." In terms of theatricality, it is at this stage that an audience is consolidated. Till now, they were all casual payers of compliments; from here on, the would-be anorectic becomes a focus of shared concern. The mysterious dimension of anorexia now sets in. A plethora of familiar explanations begin to circulate: attention deficiency, low self-esteem, the psychophysiological effects of long-term malnutrition, conformity to patriarchal ideals of feminine beauty as involving projected weakness, a desire to attain (or regain) control through punishing one's body, and so forth.

From the standpoint of dramatic interest, it is less important which of these explanations wins the day. What matters is their *proliferation*. For the purposes of drama, it is the puzzle that needs to be sustained for as long as possible. Eliciting wonder and speculation, the anorectic endorses and later invalidates some of the proposed explanations. Therapy, threats, help, and self-help (Act III) could stop the performance at this stage. Helplessness comes next (Act IV), a stage in which external intervention seems futile. From now on, the audience is compelled to sit and wait. Waiting as such is in itself dramatically important: it sets off a host of interchanging attitudes within the audience—expectations, hopes, fatigue, anger, disappointment, and self-accusation. Waiting both triggers these attitudes and mobilizes their interchangeability. Finally, (Act V), we reach the plot's dénouement: either a full-fledged tragedy, or a suspense drama in which a last-minute solution appears; the anorectic is reassimilated—momentarily or permanently—into her family's happy story.

Anorexia as Performance (B): Acting

> The theatre has always seemed to me to be the committal of a dangerous and terrible act in which the idea of theatre and performance is wiped out . . . theatre is not that theatrical display in which a myth is virtually and symbolically created but the crucible of fire and real meat in which anatomically by trampling down bones, limbs and syllables bodies are remade. . . .
>
> ANTONIN ARTAUD[9]

The anorectic does not only direct an effective plot. She *acts* in one. Grace Bowman's remark, quoted in this chapter's epigraph, exemplifies a rare moment in which an awareness of such self-theatricalization actually occurs. So does the following self-description by an anonymous blogger:

> I want to be the Poetic Waif, the starving artist, a princess, a fairy, something ethereal. I want to be Shakespeare's Ophelia, the Labyrinth's Sarah Williams, Goethe's Gretchen, a nostalgic, tragic figure, living in a world of air and dreams. Instead, I have always felt the opposite. I am logical, earthy, contained, responsible, boring. I am choosing to live in a dream world, because I cannot live in the real one.[10]

Like Bowman, this blogger is here explicitly casting herself in a role. But by and large, the metamorphosis of one's life into theater is not experienced in such explicit terms.

The acting paradigm that comes closest to capturing the specific performance which anorexia involves is Brecht's: a mode of acting that actively hampers the audience's identification with the actor/character. Brecht's "alienation effect" is designed to occasion a defamiliarization with what is seen or felt, thereby establishing a critical gap. The Brechtian actor is invited to simultaneously effect the self-transformation that identification-based acting solicits, but also to maintain and project distance and self-evaluation. Likewise, the anorectic actress does not attempt to fully merge with the character, but rather to preserve the aloofness enabling self-commentary and self-critique. The anorectic actress shifts between these two functions (identification and self-critique) at different stages of her performance. To simultaneously act and comment upon one's acting as part and parcel of the same performance sheds light on the notorious difficulties entailed in the treatment of anorexia ("referral of an eating disorders patient to a colleague is not usually considered a friendly act").[11] The problem is that therapy may easily metamorphose into yet another platform on which the anorectic's performance is staged: she reflects upon her actions and rituals, but rather than recant these routines, she, in effect, enacts them for the therapist-qua-audience:

> "How are you today?" Crossed legs, head craning towards her, the psychiatrist intrudes.
>
> "Fine, I'm fine."
>
> "How has it been going this week?"
>
> "Fine, great, a lot better."
>
> The psychiatrist shifts in his seat and raises his eyebrows. Grace pauses. She hates these frozen silences, when the masks come down and each one attempts to out-manipulate the other. She likes to think that she unnerves him, that she holds a secret control that is infallible; he can't touch her. She spills out her lies in his face, one by one, only small lies, but enough to make him feel that there is some improvement. She talks about herself as if she were a third person. Her "I" is detached from her thoughts. Her "I" is the "I" that he wants to explore; her stomach, her insides, her guts.[12]

Blurring the line between therapy and *performing* therapy, the anorectic is able to thereby preserve a core of identity that she is supposedly meant to interrogate and change. Like Severin's diminished self-narrativization, in which circumscribed description was yet another means of sexualizing reality, the anorectic establishes an "I" that can be "treated"; it is, however, an "I" that is disconnected from her actual agency, and thus a tool enabling deepening the role-playing.

The same ambiguity with relation to the constructed "I" plagues anorectic testimonials and memoirs. Such texts are *not* necessarily expressions of liberation or recovery (as they sometimes present themselves), but performances: manifestations of the self-commentary encouraged by Brechtian acting. What supports this perception for me is a personal memory of an anorectic high-school student to whom I had taught philosophy. She was highly critical of the slim-beauty ideal, gearing elaborate arguments against the ideology of thinness. She was, at the same time, confined to her home, reaching a stage of emaciation that was life-threatening. If one listened to her words, one heard a politically conscious, sophisticated, and mature individual. If, however, one looked at her body, one was bewildered by the sight of self-induced destruction— she was, at that stage, in danger of losing her teeth.

My sense of this, now, is that I was watching a performance; one that utilized pain, self-denial, and possible death as its jarring materials; one which was also audited by the performer herself, caught up in the enticing, addictive power of "being in another way." In the manner of a Brechtian actor, she was shifting between identifying with the performance and creating a critical distance from it. My own position as audience was complex too: she was, ironically, discussing philosophy with her philosophy teacher while presenting him with a body that was utterly severed from such lofty concerns—a walking counterexample to the efficacy and communicative relevance of philosophy. On one level she was studying, and thus accepting the norms of teacher-student interaction. On another level, by her ability to simultaneously recount the abstract critique against patriarchal image-consumption but, at the same time—in her own chosen articulation of her situation—be herself a "victim" of such images, she registered an embodied defiance of philosophy's effect. By creating a context in which she was studying with a philosophy teacher, she recreated in another person—an authority figure, an adult, a representative of normative expectations, a mouthpiece of a discipline associated with hyper-rationality and abstract noncorporeality, a man—the combination of understanding and impotence she was experiencing.[13] Such recreation is not accidental. I shall later suggest that anorectic performance repeatedly reproduces the anorectic's world within her audience.

Performing Suicide

Anorectics are not alone in resorting to intense pain as part of a performance. From gladiators to boxers, from acrobats to tripping clowns and "Aunt Sallys," from tragic protagonists to *castratos*, from tortured saints to fasting, pious girls ("anorexia mirabilis"), the performer's suffering was and remains inextricably woven into many kinds of performance; indeed, is itself sometimes highlighted and displayed to invite applause. The "artist's pain" is a worn cliché; but it is not so for many artists who, in interviews, go through the routine of disclosing the agonies of creative labor. To incorporate such agonies into one's self-dramatization due to the perception that such pain forms part of what is being consumed by one's audience, may metamorphose into self-destructive, even lethal, behavior.[14]

As a prolonged suicidal gesture, the anorectic performance overlaps, too, with display suicides, themselves a theatricalization of death in which real pain is integrated into a one-time performance: "I asked my family and my friends to watch me self-destructing—I made them, forced them. I sat them down in front of me and I carried on," writes Grace Bowman, admitting that "it must have been impossible to watch this, to witness this."[15] Emily Halban's mother tells her, "like so many times before, that there was nothing more painful for a mother than to see her own child literally evaporating before her eyes."[16] Like display suicides, dying becomes a communicative act: the essential privacy of death turns into a public event in which onlookers are forced to participate.[17] Like the anorectic, the display-suicide shapes uninvolved individuals into onlookers; it then imposes on them a message that becomes articulated through the act. Suicide bombers even manage to complement the communicative act typically involved in terrorism (the main message of terror being that its victims are not singled out because of their identity, but because of the political category which they represent), by an additional communicative component: someone was willing to die in order to become the message. Suicide becomes an embodiment of a political claim, (dubiously) vouching for its alleged truth through the total commitment of those undertaking it. For the individual who commits such suicide, the act forms a momentary tightening of the purchase one has over held values. One's commitment to values is thereby not merely manifested through such acts, but is further fused into them.

Kafka wrote two short stories that are relevant to this discussion. The first is obviously "The Hunger Artist," which I will later mention. But "The Penal Colony" importantly illuminates the message-related aspect of anorexia as well. The story's impact stems from its identifying the ways whereby a painful, life-compromising inscription on the body can become a cardinal feature of social power. The writing machine that performs the execution in the story materializes abstract ties between law and communication. More specifically, the machine renders explicit the latent dependency of law on the infliction of pain as its vehicle of communication. Kafka's insight is that punishment—whether conceived as retribution, deterrence, rehabilitation, or an attempt to re-prioritize established values—includes a communicative component, a message written on and through *someone's pain*. The striking twist in the tale, is that punishment is only contingently related to actual guilt: the story ends with the officer who mans the instrument executing himself on it with no connection to an alleged offence. Kafka's story suggests that the transmission of values through pain is an indispensable social function; one which *can* be associated with punishment, but is, in fact, independent of it. If someone (like the officer) dutifully perceives this deeper function, he or she can undertake to become the suffering conveyer of the painful message, without any connection to punishment as such, metamorphosing, as it were, into a mobile moral signpost. Anorexia, I will now suggest, is a communicative act of this kind: a message transmitted through bodily pain.

The "Message" of the Anorectic's Theater

> Anorexia nervosa is not about stupidity or playing up; it is an expression of something else. The body becomes a symbol to try and put across that expression, whatever it may be. The body finds a language to discuss things which cannot be articulated, or which haven't yet been acknowledged or explored.[18]

Like Kafka's convicts, the anorectic, too, is a living carrier of a message conveyed through pain. What is the precise message she enacts? To put this same question in dramatic terms: if anorexia is a five-act play, what is the play *about*? It has been suggested that anorexia is a parody of the accepted body-related norms that yoke together femininity with an enfeebled body.[19] From such perspective, the anorectic play could be regarded as a form of political theater. Yet this option is unpersuasive. There exists little resemblance between the self-conscious motivations and choices of politically-minded performers and the indifferent, highly self-centered anorectic experiences, as these are presented in the testimonials that one is likely to read. Nothing in these autobiographies suggests an outlook that genuinely looks or cares about social reality or injustice. The single, repeatedly mentioned other-oriented concern that does surface is the desire to help others avoid the route taken by the author. Such an objective, if it is believed, prevents the sense of an utter solipsism. It does not, however, overlap with the ideological conviction that typically underlies political theater.

"I am killing myself" seems to be the most rudimentary discursive meaning enacted by someone who is intentionally cutting herself off nourishment. Mandating a response, immediately implicating the onlooker with guilt or with the duty to act, this message constitutes a powerful initiation into spectatorship: Attend!—else be charged with unpardonable obtuseness. It is a message *that cannot be ignored*, and it remains unabatedly at work throughout the performance. "I am killing myself" is, moreover, not merely an invitation to witness a death, resembling the "I am dying" emanating from, say, someone languishing from a terminal disease. The suicidal message involves a distinct invitation to behold an act of self-violence. In suicidal violence, perpetrator and victim are one and the same, eliciting in the audience a threefold conflicting response: protectiveness, the respect for another's right to determine her actions (read: whether and/or how much she eats), and hostility to the perpetrator of the violence. The anorectic "play" then, is about me compelling you to behold me kill myself. Through my body, I create an experience in which you will experience a range of feelings: bewilderment, disgust, rage, compassion, impotence. By becoming exceedingly powerless next to you, I will grant you power. At the same time, I will force you into a position of helplessness. You will be unable to leave this performance. You will be unable to know its outcome. You will be aware that I, too, do not know and cannot fully determine the ending of this performance either.

The precise discursive paraphrasable content of the anorectic's message involves a further subtlety that significantly shapes the performance's inner experience. The anorectic is not simply killing herself. She lets herself die. The message "I am letting myself die" differs from "I am killing myself" in its emphasis on the subject's refusal to engage in life sustenance. Unlike the active choice of suicide, anorexia is a paradoxical form of hyperactive passivity. Its activity consists of a trying refusal to act, a refusal to accept nourishment that, if prolonged, will lead to death. Its excessive activity—grueling amounts of exercises—once it is linked with a refusal of food, is subordinated to this overarching passivity, rendering the refusal of food even more significant by exacerbating the need for nourishment. Anorexia is a strike, a protest, a manifestation of non-agency but also of strength: I am able to let myself die; I can (or at least I think I can, or at least I project to you that I can) easily intervene and stop this; but I persist in dying. The present continuous of "dying" is also important: suicide is usually an abrupt termination; dying is not. It is a gradual process in which death is freshly contemplated as it draws near. Killing oneself occurs once. By contrast, letting oneself remain in a state of dying takes place at every moment in which the state is being maintained, or acknowledged, or seen, or talked about, or casually mentioned. Dying is staged repeatedly; it is experienced anew due to the varied responses of different audiences, or due to one's own capacity to freshly experience the enacted event.

Note, too, the combination of passivity and willpower condensed into the specific verb "letting" in this context. To *let* oneself die, to restrict oneself to being an onlooker, is to effect a division of selves: part of oneself is languishing while another part will not intervene and is straitjacketed into the position of a spectator. The "spectator" part of the anorectic thus participates in what the audience is doing: anticipating, duplicating, and amplifying their own responses to a drama in which the anorectic's "watched" part is dying. Yet such self-spectating also differs from the external audience in two significant ways. Firstly, unlike all the other spectators of the anorectic's drama, *this* spectator will also die once the body being watched perishes. Secondly, while all other spectators are genuinely unable to intervene in the enacted dying, the perceiving fragment of the anorectic's self can stop the performance, and yet will not do so. In letting herself die, she *lets* the performance go on. Self-spectatorship here becomes part of the enacted drama: the audience knows that in this play the performer is also sitting among her audience, watching her own act. She is able to stop the performance. She will not. The feeling of self-empowerment repeatedly mentioned in anorectic testimonials partly results from this ability to compel others to attend a cruel spectacle, and to also hold the director's power to end it.

Suicide is often presented as a rebellion in the literature on self-harm. It is a claim staked against authority. Corroborating this view is a long history of attitudes to suicide: laws against suicide, gruesome images of afterlife punishment of suicides, debasing of suicides' corpses, bylaws sanctioning the confiscation of suicides' goods upon their death, the refusal of religious burial. "Whatever its nature," maintains Georges Minois, "power seeks to prevent and conceal suicide. The subject must dedicate his life to the king; the citizen must conserve his life for the homeland. Desertion is out of the question."[20] The anorectic's performance is a similar subversive desertion. It is a withdrawal from the unreflective perseverance in self-maintenance which keeps everyone else busy. One of the best cultural readings of suicide as such a gesture of desertion—Lisa Liebermann's *Leaving You*—enables pinpointing a further feature of this process. Liebermann presents suicidal desertion as a decision to leave others, a farewell. Guided by the prism offered by this suggestion, the anorectic's suicide is a prolonged form of leave-taking. She is not merely letting herself die, but is also leaving— for good. By *performing* a farewell, the anorectic prolongs a state in which the value of others is being crystallized and strengthened, both for her and for them.

Here, anorectic performance draws on the tragic pattern of learning through suffering, the manner whereby tragedy enables the value of our attachments to acquire a sharper meaning through loss. A performed leave-taking creates such a deepening of values for the audience but also, possibly, for the performer herself. Accessing evasive dimensions of defining attachments as they begin to recede in adolescence, the performance re-establishes formative meanings by placing them under the threatening shadow of potential loss. Empowerment in anorexia is connected to this process, too: the manner whereby role-playing revitalizes care when such attachments are felt to be waning. And this brings us to the particular stage in life in which anorexic performance typically takes place.

Projected Response

Anorexia is repeatedly understood as a refusal of adulthood via reversing the body's growth. From a theatrical perspective, by attempting to undo time's effects, the anorectic actress performs an identity that can preserve her from identifying with her metamorphosing body.[21] Such changes are not restricted to the body; ultimately, they concern love. Rather than some vying for attention, the adolescent responds to her transition from childhood—from being a source of delight and wonder—into adulthood and the more detached expressions of love that it affords.[22]

In the context of anorexia, I am proposing to understand categories such as "childhood," "adolescence," or "adulthood," as defined by distinct modalities of love, rather as fixed by age-specifications. "Adolescence" is the transition between two very different ways of being acknowledged. Anorectic performance is an attempt to regain a sense of care which is attuned to one's very existence: the love experienced by a baby or a toddler in the typically loving families described in the literature—a love usually lost to adults, who, at some stage become acknowledged for the effectiveness of their performance, not for their sheer being. Once again we encounter the manner whereby empowerment through role-playing results from *entry into care*, here being desperately re-established when it is felt to be demoting into something else. When parental performance involves a shifting from hyper-vigilance and the bestowal of limitless nourishment in infancy into enforcing expectations regarding the adolescent as a well-adapted and socialized performer, the child may experience her parents' transition between their own paradigms as overly sharp.

Perceiving anorectic performance as an attempt to reanimate receding modalities of care, harmonizes with the typical familial context notable in testimonials of anorectics. The family is warm and loving to begin with, and both parents are usually career-oriented. In such a context, the transition from unconditional love to intimidating expectations may prompt a desire to regain the lost attention by replaying a scene of parting. Note, for example, the alterations from child to adult in the following exchange between Cherry O'Neill and her parents when they confront her about her weight:

> "It's my body!" I argued. "I know how I feel, and I'm not sick! I'm not hurting anyone else by being thin, so why should it bother you? I'll tell you if I need a doctor. And why Dr. Stark? [the physician suggested by the parents] He's a pediatrician! Last time, I saw Dr. Newman, your Doctor!"
>
> "I know, honey, but you've only been to Dr. Newman once and Mommy thought you'd be more comfortable with Dr. Stark. Besides, Dr. Newman can be a little salty sometimes," my dad's soothing, less emotional tone still carried the authoritarian sternness of a protective father.
>
> "Well, if I have to see a doctor, I'll see Dr. Stark, but it's not fair!" I retorted.[23]

The alternations between the physicians stand out: despite her protests, O'Neill willingly returns to being treated by her pediatrician, rather than by the family doctor (she is seventeen at this stage). Shifting between a child and an adult also features in O'Neill's associating her skeletal figure with a child's body, or in episodes in which she is, in her own words, "spanked like a child" by her husband.[24] Emily Halban describes her fear of leaving home and growing up: "I remember skimming through old family photo albums and shedding tears over snaps of me as a little girl, laughing, with a constant twinkle in my eye."[25] "Physically," claims Grace Bowman, "the anorexic is stating that she doesn't want to be, or look like, an adult," associating this refusal with—in Bowman's own experience—a progressive disengagement from feeling.[26]

Apart from an attempt to recreate forms of care that befit a child, the anorectic performance constitutes a three-pronged attack on adulthood. Firstly, we have the attack on the efficacy of matter: a starved body is not merely a body which does not eat, but is a body that eats itself. The refusal is, on some level, a defiance of material necessity, since "[f]ood is the prototype of all exchanges with the other, be they verbal, financial, or erotic."[27] In this sense, the anorectic's disengagement from matter stages a theatrical protest against the crushing rule of matter, typically performed at the age in which the laws of the body first make themselves evident as part of the process of puberty. Anorexia constitutes a counter-thrust to the body's first substantial infringement of the boundaries of the self's conscious experience—cessation of menstruation being one of its more important manifestations (read: objectives). Cut off from its supplies, the body surrenders itself again to the mind, returning to the invisibility and to the docile subordination of a child's body.

Secondly, as we saw, the anorectic is able to instill a confusing mixture of weakness and physical strength in her audience, thereby driving home the *limitations* of adulthood. In anorectic self-consumption one takes up less and less room, physically shrinking instead of growing. Such self-disempowerment by reversing growth, leads to the other's empowerment (I felt physically powerful next to my anorectic high school student). At the same time, one is paradoxically amplifying one's personal effect upon the world, which seems to grow in direct proportion to the weakening of the body. Shrinking, the anorectic metamorphoses the adults around her into helpless giants. Their own size and adulthood become associated with impotence.

Finally, the attack on adulthood also takes the form of a deviation from one's expected performance. The anorexic resists having to perform as this or that, which is what adulthood seems to amount to. "I got tired of the feeling that I was constantly onstage, wearing someone else's clothes, saying someone else's lines," writes Marya Hornbacher.[28] Instead, the anorectic wishes to be accepted and loved as the pre-individualized wonder that she was as a child. From this perspective, resisting adulthood in the anorectic performance is an attempt to sabotage the transition from being into being a performing self. It is a performance aimed at overturning the responses one begins to receive from the world as one matures. Instead of successful assimilation into adult society by progressively realizing a limited range of the self's possibilities, by successfully becoming "this or that," one is trying to recreate the wonder sensed towards one's very existence as a limitless pool of possibilities. One achieves this by threatening to leave, by performing a prolonged farewell—warning others that one may remain unrealized. Rather than exercise the capacity of role-playing to form an imaginative gateway into an inaccessible possibility, anorectic performance manifests a desire to communicate one's entire unrealized potential through a single performance: I could be in so many ways—and the longer I perform the more you will perceive the rich promise of my range—but I may ultimately end up being nothing at all.

Acting versus Relentless Acting

The exploratory, enticing side of self-theatricalization partly accounts for the anorectic's willingness to be absorbed into her performance at the "recruiting" stage—the stage at which she still retains the capacity to reverse this process.[29] What makes this fascination particularly dangerous is the unremitting nature of anorectic role-playing. This relentlessness quality of the anorectic performance surfaces once anorexia is compared to the life-theatricalization we traced in masochistic theater.

A fantasy of total assimilation of the players into their roles animates both kinds of self-theatricalization. Dominant-submissive role-playing mobilizes scenarios of domination that intensify in proportion to the levels of humiliation attained by the actors. Scenes involving a total obliteration of the divide between the dominant/submissive role and identity thereby become a regulative ideal, guiding the more constrained scenes in which the players actually engage. And yet, such an endpoint must remain unrealized because a masochist who fully becomes the role—if such were possible—is no longer demeaned: the identity that was being humiliated is no longer there. Similarly, the anorectic cannot simply starve herself to death. She must revive herself to remain in a state of dying. Curiously, the copious literature on anorexia fails to ask *why* anorectics eat at all. Presumably, theorists relate to such eating merely as an expression of the shreds of the anorectic's retained health. But given their awareness of the long-term damages which their bodies are undergoing, the act of eating cannot be explained as an attempt to truly nourish the body. If nourishment were genuinely pursued, one would expect the anorectic's diet to retain some connection with nutritional objectives. Instead, one reads something like this:

> 9 a.m. Special K with semi-skimmed milk and a glass of hot water.
> 10 a.m. water
> 11 a.m. Diet Coke
> 12 p.m. large apple
> 1 p.m. soup
> 1.15 p.m. yoghurt
> 4 p.m. apple
> 5 p.m. Diet Coke
> 6.15 p.m. soup and a slice of bread
> 6.30 p.m. yoghurt
> 7 p.m. water[30]

Why, then, do anorectics eat rather than simply starve themselves to death? Theatrically, to be able to perform a leave-taking, the anorectic must not reach the total lack of nutrition which will result in death, but must ingest the bare minimum that will enable to remain on the verge of death for as long as possible. The masochist needs to have his identity reinstated so that it will be repeatedly humbled. Theatricalized slavery is thus sexualized, whereas true slavery is asexual, and is bound to remain merely a regulative ideal of the performance. The anorectic, too, needs to eat for her to remain in a state of theatricalized dying, rather than be altogether dead. The dietary calculations that consume so much of her time are meant to locate the precise point at which she barely exists, but is not yet dead. In this she resembles the masochist's pursuit after the infinitesimal point of being almost destroyed by his mistress—recall Severin's fascination with being looked at through eyes of stone—yet, nevertheless, remaining barely there. Ultimately though, the anorectic is playing a much tougher game. Anorexia does not allow for the temporary respites from the role available to the masochist. Any genuine relief from the role—true, life-sustaining eating of a proper nutritious meal—would ruin the anorectic's act; she would no longer be letting herself die — the heart and message of her play. Anorexia is, and must be, a nonstop, self-accelerating process.[31]

A second important difference between masochism and anorexia as forms of life-theatricalization relates to ultimate objectives. Deepening theatricality is, for the masochist, an attempt to attain more pleasure whereas for the anorectic, it is an attempt to shun blame. The prescriptive nature of anorexia, the manner whereby anorexia assumes the voice of an internal director, alerts us to the propelling force of guilt in this theater. The following letter, written by an anorectic when asked to impersonate the voice of her own anorexia, offers a glimpse into the inner experience of such guilt:

> I am a friend of Kristen Webber—her best friend. I have unselfishly dedicated myself to save her life. I tell her the truth and keep her safe. The thoughts I give her help her to become a better person. When she listens to me, she is happier and her problems disappear. Since I am the only one who tells her the truth and really wants her to be happy, I am her only friend. . . . The most important thing she needs to realize is that she is . . . overweight. I've seen her body and know that this is the truth. People tell her differently, but they haven't seen her like I have. She is the fattest person I've ever met. My job is to bring her into reality so she can see this and change . . . (pp. 66-67).[32]

Note how the anorectic voice is assuming a caring function, in which directing and scripting Kristen Webber becomes its friendly responsibility. Any act of eating is nothing but a betrayal of the role, a regression, and a theatrical failure. The same holds for time idled away without attempting to burn calories.[33]

At some stage, this more cerebral form of guilt takes the form of a somatic language: a tactile recoil from food (particularly fats) as dirty, frightening, and contaminating.[34] Once guilt turns from a role-related voice—heard in the mind either as words of guidance or of accusation—into a body-related experience in which food becomes disgusting and defiling, anorexia becomes disconnected from psychological, cultural, philosophical, or theatrical explanations. Moving from the stage that Brumberg calls "recruitment into starvation," into a second, "career" stage, the anorectic becomes sealed off from the world. Such insulation is correlated with an important shift in theatricality, to which I shall now turn.

Role-Playing Identity versus Role *Playing* Identity

> I was me, but now he's gone.
>
> METALLICA

In Goffman's theory of self-theatricalization, *sincerity* and *cynicism* are terms contextualized in relation to role-playing: one is "sincere" not if one altogether avoids acting, but if one believes in the role one is playing. "Cynicism" is the state of disbelieving one's own act.[35] Goffman's theory presupposes an actor-role binary structure that he projects onto many other forms of social role-playing. He does not, however, consider situations in which the subject is performing a nonnormative role that becomes so overwhelming that the actress/act binary structure breaks down: the "actress" is no longer believing or disbelieving her role-playing; she is overridden by it.

Anorexia, I suggest, is such a state. I already claimed that its resistance to therapy relates to the therapist's inability to address the identity beyond the role, due to therapy's transformation into yet another venue for role-playing. Full-scale anorexia may even be characterized as a state in which the distinction between identity and role no longer exists.[36] Such collapse may also explain why anorectics find it extremely difficult to participate in dramatherapy exercises, in which they are explicitly called upon to playact. Dramatherapists report that anorectics typically dislike being on stage or being perceived by others. Selecting roles from which they can maintain emotional distance, anorectics resist fully embodying their chosen role. Their acting tends to be cerebral.[37] Dramatic acting builds on a capacity to *insulate* identity from the potentially threatening role. Fuzzy borders, it seems, turn acting into a progressively challenging feat.

And then the role begins to use the actor's previous identity as a means for generating new varieties of performance:

> One night, after a full dinner at a nice restaurant, Dan [O'Neill's fiancée] delivered me to my doorstep. As we said goodnight, he warned me not to give in to any temptations to nibble my way to bed. . . . He kissed me goodnight. . . . I turned around to do Dan's bidding when my eyes fell on a mound of leftover meat scraps in Summa's dog dish. They had lamb chops tonight, I thought to myself, realizing I'd missed my favorite dinner. Suddenly, the kitchen's lingering aroma wafted its way into my nostrils and the image of the savory, glistening fat and the thought of the juicy marrow resting in the bone overwhelmed me. I couldn't stand the idea of those delectable morsels going to the dog. Without thinking, in the shadows of the laundry room between the back door and kitchen, I impulsively squatted to the floor to feast on the dinner's remnants.
>
> I started slowly, relishing the flavor and texture of each marvelous bite. Soon I was ripping the meager remains from the bones, stuffing the cold

> meat into my mouth as fast as I could detach it. Suddenly, I heard a rap on the window behind me. I spun around to see who it was. Oh my God, no! It was Dan! He was standing at the back door watching me. There was a look of horror, disbelief, and total disgust on his face. I had been caught red-handed in the betrayal of his trust, in the breaking of my promise, in an animalistic orgy on the floor, in the dark, alone. Here was the horrid truth for Dan to see. I felt so evil, tainted, pagan.
>
> Trembling, I stood up and opened the door.
>
> "What do you think you are doing?" Dan asked incredulously . . . "Do I *know* you? Do I even know you at *all*? Who *are* you anyway?"[38]

We have already seen how identity may be used by the role in masochism. Here is the anorectic counterpart of this process. What stands out is the particular way in which O'Neill devours the chops: she does not place them on a plate, but squats on the floor, at the level a dog would consume them. Notable too, is the need to get over the eating as fast as possible, as though she were tricking some guardian who might soon return. Her fiancée becomes the voice of her anorexia, astonished to find her eating in this way. The normative, supportive loved partner becomes a mouthpiece for the usurping self: the prescriptive voice, the one who will not permit O'Neill to eat. His questions are all identity-bound: "Who are you?" or "Do I know you?" externalizing her inner psychomachia (had she not been caught, she would most likely induce herself into vomiting).

Why does all this take place *after* a romantic dinner, in a state of satiety? Dramatically, the answer is the following: the anorectic role is one that either prevents the intake of food, or—if such could not be avoided—sabotages its digestion once it has been swallowed via intentional vomiting. The nonanorectic self is submerged beneath this role, struggling to peek out and eat. At some point the role assumes the capacity to mimic normative behavior, offering, as it were, a play within a play, a role playing another role (analogous to Wanda playing with Severin as if they were lovers). The romantic dinner is thus, on the part of the anorectic, a pretense. To effect the expunging of food, the role now uses the hidden self, allowing it to emerge and eat some more, but directing it to do so in such a way that will cause it to be irredeemably vilified later. The role has cultivated the capacity to feign normative behavior, and to also seem off-guard, enabling the progressive debasement of the hidden, famished self, which is manipulated into presenting itself as degradingly animalistic (she feels "pagan").

Once we realize that both roles are played by the same actress, who is torn between them and the repugnant effect elicited by the play as a whole, we cannot miss the tacit *cooperation* between the nibbling, squatting body, and the subject who immediately penalizes it. Is it possible that O'Neill somehow knew that Dan had not left? Elementary precautions such as hearing his car drive off, or looking around to see whether anyone is accidentally in the kitchen have not been taken. Could this play be intentionally performed in the hope that he is there to watch and later participate in it? A similar suspicion surfaces upon reading Peggy Claude-Pierre's account of her discovery that her anorectic daughter eats morsels that fall off the plate—which leads Claude-Pierre to intentionally place them there.[39] My daughter does not feel worthy of legitimate food, so she permits herself to consume only leftovers—such is her interpretation of this behavior. But, once again, is the daughter truly unaware of what the mother "discovers"? Could she be intentionally eating these crumbs in a conspicuous manner? Could she, thereby, be setting off a play in which the mother's wonder regarding her eating habits casts the mother in a role that, from now on, will lead into an ineffectual form of feeding (morsels) that can be easily penalized as perverse by the prescriptive voice within the anorectic's mind?[40]

Understanding anorexia as a form of dramatic performance can illuminate such potentially bewildering episodes. Anorexia is a form of role-playing in which the distinction between actress and identity crumbles. Others are drawn willy-nilly into the plays orchestrated and carried out by the performer, who is able to impose on them voices and parts drawn from her psyche. But she is not merely casting them as spectators. Because the conflict presented by the anorectic spectacle between willpower and hunger is not only displayed but also reenacted in the relations between audience and anorectic actor, the anorectic is, in fact, molding the world into her own image: the audience mimics the role of the starved body pining for nourishment whereas the anorectic incarnates the role of the all-powerful, resisting mind. The anorectic is thus able to cast an audience into the position of that which she punishes. Forcing them into a helpless counterpart to the body that she coerces becomes yet another source of the empowering potential of this theater. It also accounts for the combination of pity and anger that the anorectic elicits in her relations, since the audience is somehow aware of being scripted into a structural feature of a spectacle that generates its own reproduction: the concerned parents, "consumed" by the need to have their daughter eat, are themselves watched by friends and relatives who need to know that the daughter eats, and that the parents have been relieved of their need that she eats. The resistance to adulthood presented earlier surfaces again: instead of being assimilated into the world on its own terms as required by adulthood, one reinvents the world, sculpting it into one's own reflection, just as a child would.[41]

Repulsion and De-Theatricalization

O'Neill describes an episode in which she defecates during sleep after taking dozens of laxatives. She then describes her husband's disgust upon discovering that he is sleeping in sheets soiled by diarrhea. She watches him change the sheets, yet repeats the episode a few weeks later.[42] Inducing repulsion in this or in other ways—vomiting, eating out of bins, laxative abuse, binge eating, consuming leftovers from a dog's bowl—all seem to be another pervasive feature of anorectic theater. The emerging skeletal shape that the anorectic body becomes, itself often occasions visceral recoil from its beholders ("Compelled by her curiosity, though fearful of what she might discover, my mother reached across the bed and lifted the end of my nightshirt enough to get a look at my back. Horrified, she gasped and beckoned my dad").[43]

Theorizing repulsion in the literature tends to focus on the repugnance directed by the anorectic at aspects of her body.[44] But what explains the anorectic's attempt to induce disgust from others seems to be the function of repulsion as the flipside of the rigid perfectionism which characterizes the anorectic. Performing perfection entails a total assimilation of self into some socially sanctioned narrative, eliciting responses such as applause, respect, admiration or attraction. Awakening repulsion is the obverse: rather than fit neatly into accepted categories, one undermines categorization, in particular the differentiation between the hidden and the exposed. To put this more specifically, vomiting, defecating in one's bed, causing one's skeleton to protrude, are all different forms of making the internal external, as if some elusive inner component needed to be wrenched out and exposed. Marya Hornbacher describes what reads like an attempted suicide through vomiting: she tricks a pharmacist into selling her *Ipecac* (a vomit-inducing syrup), drinking the entire bottle on an empty stomach (she knows that the proper dose is a single spoonful); she then vomits "in insane, ripping heaves, blood spattering on the [lavatory] seat . . . quarts of water, blood." (p.171) Hornbacher is not trying to eject anything that she has eaten, so the vomiting is no longer part of the calorie intake-burning equation. It is as though her fantasy were to be turned inside out, or to eject something that she is unable to pinpoint.[45]

By eliciting disgust, the anorectic exacts the precise mirroring response that her previous theatricality of perfection instilled. An explanation that may significantly elucidate the attempt to generate such effect can be borrowed from Michael Fried's focus on overcoming theatricality. Disgust, when intended, entails an attempt *to place oneself beyond* caring for the responses of others: by becoming repulsive, even once, the subject who previously typically played at being perfect seems to lose the capacity to invoke wonder, envy, and, most importantly, empathy. Anorexia is not only a theater that undermines one's projected theatricalized life as an adult, but, through generating disgust, it is also a theater that attempts to undermine itself. By eliciting disgust, self-theatricalization may, somehow, altogether stop.

Anorexia is a life-endangering condition, often accompanied by other afflictions. It is only partly accountable by cultural causes. It is precipitated, or curbed, by physiological, familial, and psychological factors. Anorexia operates differently in women and in men, and does not affect all of its victims in a single form. It also includes stages in which it is more or less controlled by the anorectic. To reiterate: this chapter is not an attempt to unravel all of its mysteries. And yet, a substantial range of anorectic experiences, actions, and regulative principles could be accounted for when anorexia is perceived as a form of theater. The anorexic theater includes a decipherable, paraphrasable message. It can be associated with a particular school of acting. It also configures a specific response in its audience, and creates and disseminates a particular spectacle. Anorexia demands relentless role-playing, in which any lapse in the act immediately undermines it. The anorectic voice orchestrates theatrical effects by manipulating the anorectic's pre-usurped identity. Finally, the anorectic's theater also encompasses a wish for a release from theatricality, exploiting the aversion that it induces.

It is not up to a philosopher to determine whether or not this explanatory scheme can be harnessed to accomplish a more effective therapy. A possibility that therapists might consider in light of this discussion is that the therapist willingly assume the role of the anorectic's audience, but then attempt to shape the performance itself. A therapist can perhaps prolong episodes of non-theatricality in the anorectic's experience (isolating the anorectic from her friends and family, removing mirrors, creating impartial and unmoved spectatorship, all seem to be measures routinely taken in clinics anyway), and also undermine the performance as such by intimating that it is *artistically flawed* (for example, that it lacks humor or originality). Emily Halban describes an experience of *humiliation* when she was initially diagnosed as anorectic by her physician upon realizing that she conformed to all of the typical criteria.[46] Grace Bowman writes: "I liked to think of my case as unique, I liked to think of my illness as having its own terms," though she was humbled when discovering that her very words and metaphors were recited by other anorectics.[47] Using the anorectic's lack of originality as an aesthetic critique against her performance is, thus, a therapeutic possibility for disrupting this role-playing.

It is difficult to predict whether such therapeutic orientation can yield an effective intervention. Some believe in the dictum that there is no show without an audience. If this is true, then guarded optimism is warranted regarding one's capacity to intervene and hamper the development of anorexia by intentionally becoming the wrong kind of audience. Yet we also know that Kafka's hunger artist persists in his art and starves to death, even though the audience is no longer there.

CONCLUSION

A young man enters the stage carrying his old servant on his back. The servant has beseeched him to go on without him, so that he would raise his own chances of survival. The young man refuses. He is fervently looking for food to nourish the servant. Because all this takes place immediately after one of the most celebrated speeches in Western drama, the episode tends to be overlooked. The oversight is unfortunate. If the word *genius* is applicable anywhere, this entrance constitutes one of its strongest contenders. More precisely, genius resides in the clash between what the young man's loyalty stands for, and the pseudo-wisdom conveyed by the famous speech.

The speech tells us that this world is only a stage, and that men and women are mere players. It catalogues the seven ages of man, moving from infancy to old age—itself imaged as nothing more than a non-endearing form of childhood, in which one merely lacks all that was had before. The speech is often presented as conveying Shakespeare's own views. But Shakespeare's real attitude to this sweeping identification of life with theater can be fathomed from his placing it in the mouth of Jacques: a shallow, seemingly witty melancholic who lacks true penetration and insight. Uncommitted, half-hearted, somewhat disembodied, Jacques is unceremoniously dismissed by the play's more impressive characters as soon as they meet him. His impoverished understanding of old age—seeing it as mere dependency—is being contrasted to Orlando's entry and what it stands for: old age as an opportunity to receive the kindness of the young. Such kindness is not repayment. It amounts to an acknowledgment of what the old bestowed on the young in the past. By receiving kindness, one does not merely become a helpless pathetic baby, which is all Jacques sees. Rather, one reconnects with one's history: the lasting value of past acts is discerned and taken in, as this value is reflected in the actions of those who are, now, manifesting the kindness. The shallowness of Jacques's reductive, seemingly plausible claims is brought out by them being followed by a touching gesture, in which old age becomes far more than a mere loss.

Unlike Jacques, Shakespeare, it seems, did not think that life is a stage. Too much generosity, kindness, beauty, cruelty, and misery take place for the life-as-stage formula to convince anyone but lugubrious cynics who lack comprehensive insight. While self-theatricalization occurs in multiple ways, identities do interact meaningfully and directly. Intimacy, friendship, duty, revenge, grief—all emanate from something that cannot be reduced into role-playing. When Orlando enters with Adam on his back, he is not acting. When Ganymede instructs Orlando on how to woo Rosalind, the love and erotic energy of the scene is not acted. Behind the multiple masks that the scenes involve, behind the fact that the episodes are themselves performed, something genuine is being discovered and disclosed. At the same time, while men and women are not merely players, the stage is also not simply the place where truth comes to die. For Shakespeare, the opposition between truth and falsehood does not neatly harmonize with the opposition between theatricality and identity: truths, genuine experiences, are often discovered and enabled by masks.

Philosophers would wish to know more about the meaning ascribed to "genuine" in such contexts, as well as the manner whereby theatricality facilitates truth. This book has sought to respond to both these questions. Tying together the spheres we have travelled through—acting, puppetry, masochism, pornography, anorexia—is the surfacing of an intense experience that is felt to be a genuine manifestation of who one is. All such contexts involved theatricality. But instead of the skepticism that this recognition should have evoked, we encountered lasting, identity-related experiences: the masochist and the pornographic performer seem to really be able to experience intimacy; actors could be personally exploited even while merely performing; anorectics could actually die as part of their own performance; acting as such appeared as a gateway into more intense living. In all, fictional role-playing did not undermine the discovery of important unrevealed aspects of one's identity. On the contrary, it generated the impetus for this process and then provided its structure.

The theory of acting presented in the first half of this book should prevent the claim above from collapsing into the idea that agency is constituted by performativity, a staple of postmodernism. To oppose between assumptions regarding a real self on the one hand and performed subjectivity on the other, could only persuade someone who sees performance as pretense or mimicry— both forms of role-playing in which distance from experience is sought. But if one takes a closer look at performance, recognizing how acting cannot be reduced to repeated mimicry, the anti-essentialism and playful skepticism with which performative agency tends to be implicated in post-humanist theory becomes less persuasive. Identity and performativity are interlinked. Yet, since performance includes forms of role-playing that establish entry points into experience rather than a withdrawal from it, self-theatricality is not simply oppositional to assumptions regarding a real self.

Several meanings of such reality have been identified in the previous inquiries. First, we have the reality of the self's possibilities, the manner whereby these can grow and diminish, and the way in which acting forms a bridge into a momentary realization of that which is unavailable. Second, we have the reality of inhabiting one's lived possibility, fluctuating between distance and full-blooded immersion in it. Third comes the reality of the contingency of one's actual lived configuration, and the desire to withdraw from identity and to become another, enjoying the flexibility of the pre-subjective self. Fourth is the further plunge into the object within—the unformed, non-experiencing dimension of being that is really there, out of which subject-effects emerge. Fifth are the networks of care in which interpersonal values determine the self in a manner that theatrical role-playing cannot always relax. Sixth come links between embodiment and value, establishing what one is by what one does, regardless of conscious intent, thereby setting a limit to role-playing. Seventh are forms of intimacy that emerge only as part of theatrical role-playing. In these, the most potent moments of touching another person in love materialize as episodes within a planned performance. Eighth are forms of being in which a wholesale transformation of one's life into a prolonged act takes place, identifying a role with who and with what one is. In all these different senses of *real*, the reality of lived experience is tapped by acts of self-theatricalization. The postmodernist's mistake is revealed as a precise inversion of Plato's error: the latter vilified acting because it is oppositional to truth; the former applauds it for the same reason. In reducing acting to pretense, both miss the capacity of acting to become a vehicle of truth.

That being said, there is in self-theatricality something that altogether evades the vocabulary of truth and subjectivity—a call for an intensification of experience. As one acts, one is not concerned with discovering truth, but delights in operating within a magical sphere, somehow detached from life, yet wholly absorbed in it. This book does not intend to present the actor as an inquirer, or as therapeutically releasing suppressed content in public. But in bringing out the points at which acting and truth touch, a description of the underpinnings of acting's magic is proposed. In amplifying existence, acting is first and foremost an experience rather than a mode of knowing. Yet the hold exerted by such experience on an actor, its power, its meaning, arise from touching what really exists. Acting is an artificial mechanism that cuts through appearances, revealing hidden dimensions of the living process. Its overlap with philosophy consists of this reach into an evasive reality. Its distance from philosophy relates to orientation: philosophy justifies, whereas acting realizes; philosophy thinks, acting does; philosophy articulates, acting situates.

Philosophy, in short, is a rigorous expression of the wish to know—acting, a committed manifestation of the desire to be. For too long and for the wrong reasons, these undertakings have been considered as standing for opposed orientations. We are, perhaps, ready to begin taking in their mutual complementariness. This should not read as a plea for interdisciplinarity: disciplines are aspects of knowledge, not of being, and acting is not a discipline. In spotlighting significantly different encounters between the desire to know and the need to be, this book calls for a meeting of *vocations* rather than for an interpenetration of disciplines. To be in another way illuminates what one knows. To know intensifies what one becomes. A "cross-vocational" experience is the result.

Vocations are important: a meaningful response to life is served by allowing one's outlook and experience to be determined by a commitment to them. But this only goes so far. Whether one is a seeker of understanding or of experience, an actor, a philosopher, a theater scholar—such hats sometimes need to be transcended. We are more. This should *not* be construed as a call for liberation. Allowing oneself to step outside one's vocation is not a betrayal. Ultimately, it enables a recreation of one's commitment *to* one's vocation, a reassessment of its meaning, a broadening of its scope. Such a conclusion follows from what acting teaches: becoming another can serve rather than undermine the attempt to fully be who one is.

Notes

Introduction

1. David Z. Saltz, "Why Performance Theory Needs Philosophy," *Journal of Dramatic Theory and Criticism,* 2001.

Intro to Part One

1. Paul Thom's main contemporary exemplifier of the older view, according to which performance constitutes a mere support for some other work of art, is Susanne Langer. See Paul Thom, *For an Audience: A Philosophy of the Performing Arts,* 1993, ch. 6. For the claim that Aristotle is the originator of this view, see David Osipovich, "What Is a Theatrical Performance?," *Journal of Aesthetics and Art Criticism,* 2006. James R. Hamilton, *The Art of Theater,* 2007, is a detailed and careful disengagement of theater from literature. For the dissociation of theater from literature from the perspective of the history of theater, see William B. Worthen, *Drama: Between Poetry and Performance,* 2010, ch. 1.

Part 1—What Actors Do

1. The remark is by François Ricobboni in his *The Art of the Theatre* (1750), and is quoted in Jean Benedetti, *The Art of the Actor: The Essential History of Acting, from Classical Times to the Present Day,* 2005, pp. 73–4.

2. Mel Gussow, *Michael Gambon: A Life in Acting,* 2004, p. 199.

3. Four further clarifications of this definition are called for: First, I regard this definition as providing both a necessary and a sufficient characterization of dramatic acting. This implies that a broad range of actions performed outside the theater—a parent pretending to be a roaring lion for a delighted toddler, or someone mimicking a politician as part of a joke—are acting (though not necessarily good acting). It also implies that some theatrical parts, or some enacted episodes of theatrical parts, do not involve acting, but are, rather, forms of *participation* in a theatrical event. A play may require that an actress be an invisible part of the audience for a while, or that she walk on stage merely to remove a prop. Such actions do

not constitute acting. Secondly, in relatively rare cases, actors are called upon to "act themselves" (as when a famous movie-star is cast to play a movie-star resembling his or her own biographical persona, or when an actor dying from cancer enacts a character similarly afflicted). Such cases *do* constitute acting rather than live testimonies, and are, accordingly, not counterexamples to the definition: even if the imaginative transformation is minimal, by being embedded in an aesthetic offering, the interplay between enacting who one is supposed to be in life and accomplishing aesthetic objectives on screen or stage, sets apart such cases from biographical documentaries (for several examples of such self-acting, see Steven Dedalus Burch, "Imitation of Life: A Meditation on 'Victim Art,'" *Journal of Dramatic Theory and Criticism*, 1997). Thirdly, aesthetic control includes legal and moral monitoring, as highlighted in the slave-killing example: blatantly illegal or immoral acts on stage immediately annul the ability of an audience to relate to the staged context *qua* aesthetic offering. It becomes something else—the forms of attention appropriate for an aesthetic offering are replaced by non-aesthetically attuned responses. Fourthly, the reader will note that distinctions between acting and overlapping notions such as "pretense" or "performativity" are not yet introduced. The distinction between acting and pretense will be later addressed in this part of the book. The difference between acting and other forms of self-theatricalization will be postponed to Part IV.

4. For the mechanistic tradition, see E. J. Dijksterhuis, *The Mechanization of the World Picture,* 1961, and , L. Davidson Rosenfield, *From Beast-Machine to Man-Machine: The Theme of Animal Soul in French Letters from Decartes to La Mettrie,* 1940. For contemporary challenges of the predominance of this tradition as well as expositions of the counter-tradition, see Shaun Gallagher, *How the Body Shapes the Mind,* 2005; Mark Johnson, *The Meaning of the Body: Aesthetics of Human Understanding,* 2007, and Richard Shusterman, *Body Consciousness: A Philosophy of Mindfulness and Somaesthetics,* 2008. For Continental philosophy's rethinking of the mechanized body, see Donn Welton, ed., *The Body: Classic and Contemporary Readings,* 1999. Cognitive science has prompted such rethinking within theater studies as well. For such work, see articles in B.A. McConachie and F.E. Hart, eds., *Performance and Cognition: Theatre Studies and the Cognitive Turn,* 2006).

5. For two actor-related implications of rethinking embodiment and adopting the non-mechanistic approach, see B. Merlin, *Beyond Stanislavsky: The Psycho-Physical Approach to Actor Training,* 2001, and P.B. Zarrilli & P. Hulton, *Psychophysical Acting: An Intercultural Approach after Stanislavski,* 2009. For the manner whereby accounts of the body have historically shaped approaches to acting, see Joseph R. Roach, *The Player's Passion: Studies in the Science of Acting,* 1993.

6. To describe the debate in this way is to simplify it in four ways. Firstly, it involves lumping together all non-Stanislavsky oriented approaches—e.g. Brecht's ideological approach to acting or Lecoq's emphasis on physical action as establishing inner experience—as if all they shared was their opposition to Stanislavsky. Sec-

ondly, it assumes that Stanislavsky neatly belonged to the camp I have situated him in, a point contested by authors who have repeatedly argued against the false appropriation of Stanislavsky through his American domestication by Strasberg and his Method. Thirdly, it ignores non-Western acting traditions. Fourthly, it assumes that the debates between "feelers" and "presenters" began with Stanislavsky, whereas in actuality they are perceptible at least as far back as Diderot. My response to the first and third objections is that: a) what I plan to say will not be applicable to each and every school of acting, but b) it will nevertheless pertain to a substantial part of the practice both in Western and non-Western contexts. The second and fourth objections will not affect my argument. According to Gordon—who also provides a far more detailed map of approaches to acting than the one sketched above—Strasberg's Method remains the most popular approach to actor instruction in the English-speaking world (see Robert Gordon, *The Purpose of Playing: Modern Acting Theories in Perspective,* 1996, pp. 354–6). A falsification of Stanislavsky—if Strasberg is, indeed, guilty of one—can nevertheless become the reigning position and the one that should accordingly be discussed. Anti-Strasberg sentiment is strong among some circles (see ch. 5 in John Harrop, *Acting,* 1992, and ch. 2 in Richard Hornby, *The End of Acting: A Radical View,* 1992.) Method-acting has also been analyzed as an ideological tool through which a specifically American version of the self is disseminated and consolidated (see Michael L. Quinn, "Self-Reliance and Ritual Renewal: Anti-Theatrical Ideology in American Method Acting," *Journal of Dramatic Theory and Criticism,* 1995). For a useful corrective, see David Krasner, "I Hate Strasberg: Method Bashing in the Academy," in *Method Acting Reconsidered: Theory, Practice, Future,* edited by. David Krasner, 2000, pp. 3–33). For my largely ahistorical purposes, the remarks above relating to experience-oriented acting can be assigned to Strasberg rather than Stanislavsky and can be traced back to the two protagonists in Diderot's *The Paradox of Acting* ,or even earlier.

7. Don Richardson, *Acting without Agony: An Alternative to the Method,* 1988, p. 11.

8. See Hornby, *The End of Acting,* p. 65; see also Harrop, *Acting,* p. 126.

9. Simon Callow, *Being an Actor,* 2004, p. 31.

10. Hornby, *The End of Acting,* p. 57.

11. Charles Marowitz, *The Act of Being: Towards a Theory of Acting,* 1978, p. 100.

12. Antony Sher, *Year of the King: An Actor's Diary and Sketchbook,* 1997, p. 196.

13. See Benedetti, *The Art of the Actor,* p. 60; p. 64.

14. See Mel Gordon's introduction to Michael Chekhov's *On the Technique of Acting,* 1991, pp. ix-x.

Part I—Three Kinds of Existential Amplification

1. Alexander Nehamas associates such a view of personal experience with Aristotle, in his *Nietzsche, Life as Literature,* 1985.

2. Nicholas Rescher usefully delineates four alternative metaphysical render-

ings of the possible within Western philosophy: Nominalism (possibilities exist in language), Conceptualism (they exist in the mind), Conceptual Realism (they exist in the mind of God), and Realism (they exist independently of human thought). Because foregrounding the centrality of possibilities for subjectivity can be alternatively formulated in each of these competing ontologies, it is unnecessary to couch these remarks in a more specific ontology of possibilities. See, Nicholas Rescher "The Ontology of the Possible," in *The Possible and the Actual: Readings in the Metaphysics of Modality*, ed. Michael J. Loux, 1979, pp. 166–81. The perceptual claim above—we *perceive* possibilities—is contested in discussions within the philosophy of perception. For a recent advocating of it (via a distinction between what one sees and what one's perceptual state involves); see also Bence Nanay, "Do We Sense Modalities with Our Sense Modalities?," *Ratio*, 2011.

3. Jorge Luis Borges's short story *The Zahir* articulates this idea in relation to money.

4. I am here distancing existential amplification from a more limited version of this idea, put forth by Augusto Boal, who talks of "inner cops" that monitor and hamper the actor from releasing some unrealized possibilities, an interior police that Boal's own theatre hopes to overthrow. See Augusto Boal, *The Rainbow of Desire: The Boal Method of Theatre and Therapy,* 1995, pp. 35–36.

5. Callow, ibid., p. 84 (italics mine).

6. There are several questions discussed in the literature on the so called "paradox": (a) Does one experience genuine emotions in response to fictional events? (b) If such are experienced, are they the same as real emotions; if not, how do they differ? (c) Is it rational to experience such responses? In the above, I am assuming a positive response to (a), elaborating on (b), and ignoring (c). For a useful discussion (though in the context of literary fictions, not in that of acting), see Berys N. Gaut, *Art, Emotion and Ethics,* 2007, pp. 208–26.

7. Phillip Zarrilli exemplifies this conviction. He prefers to regard acting in terms of "dynamic energetics" and not in terms of representation. He speaks of the "actor's immediate and appropriate deployment of her energy in the act of performance and the spectator's experience of that performance" Zarrilli, *Psychophysical Acting*, p. 50; see also Lehmann's description of "energetic theatre" in Hans-Thies Lehmann, *Postdramatic Theatre,* 2006, pp. 37–8. For further examples of energy-oriented approaches to actor-training, see Jane Goodall, *Stage Presence,* 2008, ch. 1.

8. There have been attempts within theater studies to situate or contextualize articulations of such terms. See Goodall, *Stage Presence* and Joseph R. Roach, *It,* 2007. Conceptually, what Goodall proposes is that 'presence' encapsulates a force that is simultaneously controllable and mysterious (p. 20). For Roach, "it" is the ability to embody simultaneously contradictory qualities (p. 8).

9. While the bias against metaphysical or theological nomenclature within Anglo-American aesthetics is strong, it is unclear whether it is deep ("deep" in

the sense of genuinely purging aesthetic experience from such concepts, either by elimination or by reinterpretation) or superficial (merely offering apparently "safe" interchangeable words, thus constituting no more than a shift between vocabularies). Dance theory in particular has given rise to some exceptions to this bias. Susanne Langer has analyzed dance as embodiment of "virtual powers"—the vital force emanating from dancers (see Susane K. Langer, *Feeling and Form: A Theory of Art,* 1953, ch. 11.) Beardsley's account of dance, involved an attempt to credibly formulate a general truth he found in a remark by Merce Cunningham, who said that dance provides "an amplification of energy." Beardsley accounted for this amplification by postulating "intense volitional qualities": properties that are perceived and expressed in dance, see Monroe C. Beardsley, "What Is Going on in a Dance?," *Dance Research Journal,* 1982. Some of the literature on "presence" in performance attempts to engage features such as energy by translating them into a parallel vocabulary. See, for example, the chapters by Jaeger and Erickson in D. Krasner and D.Z. Saltz, eds., *Staging Philosophy: Intersections of Theater, Performance, and Philosophy,* 2006.

10. Paul Woodruff's account of character as "a person whose story is worth following" (due to the ability of the story to evoke various kinds of care from an audience) may be useful as a guide to literary characters and to the plot-related aspects of theatrical spectatorship. But it does not include that which actors distinctly add to the life-stories they present. See Paul Woodruff, *The Necessity of Theater: The Art of Watching and Being Watched,* 2008, ch. 5, p. 95.

11. David Davies follows Wollheim's claims regarding successful performance as one that manages to render the vehicle an object of ever-increasing attention. The attempt is then made to explain such "regard" by virtue of attributing significance to every *movement* of the performer, coupled to an attempt to relate such movements to a point being made (David Davies, *Philosophy of the Performing Arts,* 2011, esp. p. 15.). This covers well the interpretative dimension of spectatorship: the meaning-making operations that an attentive audience engages in. But response to a performance includes additional layers that are unrelated to meaning-making. Amateur actors can come up with a semantically rich performance that, nevertheless, utterly fails to move the audience. What they often miss is not the capacity to convey the meaning of movement, but additional layers that consist of infusing a gesture with non-semantic significance, a quality that an audience is able to pick out and respond to.

12. Michael Goldman, *The Actor's Freedom: Toward a Theory of Drama,* 1975, p. 5.

13. John Gielgud, *John Gielgud: An Actor and His Time,* 1997, p. 39.

14. Lee Strasberg, *A Dream of Passion: The Development of the Method,* 1988, pp. 22–3.

15. Richard B. Onians, *The Origins of European Thought About the Body, the*

Mind, the Soul, the World, Time and Fate: New Interpretations of Greek, Roman and Kindred Evidence Also of Some Basic Jewish and Christian Beliefs, 1988, pp. 50–52.

16. The typology is by Peter Kivy, who traces the first tradition (the "possessed") back to Plato's *Ion* and the second (the "possessor") to pseudo-Longinus, arguing that both traditions underpin the ideal of artistic genius. See Peter Kivy, *The Possessor and the Possessed: Handel, Mozart, Beethoven, and the Idea of Musical Genius,* 2001.

17. Bert States offers testimonials of the mesmerizing effect of performances by Sarah Bernhardt and Eleonora Duse, associating the latter with a capacity to become her role, and the former with presenting two whole women in one body, Bert O. States, *Great Reckonings in Little Rooms: On the Phenomenology of Theater,* 1985, 166–70.

18. In Toby Cole, ed., *Actors on Acting: The Theories, Techniques, and Practices of the Great Actors of All Times as Told in Their Own Words,* 1970, p. 483.

19. Sanford Meisner and Dennis Longwell, *Sanford Meisner on Acting,* 1987, p. 68.

20. Jacques Lecoq's approach is the best-known in this context, but see also Merlin, *Beyond Stanislavsky,* and Zarrilli, *Psychophysical Acting.*

21. Hornby, *The End of Acting,* p. 21.

22. For such a view see Hornby, *The End of Acting,* ch. 2.

23. Harrop, *Acting,* p. 111.

24. For the kind of criticisms I have in mind, see Philip Auslander, "'Just Be Your Self': Logocentrism and Difference in Performance Theory," in *Acting Reconsidered: A Theoretical and Practical Guide,* edited by Phillip B. Zarrilli, 2002, pp. 53–60; see also Cynthia Bishop Dillon, "Active Interpretation/Deconstruction Play: Postmodern Considerations of Acting," *Journal of Dramatic Theory and Criticism,* (1993). For one influential exposition of the process described above, see E. Fuchs, *The Death of Character: Perspectives on Theater after Modernism,* 1996.

25. Elizabeth Burns maintains that the actor "realiz[es] theatricalized versions of the residue of unrealizable potentialities of existence," a formulation that she then unpacked in terms of "depersonalization"—the actor's ability to momentarily incarnate personality fragments rather than full-blown "characters," thereby momentarily "being without the continuous, coherent, identity we associate with the idea of "character."" My account of existential amplification is clearly broader than this, but Burns's formulation enables noting how it may include nonidentity committed versions of the self. See, Elizabeth Burns, *Theatricality: A Study of Convention in the Theatre and in Social Life,* 1972. For the citations see p. 150 and p. 174; for her discussion, see pp. 174–83.

26. Tzachi Zamir, *Double Vision: Moral Philosophy and Shakespearean Drama,* 2007, ch. 3.

27. Stanton Garner presents an analogous argument regarding the complemen-

tarity (rather than rivalry) between post-humanist criticism and phenomenology: the manner whereby both can and do powerfully harmonize rather than necessarily clash. See esp; Stanton B. Garner, *Bodied Spaces: Phenomenology and Performance in Contemporary Drama,* 1994. ch. 1

Part I—The Experience of Amplification

1. Uta Hagen Haskel Frankel, *Respect for Acting,* 1973, p. 12. Salvini's wry reflections on Coquelin's oft-quoted remark (reproduced in Cole's anthology) are well-worth reading in this context.

2. Michael A. Morrison, *John Barrymore, Shakespearean Actor,* 1997, p. 115.

3. Brecht's precise position regarding "alienation effects" is unclear. In some versions of his approach (based on texts like "The Street Scene" or "A Short Description of a New Technique of Acting which Produces an Alienation Effect"), Brecht is radically opposed to any form of actor-role identification. In others, he encourages such identification, asking his actor to comment on the role *after* embodying it. For a nuanced account of developments in Brecht's position as well as discrepancies between his theories and practice, see Gordon, *The Purpose of Playing,* ch. 8.

4. John Gielgud, *Early Stages,* cited in Cole, ed., *Actors on Acting,* p. 398.

5. Laurence Olivier, *Confessions of an Actor: An Autobiography,* 1984, p. 20. For Gambon's comment, see Gussow, *Michael Gambon: A Life in Acting,* p. 155.

6. Declan Donnellan, *The Actor and the Target,* 2002, p. 81.

7. On this point and for a different possible articulation of the being/pretending/acting distinction, see David Z. Saltz, "How to Do Things on Stage," *The Journal of Aesthetics and Art Criticism,* 1991.

8. Truth *claim* rather than "truth" per se, better captures the relationship between art and truth. An aesthetic offering is (sometimes) a proposal regarding the state of things—a claim rather than an assertion. For further elaboration of further distinction (in the context of literature), see Tzachi Zamir, "Philosophy," in *The Oxford Handbook of Shakespeare,* edited by A.F. Kinney, 2012, pp. 623–40.

9. M. Brando and R. Lindsey, *Brando: Songs My Mother Taught Me,* 1994, pp. 127–8.

10. K. Branagh, *Beginning,* 1989, p. 211.

11. Strasberg, *A Dream of Passion,* p. 35. For other references, see Roach, *The Player's Passion,* pp. 16–17.

12. J. Derrida, "The Theater of Cruelty and the Closure of Representation," in *Mimesis, Masochism, & Mime: The Politics of Theatricality in Contemporary French Thought,* edited by. T. Murray, 1997, pp. 40–61, p. 54.

13. Cited in Cole, ed., *Actors on Acting,* p. 402.

14. Sanford Meisner presents many such repetition exercises, providing the rationale above for doing them: "I'm trying to eliminate a habit that, as you said, you've done all your acting life. In order to build up performances which are com-

ing out of you, which are coming out of your emotional grasp of the material, I choose to reduce you to a neutral, meaningless, inhuman object—a robot, call it what you like. In order to fill those words with the truth of your emotional life, you're first going to learn the text coldly, without expression, in a completely neutral way." See Meisner and Longwell, *Sanford Meisner on Acting*, p. 68.

15. I am thinking here of Ciana Fernandes's analysis of the role of repetition in the dance theater of Pina Bausch. Fernandes argues that the centrality of thematic repetition in Bausch's work foregrounds political claims about dance and its regimentation of the body, undermining the idealization of dance as constituting a spontaneous expression; see C. Fernandes, *Pina Bausch and the Wuppertal Dance Theater: The Aesthetics of Repetition and Transformation,* 2001. For a different discussion of another dance piece ("Both Sitting Duet") in which repetitive patterns disclose Deleuzean insights regarding repetition, see Valerie A. Briginshaw, "Difference and Repetition in 'Both Sitting Duet,'" *Topoi: An International Review of Philosophy*, 2005.

16. The criticism is by Arthur Hopkins, and it is cited in Morrison, *John Barrymore, Shakespearean Actor*, p. 144–45.

Part I—Watching Actors

1. Marowitz, *The Act of Being*, pp. 39–41.

2. For additional arguments regarding the variety of the audience and the implications of considering it as a constructed rather than a given entity, which is "initiated" into being by the performance into particular acts of meaning-making, see Herbert Blau, *The Audience,* 1990, and William B. Worthen, *Modern Drama and the Rhetoric of Theater,* 1991. Both books develop and contextualize this idea in relation to its anticipations. Such studies enable an ideological reading of the proposal I am about to present: the audience is constituted and initiated into an ideologically significant participation with the acting process. Such a reading will regard what I present above as proposed truth-claims as constructions of a fantasy. While I am less impressed by this line than many of my colleagues, it is not necessary to choose between truth-talk and fantasy-talk: preserving the mutual translatability of these vocabularies is an advantage for a theory of spectatorship that is able to accommodate both.

3. "Theatre means the collectively spent and used up lifetime in the collectively breathed air of that space in which the performing and the spectating take place. The emission and reception of signs and signals take place simultaneously." In Lehmann, *Postdramatic Theatre*, p. 17. The distinction between the art of watching and the art of being watched is developed by Woodruff, who defends a definition of theater as "the art of making human action worth watching" (p. 67). Woodruff presents what I describe above as a content-related theory of theatrical response in the second part of his book (Woodruff, *The Necessity of Theater*). For him, theater

depends on an audience that cares and is emotionally involved in the performance; see p. 154). Brecht endorses a non-emotionally oriented, yet, nevertheless, content-directed account of spectatorship: the audience is supposed to think, but not necessarily be moved, by the enacted content. "Alienation effects" are meant to assist in achieving this.

4. Here are four such approaches. Bruce Wilshire focuses on the concept of "standing in": the actor populates both the non-fictional and the fictional world. Using his "dual citizenship" (as character and as actor), the actor "stands in" for the audience in the other world. "Standing in" touches the audience "because it is the problem par excellence of our own identity as selves" (see Bruce Wilshire, *Role Playing and Identity: The Limits of Theatre as Metaphor,* 1982, p. 43.) Michael Goldman regards the actor as bridging the gap between self and the world's otherness: "You are merely a self . . . assaulted by otherness from within and without. In taking on the spirit of another body, the actor leaps the gap between the fearful self and frightful other. . . . The actor is a figure of power and danger, of pity and fear, because he is at once the otherness that threatens—now uncannily animate—and the threatened self, daring in its exposure and ambition" (Goldman, *The Actor's Freedom*, p. 122.). The potential of acting to disclose the otherness within the actor is also described by Josette Féral in her introduction to a special issue of *SubStance* devoted to theatricality: "[T]he spectator's gaze is double: he sees in the actor both the subject that he is and the fiction that he incarnates (or the action he performs); he sees him as both master of himself and subject to the other within him. He sees not only what he says and what he does, but also what escapes him—what is said in himself and in spite of himself" (Josette Féral, "Foreword," *SubStance*, 2002). A fourth option with regards to the subliminal links between audience and actor involves endorsing Richard Hornby's account of the psychosexual basis of acting. Hornby associates the dissipating borders of identity which acting involves (the collapse of self into role) with the regression into the oceanic state described by Freud (Hornby, *The End of Acting*, ch. 2). In beholding an actor, the audience is partaking of a quasi-masochistic pleasure in identifying with a disintegration of selfhood. For Wilshire, the self's construction through awkward participation in fictional roles is a salient problem of modern identity. For Goldman and Féral, what is central is the separation of self from others. For Hornby, it is the self's desire to withdraw from identity, dissolving into non-differentiation and the allure of self-shattering.

5. Kendall L. Walton, *Mimesis as Make-Believe: On the Foundations of the Representational Arts,* 1990, p. 243.

6. The various layers that make up the audience's manner of relating to a fiction specifically through an actor's work require a preliminary analysis of the status of language in the theater, particularly its transition from written to performed language. An attempt to delineate these layers will be undertaken in the next section of the book.

7. Cited in Cole, ed., *Actors on Acting*, p. 494.

8. For an argument that takes the audience's own performance further than this, suggesting that an ethical bond is attempted in the theater when an audience is invited to listen to an actor (or, ideally, when an audience even respects an obligation to perform such listening), see Alice Rayner, "The Audience: Subjectivity, Community and the Ethics of Listening," *Journal of Dramatic Theory and Criticism*, 1993.

9. David Davies argues against Woodruff and Thom, who claim that theater necessitates an audience. He nevertheless misses the distinction between three different ways in which the status of the audience can be examined: a) whether a theatrical performance necessitates an actual audience (which he plausibly denies); b) whether a theatrical performance is not somehow guided by a projected audience, whether or not it exists (which he plausibly affirms), and c) the role an actual audience plays for a performer, and why the latter may be interested in the former at all (a question he does not discuss). See Davies, *Philosophy of the Performing Arts*, pp. 172–89.

10. For a typology of such implicit interactions, see C. Neuringer & R. A. Willis, "The Psychodynamics of Theatrical Spectatorship," *Journal of Dramatic Theory and Criticism*, 1987.

11. For other responses to Philip Auslander's critique regarding the importance of live performance, see Osipovich, "What Is a Theatrical Performance?" and Noël Carroll, "Philosophy and Drama: Performance, Interpretation and Intentionality," in *Staging Philosophy: Intersections of Theatre, Performance, and Philosophy*, eds. David Krasner and David Z. Saltz, 2006, pp. 104–21. Note that the response above does not deny that numerous aesthetic merits of a theatrical performance can be communicated in ways that do not depend on live performance. The claim is, rather, that due to the participation of an audience in a process of validation which touches the performer's act while it is being performed, but also due to the audience's need to be part of such act in relation to a particular performer, live performance is able to establish a unique experience that, by comparison, watching a digitized copy of the performance will not create. Note, however, that if an audience watches a live performance on a screen, and its responses are somehow felt by the performer, the technological mediation does not disrupt the process I am describing. Participating in a *live* performance remains unique, but it does not depend on a non-mediated perception of the performance.

12. From *Early Stages*, cited in Cole, ed., *Actors on Acting*, p. 402.

13. To be more (technically) precise: a token of a performance might be enacted specifically for the purposes of filming it, and that token would not have been staged without the projected recording of it, but the *performance* as such is *independent* of its recordings.

14. For the same claim defended by a different argument, see Richard Hornby,

"The Camera, the Actor and the Audience," *Journal of Dramatic Theory and Criticism*, 2003. Stanton Garner calls attention to the manner whereby the gaze of the actor when looking at the audience performs a radically different function in live versus filmed performance, bringing out the different forms of participation being mobilized: in the latter the audience *imagines* being looked at, whereas a live actor can actually momentarily turn the audience into an object of spectatorship: "Alone among the elements that constitute the stage's semiotic field, the body is a sign that looks back." (Garner, *Bodied Spaces*, p. 49.)

15. The debate over the importance (or lack of it) of live performance currently suffers from generalizing over distinct forms of performance. My following comments should be understood as applicable only to *theatrical* live performance. To extend them to dance may be illuminating, but the underlying experience of dance and its spectatorship would first have to be clarified. For a critical discussion of Philip Auslander's challenge of the idea that live action matters, see the exchange between him and Noël Carroll in Krasner Saltz, eds., *Staging Philosophy*. Relevant, too, is Osipovich, "What Is a Theatrical Performance?" Osipovich underscores the import of audience-performer interaction as non-repeatable dimensions underlying, for him, the unscripted dimension of performance. For an attempt to invoke Walter Benjamin's notion of aura in order to pinpoint the essential feature of watching a repeated live performance in contrast to viewing a televised rerun, see Sarah Ruhl, "Re-Runs and Repetition," *Contemporary Theatre Review: An International Journal*, 2006. For the debate over live performance in the context of music and the distinction between live versus recorded music, see Lee B. Brown, "Phonography, Repetition and Spontaneity," *Philosophy and Literature*, 2000.

Part I—Listening to Actors

1. Konstantin Stanislavsky, *Building a Character,* 2003, p. 100.
2. Charlie Chaplin, *My Autobiography,* 1964, p. 397.
3. For the centrality of this training to Barrymore, his anguish over the poverty of his voice ("I went out into the woods . . . and recited the entire play, and then threw the book away. It could not be done. My voice had a high, nasal tone and I recited 'A horse, a horse, my kingdom for a horse!' like a terrified tenor trying to escape from a couple of blondes"), and his pride over "finding a voice," see Morrison, *John Barrymore, Shakespearean Actor,* pp. 75–9; pp. 126–9; and citation on p. 74.
4. Callow, *Being an Actor*, pp. 260–61.
5. Cicely Berry, *Voice and the Actor,* 1973, p.15.
6. Stanislavsky, *Building a Character*, p. 88.
7. This is not proposed as a substantive definition of the process of thought as such, but as a *stipulation* of terms meant to set apart two distinct mental operations. The above characterization of thought has been defended as a substantive one by

many philosophers of language, for example, Michael Dummett, *Truth and Other Enigmas,* 1978, for whom perceiving thoughts as essentially linguistic is the basis for analytic philosophy as such (see pp. 437–58). But the actual relations between language and thought need not concern us.

8. Brando and Lindsey, *Brando: Songs My Mother Taught Me,* p. 316.

9. Simon Callow, *Charles Laughton: A Difficult Actor,* 1987, p. 137.

10. Chaplin, *My Autobiography,* p. 210.

11. *Korol Lir Po Tragedii Shekspira,* directed by Grigorii Mikhailovich Kozintsev, 1971. Lester's performance of this scene can be watched in *As You Like It,* dir. Fiona Shaw, 1996.

12. The kind of gaps between characters and language that I will describe as part of the next three operations of voice can be transcribed into vocabularies that stress action through language: speech-acts can be performed in various qualitatively distinct ways, manifested by distance between agents and their speech-acts. I nevertheless regard the typology above as more informative than the vocabulary proposed by speech-act theory, since it captures not only distance from one's spoken acts, but also what underpins such distance.

13. "The actor must shake loose the acquired, unconscious patterns in order to allow the imprint of a completely different pattern of speech, belonging, for instance, to a character in a play quite unlike him or herself. We have a myriad of possible rhythms in our brains, and exercising them releases varying shades of communication and varying shades of identity. Anyone who says, 'This is who I am and how I speak' has locked the door on 'I wonder who I really am and what I might become, and what my real voice is, and what I might say if I spoke my thoughts out freely through my real voice.'" (Kristin Linklater, *Freeing Shakespeare's Voice: The Actor's Guide to Talking the Text,* 1992, p. 128). I came across this quotation in David Farrell Krell, "The Moment of Nothing: A Philosophical Note on the Work of Kristin Linklater," *Mosaic,* 2011,: p. 118. The entire *Mosaic* issue is devoted to voice work with a particular emphasis on Linklater's approach.

14. Kristin Linklater, *Freeing the Natural Voice,* 1976, p. 2. In her later book on Shakespeare, Linklater also claims that the adult voice has been "conditioned to talk about feelings rather than to reveal them" (Linklater, *Freeing Shakespeare's Voice,* p. 5). The idea of freeing the speaking voice in order to reach into one's inner uncontaminated "essence" was endorsed by a previous influential voice teacher, Margaret Carrington. See Morrison, *John Barrymore, Shakespearean Actor,* p. 75.

15. Vincent Canby, "The Elephant Man," *The New York Times,* October 3, 1980.

16. *King Lear,* directed by Peter Brook, 1970.

17. *Sophie's Choice,* directed by Alan Pakula, 1982.

18. For an extended analysis of the intellectual dimensions of stuttering as both a condition and a trope, see Marc Shell, *Stutter,* 2005. For a reading of fast-talkers

(though mostly limited to women as fast-talkers), see Maria DiBattista, *Fast-Talking Dames*, 2003.

19. *The King's Speech*, directed by Tom Hooper, 2010. *The Prince of Tides*, directed by Barbra Streisand, 1991.

Part II—Staging Words

1. In J. Dench J. Miller, *And Furthermore*, 2011, p. 57. For several other examples of script-performance deviations, see J. Garfein, *Life and Acting: Techniques for the Actor*, 2010, pp. 61–65.

2. Simon Callow's biography of Charles Laughton pursues in touching detail Laughton's struggles and (in Laughton's own experience) apparent failure to enact Shakespearean roles. Significantly for my claim above, Callow suggests that the cause of this was Laughton's inability to "draw energy or sense" from verse, concluding that Laughton in verse was "Laughton muzzled" (Callow, *Charles Laughton: A Difficult Actor*, p. 75); see also the chapter on Laughton playing Lear, pp. 250–70.

3. From "The Art of Speaking" in Cole, ed. *Actors on Acting*, p. 464.

4. For such positions, see Hamilton, *The Art of Theater*, Osipovich, "What Is a Theatrical Performance?" Osipovich actually believes that the interpretation of a play is sometimes an important aspect of theatrical work, but nevertheless dismisses the idea that theatrical events are interpretations. For him, a theatrical event ultimately exists in the partly un-scriptable encounter between performers and audience. Another opponent to identifying productions with interpretations is Saltz (David Z. Saltz, "What Theatrical Performance Is (Not): The Interpretation Fallacy," 2001.) He too, recognizes the possibility that some theatrical works are interpretations, but resists the subordination of performances to scripts. The typology to be presented below will not be vulnerable to the arguments made by these critics, while simultaneously attempting to facilitate rather than marginalize the creative interface between performance and literary interpretation.

5. To regard a performance as an interpretation of a work in this sense—that is, as a claim regarding meaning, significance and potential relevance for an addressee—differs from some other influential ways in which such 'interpretation' has been cast by aestheticians. David Saltz presents views by Wollheim and Scruton for whom the interpretation of performers consists in what they necessarily *add* to what may be scripted (given that a token necessarily possesses properties that are not part of the type). Carroll advocates such a view too, writing that "all performances involve interpretations of play texts or play plans in the sense that dramatic performances must go beyond what is given in the text or play plan . . . there is always some scope for invention in putting flesh on a performance plan." In the formulation preferred above, interpreting demands more than instancing: an actress *interprets* a script even if she *adds* nothing to it. Alternatively, she can add creatively

to it, or "fill it out" without interpreting it at all. For Saltz's presentation of these views, see Saltz, "What Theatrical Performance Is (Not): The Interpretation Fallacy." For Carroll's view, see Carroll, "Philosophy and Drama: Performance, Interpretation and Intentionality," in *Staging Philosophy: Intersections of Theatre, Performance, and Philosophy*, Krasner and Saltz, eds. 2006, p. 108.

6. For a discussion of non-scripted theater, see Hamilton, *The Art of Theater*, ch. 3.

7. David Saltz has theorized this terrain by distinguishing between the play's supplying of the fictional coordinates within which the actors operate (he calls this the "infiction"), and the audience's ability to "read off" the play from the work of the actors ("outfiction"). The tripartite distinction proposed above suggests that "reading off" should itself be broken down further into what the play is interpreted as *meaning*— as this can be gathered from an actor's work— and the *potency* in which this interpretation is realized in a particular performance. For Saltz's distinction, see David Z. Saltz, "Infiction and Outfiction: The Role of Fiction in Theatrical Performance," in *Staging Philosophy: Intersections of Theater, Performance, and Philosophy*, edited by Krasner and pp. 203–20.

8. The analogy to recipes has been offered by Noël Carroll in his *A Philosophy of Mass Art*. He invokes it again in Carroll, "Philosophy and Drama: Performance, Interpretation and Intentionality," in *Staging Philosophy: Intersections of Theatre, Performance, and Philosophy*, Krasner and Saltz, p. 108. For a critical discussion, see Saltz, "What Theatrical Performance Is (Not): The Interpretation Fallacy."

9. For Carroll's version of the type/token view in relation to performance, see Carroll, "Philosophy and Drama: Performance, Interpretation and Intentionality," in *Staging Philosophy: Intersections of Theatre, Performance, and Philosophy*, Krasner and Saltz, 2006. For Thom's view, see Thom, *For an Audience*, p. 3. For more extensive discussions of the ontological debate, see Davies, *Philosophy of the Performing Arts*, and Hamilton, *The Art of Theater*.

10. The ability to generate hypothetical counterexamples to this claim—e.g. a troupe of actors that erroneously believe they are performing a particular play when they have mistakenly used the text of another play—takes very little substance from this claim.

11. The citation is from *The Unbearable Lightness of Being*, and it is quoted in Gaut, *Art, Emotion and Ethics*, pp. 146–7.

12. Shusterman is citing the *Chambers 21st Century Dictionary* (Richard Shusterman, *Surface and Depth: Dialectics of Criticism and Culture*, 2002, p. 234.). Shusterman harnesses this insight to an ambitious attempt to perceive dramatization as capturing a vital aspect of all art (the chapter is entitled "Art as Dramatization"), which, when reaching its most rewarding potency, does not merely mirror life but is a means of framing heightened experience. For a recent attempt to perceive the

reading of literature as itself a form of dramatization, see John Gibson, *Fiction and the Weave of Life,* 2007, ch. 3.

13. All quotations from Shakespeare's plays (here and elsewhere in this book), are to *The New Cambridge Shakespeare* editions.

14. For a classic presentation of this idea, see the discussion of the "concrete universal" in W.K. Wimsatt, *The Verbal Icon: Studies in the Meaning of Poetry,* 1967. For a contemporary attempt to articulate and defend its philosophical viability, see Zamir, *Double Vision,* ch. 2.

15. For additional aspects of literary intensity without relation to acting, see Zamir, "Philosophy," in *The Oxford Handbook of Shakespeare,* 2012.

16. Embodying a text brings out some of its meanings, as I shall immediately describe. But once this understanding is informed by the realization that some features of reading are also lost through this process, one avoids the prioritization implied by proposals according to which acting is a physicalization of the reading process. For a book-length presentation of such a proposal, see David Cole, *Acting as Reading: The Place of the Reading Process in the Actor's Work,* 1992.

17. Bence Nanay offers a useful summary of existing accounts of identification and the problems that beset them, formulating an intriguing account of theatrical identification predicated on the relations between action and perception ("Perception, Action, and Identification in the Theater," in Krasner and Saltz *Staging Philosophy*, pp. 244–54.) David Krasner's essay in the same collection ("Empathy and Theatre") offers an erudite discussion of the relations between empathy, identification, sympathy, compassion, and understanding, which he sees as significantly different processes that, while interlacing in various ways, should be set apart.

18. In defending actors from Plato's warning that decent people should not act, Paul Thom writes that "it must be remembered that it is perfectly possible to give representations, even repeatedly, without identifying with what is represented" (Thom, *For an Audience*, p. 131.). I disagree: it is impossible to act without identifying with the represented state, but it is certainly possible to identify (in art or life) without personally endorsing that with which one identifies.

19. Konstantin Stanislavsky, *An Actor Prepares,* 2003, pp. 76–7.

20. J. M. Coetzee, *Elizabeth Costello,* 2003, pp. 22–23.

21. *William Shakespeare's the Merchant of Venice*, directed by Jack Gold, 1980.

22. *William Shakespeare's the Merchant of Venice*, directed by John Sichel, 1973.

23. Bert States describes the actor as, in this sense, "validating" the playwright's words: "[A]ll dramatic texts are hypotheses, yearnings. The poet records his vision of the world as an imitation of a possible truth. And behold, the actor appears and validates his vision, as nature validates the vision of the physicist by behaving naturally. The actor is living proof that the play is true" (States, *Great Reckonings in Little Rooms,* p. 127). It is interesting to harmonize such a proposal into the various other

forms of validation that are at play in the theater which were explored earlier in this book. But what is missing from such a formulation is how actors may instantiate something that is a possibility of the text, but one that has *not* been imagined by its author. Once again, to conceive of plays as recipes awaiting realization underestimates the creative function of performers: by bringing out latent possibilities, actors do more than validate what the author has always imagined.

24. Cited in Worthen, *Drama*, p. 5.

Part II—Staging Literature

1. For a description of the main contours of this view, see Thom, *For an Audience*, pp. 144–70.

2. Two additional exceptions that should be mentioned are James Calderwood and Lionel Abel. Calderwood's metadramatic readings of Shakespeare assume that a gifted dramatist tends to be substantially preoccupied with the meaning of his art, and that such concerns filter into his work. Calderwood extracts many fine points regarding the possible meaning of theater for Shakespeare that are latent in the themes and words within his plays. For such, see James L. Calderwood, *Shakespearean Metadrama: The Argument of the Play in Titus Andronicus, Love's Labour's Lost, Romeo and Juliet, A Midsummer Night's Dream, and Richard II*, 1971. Lionel Abel claimed that a character's awareness of its own collaboration with an author forms a significant part of drama. He historicized this claim, arguing that Hamlet constitutes a transition point: a character aware of its own theatricalization and responding accordingly: "[Hamlet] is the first stage figure with an acute awareness of what it means to be staged" (Lionel Abel, *Metatheatre: A New View of Dramatic Form*, 1963, pp. 57–8).

3. The primary source for his approach is to be found in Goldman, *The Actor's Freedom*. He has developed and exemplified his insights further in his books on Shakespeare and Ibsen. For the purposes of this discussion of drama, his most significant book is Michael Goldman, *On Drama: Boundaries of Genre, Borders of Self*, 2000, in which Goldman takes up explicitly the question of genre. His main insight remains that "there is a basic way in which the action of plays tends to reproduce the acting process" (p. 18). While I wish to appropriate this claim, my own understanding of the acting experience and what it taps in its beholder leads me to perceive different correlations between the plot of a play and the audience's projected response.

4. Michael Goldman sees this over-tight identification as an aspect of all successful acting. For Goldman, any good performer presents "a definiteness of projected identity, a presentation of self that seems surer and sharper than anything we encounter in ordinary life" (Goldman, *On Drama*, p. 22). While I think that Goldman correctly picks out how powerful acting affects the audience in the sense of watching an enactment of tight identification, I think that such responses also

depend upon the *kind* of role being played. Heroes tap role-identity tensions differently than other character types, because, as characters (and not merely as actors playing characters) they exhibit the smooth role-identity unification that the audience is fascinated by.

5. Rupert D. V. Glasgow, *Madness, Masks, and Laughter: An Essay on Comedy,* 1995, pp. 33–73, discusses numerous ways in which comedy involves social and other masks that are maintained or dropped.

6. Gussow, *Michael Gambon: A Life in Acting*, p. 199.

7. P. Berliner, *Thinking in Jazz: The Infinite Art of Improvisation,* 1994, p. 166.

8. Compare Goldman, *On Drama*: "It would be a grave mistake to assume . . . that literature is the larger category, of which drama is a specialization. Many problems not only in dramatic but literary theory would take on a sharply new perspective if . . . we were to reverse the process and think instead of drama as the most general case of literature, with poetry, the novel, and so forth as specializations" (p. 6).

9. Early-modern anti-theatrical authors called attention to the potential sin involved in incarnating non-Christians like Shylock. In *A Mirror of Monsters* (1587), William Rankin declares that "[p]layers, when they take upon them the persons of heathen men, imagining themselves (to vainglory in the wrath of God) to be the men whose persons they present; wherein, by calling upon Mahomet, by swearing by the temples of idolatry dedicated to idols, by calling on Jupiter, Mars, Venus, and other such petty gods, they most wickedly rob God of his honor, and blaspheme the virtue of his heavenly power." Portia's transgression (a woman in disguise appropriating the authority of practicing law) thus duplicates the actor's, potentially far more serious transgression of voicing heretical words and oaths by embodying Shylock. The Rankin citation is from T. Pollard, *Shakespeare's Theater: A Sourcebook,* 2004, p. 132.

10. Marvin Rosenberg, *The Masks of King Lear,* 1972, p. 69.

Part II—Staging Objects

1. For an opposite view, see Michael Meschke, *In Search of Aesthetics for the Puppet Theatre,* 1992 Ch. 4.

2. Sivory-Asp writes: "First there is an idea, a theme for the play. I believe that the puppeteer who designs and makes a puppet herself lives through that creative step connected with the play. The idea is an embryo and, while working on it, the puppeteer gives birth to a baby, the puppet. The puppet is an object of the designer-puppeteer's thoughts, like a painter's picture. She has transferred part of herself into the puppet. Strangely enough, one can very often find a resemblance between the puppeteer and her puppet; they have become deeply acquainted with each other during this process." (Sirpa Sivory-Asp, "The Presence of the Gods," in *The Language of the Puppet*, eds. Laurence Richard Kominz and Mark Levenson, 1990, p. 3).

3. There is also an ideological dimension to a puppeteer operating several roles or several puppeteers operating a single one. Having a single large puppet operated by several puppeteers has been heralded as politically important in anarchist demonstrations, since such a form of protest manifests the capacity of a collective to mobilize protest without relying on a single source of volition, a leader. The giant puppets in anarchist interventions thus demonstrate a point regarding the independence of action upon hierarchy; the effectiveness of a diffusion of individual wills into a collective imagination. For such an argument, see David Graeber, "On the Phenomenology of Giant Puppets: Broken Windows, Imaginary Jars of Urine, and the Cosmological Role of the Police in American Culture," in *Possibilities: Essays on Hierarchy, Rebellion, and Desire*, 2007, pp. 375–418, esp. 383. A different ideological reading of puppetry as a medium holds that modernist puppetry enables authors to address an audience outside market relations, by avoiding the mediation of the commodified pseudo-personalities of live performers. For this argument, see William B. Worthen, "Of Actors and Automata: Hieroglyphics of Modernism," *Journal of Dramatic Theory and Criticism*, 1994.

4. Peter D. Arnott, *Plays without People: Puppetry and Serious Drama,* 1964, here p. 58.

5. C. Collodi, [Carlo Lorenzini],*The Adventures of Pinnocchio, 1883.*

6. Reading the episode in this way adopts Geppetto's perspective. It thereby taps themes of paternity and aging. Pinocchio-centered readings bring out different meanings. In her reading of Pinocchio as a detailed exemplification of a new modality of Italian agency, Suzanne Stewart-Steinberg associates Pinocchio's resistance with a "radically new" understanding of ideology, in which one is at once a product/producer of ideology, but also manifests a remainder that will not be subsumed under this process. Geppetto is encountering this residual in his puppet. See Suzanne Stewart-Steinberg, *The Pinocchio Effect: On Making Italians 1860–1920,* 2007, pp. 45–47. Scott Shershow's analysis (centering on the transition from the book to the Disney film) is more pessimistic: the film (unlike the book) is forced to convey the domination that underlies bourgeois values, without any unassimilated remainder. See Scott Cutler Shershow, *Puppets and "Popular" Culture,* 1995, p. 232. For Harold Segel, Pinocchio's ultimate condescension towards the puppet that he was (once he becomes a real boy), ironically conveys his inability to fathom his entry into the far more scripted existence involved in successful adulthood, See Harold B. Segel, *Pinocchio's Progeny: Puppets, Marionettes, Automatons and Robots in Modernist and Avant-Garde Drama,* 1995, pp. 42–43.

7. Hadas Ophrat, *Conversations with a Puppet: On Contemporary Puppetry,* 2008, pp. 52–3 [in Hebrew].

8. Puppetry has been linked with theology in various ways. For the puppeteer as metaphorically standing for a prime mover, see Shmuel Moreh, "The Shadow Play (Khayāl Al-Zill) in the Light of Arabic Literature," *Journal of Arabic Litera-*

ture, 1987. For the puppets as latently conveying divine forces that previously were encapsulated in idols, see Victoria Nelson, *The Secret Life of Puppets*, 2001. I shall mostly ignore this dimension of puppetry (though it does pertain to my analysis of the subject-object transition below).

9. Peter Schumann, "What, at the End of This Century, Is the Situation of Puppets and Performing Objects?," in *Puppets, Masks, and Performing Objects*, edited by J. S. Bell, 2001, pp. 46–51; here p. 48.

10. Gianfranco Poggi, *Money and the Modern Mind: Georg Simmel's Philosophy of Money*, 1993, ch. 3.

11. Fyodor Dostoyevsky, *Notes from Underground*, 1961, p. 115.

12. On such conceptions, see the opening chapters in Cynthia Marshall, *The Shattering of the Self: Violence, Subjectivity, and Early Modern Texts*, 2002. For what could be read as an intriguing application of Marshall's thesis to puppetry, see Matthew I. Cohen, "Puppetry and the Destruction of the Object," *Performance Research*, 2007. Cohen's thesis is inspired by Winnicot's theory (rather than by postulations of primary masochism) in its claim that puppets facilitate violence to objects. Cohen surveys several examples for puppet performances that highlight such violence. To the interesting suggestions he makes regarding the meaning of such violence I would like to add that the violence to puppets registers a resistance to the inner object. Relevant to the theme of destabilizing the subject-object divide is also Victoria Nelson's discussion of Bruno Shulz's work, in which, Nelson claims, the merging with internal thinghood is an explicit objective. See Nelson, *The Secret Life of Puppets*, pp. 70–4.

13. Max von Boehn, *Puppets and Automata*, 1972, p. 15.

14. A. A. Milne, *The House at Pooh Corner*, 1992, p. 172. For an extended (and truly lovely) interpretation of this dimension in Milne's Pooh novels, see W. Meadowlark's "A La Recherche du Pooh Perdu," in Fredrick Campbell Crews, *The Pooh Perplex: A Freshman Casebook*, 1963, pp. 75–83. The reading is actually by Crews, and is considered a parody. One can only hope that non-satirical criticism would attain more frequently the insight, intelligence and reach of this parody.

15. Eric Bass's solo puppet-and-mask performance "Autumn Portraits" offers a good example of a puppet's confrontation with death. Another is Bruce Schwartz's "The Farmer's Cursed Wife." Hebrew readers may find many more examples and a discussion of the death motif within puppet theater in Ophrat, *Conversations with a Puppet*, ch. 1.

16. Tadeusz Kantor seems to run together the fear of death and the fear of becoming an object in his rationalization for his use of puppets as he articulates it in his "The Theater of Death": "[the puppet's appearance in my thoughts] complies with my ever-deepening conviction that it is possible to express life in art only through the absence of life, through an appeal to death, through appearances, through emptiness and the lack of a message." The remark is quoted, discussed, and related to

Kantor's theatre in Segel, *Pinocchio's Progeny*, p. 327. While the fear of matter and the fear of becoming matter (death) are interrelated, there is a distinct resistance I am trying to bring out, *not* to non-living as such, but to the idea of an internal, consistently present objecthood out of which subjectivity repeatedly emerges.

17. Compare Kenneth Gross's discussion of Dennis Silk's view of puppets as "pilgrim[s] to human beings from the world of things. . . . The puppet reminds us of our powers of animation. It may remind us by contrast of our human tendency to turn ourselves, our thoughts, our memories, and our words into fixed, frozen, inanimate, or mechanical things" (Kenneth Gross, *Puppet: An Essay on Uncanny Life,* 2011, p. 33).

18. For a book length exploration of the meaning and implications of the ascription of inferior cultural status to puppets, see Shershow, *Puppets and "Popular" Culture.*

19. Ovid, *Metamorphoses,* 1977, book X, ii.

20. Kenneth Gross, *The Dream of the Moving Statue,* 1992, p. 74, p. 81.

21. Thomas Nagel, "Sexual Perversion," *The Journal of Philosophy*, (1969). Valérie Guignabodet's film *Monique* can be usefully contrasted to the Pygmalion tale in presenting an unabashed preference for a statue (an erotic love doll) over a human, alongside a non-apologetic attempt to foster a relationship with the former. Websites such as Realdoll.com specialize in producing such love dolls. In testimonials presented in these sites and elsewhere on the internet, it is interesting to notice, in the context of the claims above, how such dolls are conceived by purchasers as fulfilling not merely a sexual need, but are claimed to become partial partners. See, for example, an episode devoted to such relationships in the television series *My Strange Addiction*, directed by R. Joseph Fitzgerald, 2010.

22. Both quotations are from Albert Camus, *The Myth of Sisyphus, and Other Essays,* 1955, p. 89.

23. Personal communication, June 8, 2007.

24. Cited in Arnott, *Plays without People*, p. 13. For Arnott's own elaboration of this idea, see pp. 64–45.

25. G. B. Shaw, "Note on Puppets," in Von Boehn, *Puppets and Automata*, p. vi.

26. Those who accept Derrida's criticism of presence may take this point further, holding that puppetry is a medium that undermines the Western default metaphysical stance. Puppetry's systematic infantilizing as an expressive genre is related to its capacity to unsettle an entire organizing structure. They would say that in actor-based theater, this correspondence between performance and offering a counter-metaphysics is rarely achieved, though it may have been attempted by some playwrights (e.g. Beckett). For such a view (though not in the context of puppetry), see Dillon, "Active Interpretation/Deconstruction Play: Postmodern Considerations of Acting" 1993. For an argument according to which many dominant forms of actor-

training have not taken in the significance of the Derridian critique of presence, see Auslander, "'Just Be Your Self': Logocentrism and Difference in Performance Theory," in *Acting Reconsidered: A Theoretical and Practical Guide*, Zarrilli, 2002. As claimed earlier in this book, the identification of acting with a realization of possibilities or the idea of self-animation do not necessarily assume a metaphysics of presence, or a robust subjectivity that exists prior to its effects. Such ideas can harmonize with a vocabulary that emphasizes acts of selfing, repeated performance, and self-effects.

Part III—Unethical Acts

1. Richard Schechner, *Environmental Theatre*, 1973 p. 191.

2. From *Strasberg at the Actors Studio*, in Cole, ed., *Actors on Acting*, p. 623.

3. Jonas A. Barish, *The Antitheatrical Prejudice*, 1981, both citations are from p. 2.

4. A. Villiers, *La Prostitution de l'acteur*, 1946, is devoted to the exploration of this claim and its different defenses (see esp. ch. 3). See, too, the citation Barish provides from Caïn Marchenoir (1887) in pp. 321–22. For more recent work, specifically on the actress/whore overlap, see Kirsten Pullen, *Actresses and Whores: On Stage and in Society*, 2004. In his study of the overlap between theater and prostitution on the earlymodern English stage, Joseph Lenz adds to the predictable arguments—that either emphasize the interpenetration of brothels and theaters in the period or bring out the alleged capacity of theater to sexually stimulate its audience—the idea that a theatrical performance was implicitly conceived *as* an intercourse in which the spectators internalize a sexual image orchestrated by the actors, see Joseph Lenz, "Base Trade: Theater as Prostitution," *Elh*, (1993). As supportive evidence for this claim, consider William Prynne's *Histrio-Mastrix* (1633). Prynne approvingly cites Clement of Alexandria, who informed his readers that if they audited a play they should realize that "their eares had committed whoredome, their eyes had played the harlots with them and, which is more strange, that their very sight had committed adultery before any actual embracement by reason of the obscene Picturers and filthy Enterludes" (William Prynne, *Histrio-Mastix*, 1633, Part I, Act 6.3 p. 329 in Early English Books [EEBO] edition). Histories of prostitution, too, include discussion of the flexible boundaries between prostitution and performance. For references to this literature, see Pullen (ibid) p. 3.

5. "Then these goodly Pageants being done, every one sorteth to his mate, each bring another home-ward of their way: then begin they to repeate the lascivious acts and speeches they have heard, and thereby infect their minde with wicked passions, so that in their secret conclaves they play the sodomites, or worse" (from Greene's "*A Refutation of the Apology for Actors*," EEBO. P. 61). There are numerous examples of such claims (Prynne devotes entire chapters to the links of theater with

prostitution and fornication). For Rousseau's antitheatrical arguments that exemplify this critique (along with its own dependency on unsupportable assumptions), see Barish, *The Antitheatrical Prejudice*, p. 282.

6. In his 1580 *A Second and Third Blast of Retreat from Plays and Theaters*, Anthony Munday writes: "As for those stagers themselves . . . ask them, if in their laying out of their parts, they choose not those parts which are most agreeing to their inclination, and that they can best discharge? And look what every of them doth most delight in, that he can best handle to the contentment of others. If it be a roisting, bawdy, and lascivious part, wherein are unseemly speeches, and that they make choice of them as best answering and proper to their manner of play: may we not say, by how much he exceeds in his gesture, he delights himself in his part? And by so much it is pleasing to his disposition and nature? If it be his nature to be a bawdy player, and he delight in such filthy and cursed actions, shall we not think him in his life to be more disordered, and to abhor virtue?" Quoted in Pollard, *Shakespeare's Theater*, p. 80.

7. Brando and Lindsey, *Brando: Songs My Mother Taught Me*, p. 115.

8. For a detailed exploration of the relationship between acting-theory and theories of the body, see Roach, *The Player's Passion*. Physically oriented actor-training systems mentioned earlier in this book such as Zarrilli's, or the one described by Merlin, are selective: while obviously much more attuned to the self-shaping capacities of the body and while they would resist a view in which the body is mechanized, such theories, like their psychologically-attuned counterparts, have said nothing about the ethical implications that such self-shaping may entail.

9. References for such reappraisal of the body were provided earlier in this book. Within Anglo-American aesthetics these include Gallagher, *How the Body Shapes the Mind*; Johnson, *The Meaning of the Body*; and Shusterman, *Body Consciousness*. Within Continental philosophy, such rethinking can be found in Welton, ed., *The Body: Classic and Contemporary Readings*. Within theater studies such reappraisals have recently been facilitated via incorporations of cognitive science. For work on theatrical embodiment from this perspective, see Amy Cook, "Interplay: The Method and Potential of a Cognitive Scientific Approach to Theatre," *Theatre Journal*, 2007, and McConachie and Hart, eds., *Performance and Cognition: Theatre Studies and the Cognitive Turn*.

10. Suzanne Burgoyne, Poulin, Karen, and Ashley Rearden, "The Impact of Acting on Student Actors: Boundary Blurring, Growth, and Emotional Distress," *Theatre Topics*, 1999, p. 161.

11. By "harming others or the practice" I have in mind the inequity one may sense in turning one's looks or tragedy into professional assets: other lawyers or factory workers may plausibly resent that their own lack of good looks or a personal misfortune may discourage professional favoritism. Moreover, good looks or personal disasters are also irrelevant to the professional decisions taken by the fac-

tory proprietor or the judge, and such a conclusion is likely to be conceded even by those who exploit these to obtain an edge. Accordingly, when someone manages to turn them into assets, one also manipulates another professional (the judge or the factory supervisor), and also distorts implicit features of the practice by introducing elements which, if explicitly considered, would be excluded: a judge should be able to ignore a lawyer's looks, and if a factory manager wished to take into account the personal circumstances of those who are being let off, this information should be made available to anyone who is liable to lose a job.

12. Avishai Margalit, *The Ethics of Memory,* 2002. Margalit does not argue that memory is a necessary condition for caring (one may care deeply about a mother one has never met and, accordingly, does not recall). Nor does he claim that caring is a necessary condition for memory (we remember some who we do not care for). He advocates what he calls a "conditional necessity": if I both remember X and care for her, forgetting X or an important aspect of X (such as her name) amounts to caring for her no longer.

13. Margalit, *The Ethics of Memory*, pp. 28–30. I intend to draw on Margalit's insight regarding a connection between some ethical violations and a withdrawal from care but only in its more general form. Regarding the specific articulation Margalit argues for—withdrawal from care as unethical in the context of forgetting—his account: a) should be supplemented with a distinction between forgetting X and merely not thinking about X; b) seems to involve an overly simple transition between forgetting and not caring (one can recall and then immediately forget a name; care, on the other hand, is a presumably more stable state); c) must incorporate the recognition that forgetting can itself be a meaningful response rather than an ethical failure. In Margalit's example, the colonel can presumably be constantly haunted by the death of the soldier and yet fail to recall his name. It can reasonably be suggested that the colonel is in denial due to the overwhelming effect of being asked about this, or even that forgetting is induced by a subliminal wish to be punished: the colonel cares so much about the young man's death that he subconsciously orchestrates the outrage against him.

14. The primary theorists here include Carol Gilligan, Nel Noddings, Virginia Held, and Michael Slote. For a survey of the literature on care, Virginia Held, *The Ethics of Care: Personal, Political, and Global,* 2006, ch. 2.

15. The site is called DearCupid.org, and the entry is from November 28, 2009 under a question entitled "How do husbands/wives of actresses/actors deal with this jealousy?" (page accessed on November 23, 2011). Many other entries in the page discuss such frustration by other partners of actors and actresses, including a relationship that has broken up because of such issues.

16. "The audience watching a character stripping is well aware that the private parts revealed are the actor's own, closing the gap between representation and presentation. Reaching the body itself, bare and wordless, the gesture of stripping

touches the limits of theatrical expression." (Hanna Scolnicov, "Stripping as Gesture," *Assaph*, 2010, p. 150).

17. Michael Caine, *Acting in Film*, 1990, p. 94.

18. Gordon, *The Purpose of Playing*, pp. 354–56.

19. François Joseph Talma: *Reflections on the Actor's Art* (1825), in Cole, ed., *Actors on Acting*, p. 186.

20. Chaplin, *My Autobiography*, p. 101.

21. Some important work includes Elaine Aston, *Feminist Theatre Practice: A Handbook*, 1999; Sue-Ellen Case, *Feminism and Theatre*, 1988; and Elin Diamond, *Unmaking Mimesis: Essays on Feminism and Theatre*, 1997. For a critical discussion of these contributions in relation to performance, see J. Ellen Gainor, "Rethinking Feminism, Stanislavsky and Performance," *Theatre Topics*, 2002.

22. For an elaboration of this option, see Diamond, *Unmaking Mimesis*, ch. 2.

23. For such a combination of ideologically aware performance accompanied by unease regarding Brechtian acting as a satisfactory solution, see Jill Dolan, *Presence and Desire: Essays on Gender, Sexuality, Performance*, 1993, ch. 4.

24. David Wiles, "Burdens of Representation: The Method and the Audience," in *Method Acting Reconsidered: Theory, Practice, Future*, edited by David Krasner, 2000, pp. 169–78, p. 175.

25. Eric Bentley, *Theatre of War: Comments on 32 Occasions*, 1972, p. 374.

26. Wilshire, *Role Playing and Identity*, p. 43.

27. This co-creative function of the actor in relation to the audience sets apart the "imaginative resistance" unique to acting from other kinds of resistance discussed in the literature. The actor may resist imagining states that would prompt others (his audience) to adopt objectionable attitudes. Additional differences that distinguish the imaginative resistance of actors from those of, say, readers, relate to the scope and intensity of the imagination required in acting as specified earlier in this book: detail of imaginative participation, duration and repetition. To ponder whether or not to read a novel about a lovable Nazi is different than to consider an offer to perform such a role in a play involving a two-month rehearsal period and an expected two-season run. The difference is analogous to the one between touring a country with objectionable politics and living and paying taxes in it for several years.

28. For a discussion of this performance and the controversy it elicited, see Burch, "Imitation of Life: A Meditation on 'Victim Art,'"

29. Bilha Feldman, *Three Approaches to the Art of Acting: Stanislavski, Chekhov, Grotowski: Theories & Exercises*, 2011, p. 85 (my translation).

30. See, for example, Martha C. Nussbaum, *Sex & Social Justice*, 1999, ch. 11.

31. Eric Bentley writes of the naked actor "for the actor knows he is a whore and that violation by the eyes is humanly as thoroughgoing as any other" (Bentley, *Theatre of War*, p. 377). Richard Schechner, in the cryptic remark quoted in this

chapter's epigraph, even identifies prostitution and theater. Schechner continues, "Those who wish to end prostitution need only perfect theater—and vice versa" (Schechner, *Environmental Theatre*, p. 191). By contrast, there are those who invoke the figure of the courtesan to argue for a distinction between genuine acting and prostitution. Jerzy Grotowski attempts this by distinguishing between the "courtesan actor" (the actor who is motivated by money and giving pleasure to an audience) and the "holy actor" who is truly "giving and receiving" from an attitude of "true love" through self-sacrifice (Jerzy Grotowski, *Towards a Poor Theatre*, 1968, pp. 32–5).

32. Note that the point is unrelated to defending or attacking sex work. A psychologically sensitive defence of sex work should recognize and respond to the ability of prostitution to remake those who practice it. The prostitute's capacity to experience intimacy is prone to be strongly undermined. Progressively crippling its practitioner, sex work cannot be fairly compared with other unappealing jobs, since in other occupations such linkage between values and acts remains largely unaffected.

33. *Shortbus*, directed by John Mitchell Cameron, 2006; *Intimité*, directed by Patrice Chéreau. 2000. A similar demand is apparently made of actors in Lars von Trier's *The Nymphomaniac*.

34. Sabina Krüger, "Die Evokation der Monster: Grenz und Schwellenerfahrung als Probenverfahren Bei La Fura Dels Baus," in *Chaos und Konzept: Proben und Probieren im Theater*, edited by Melanie Hinz, 2011, pp. 262–85.

35. In Krüger's article, the ideal of breaking the will of the actor is cited as an explicit objective of actor training by Bernd Stegemann, a professor at the Ernst Busch Academy of Dramatic Arts in Berlin (ibid., p. 283). In a film documenting the progress of four students in this academy over seven years, one of the four, Prodromos Antoniadis, complains repeatedly that he feels that teachers are attempting to break him as a person (*Die Spielwütigen*, directed by Andreas Veiel 2004.). Many of Schechner's exercises, particularly those relating to nakedness, are motivated by far-reaching goals of remaking the performer (Schechner, *Environmental Theatre*, ch. 3). Grotowski invites his actor to spiritually dissect and sacrifice himself, identifying and removing inner blocks and thereby offering himself up as a gift (Grotowski, *Towards a Poor Theatre*, pp. 33–5).

36. Schechner, *Environmental Theatre*, p. 42, p. 117.

37. Axson-Flynn v. Johnson. United States Court of Appeals for the Tenth Circuit, 2004.

38. In 1587 William Rankin wrote in his *A Mirror of Monsters*: "Players, when they take upon them the persons of heathen men, imagining themselves (to vainglory in the wrath of God) to be the men whose persons they present; wherein calling upon Mahomet, by swearing by the temples of idolatry dedicated to idols, by calling on Jupiter, Mars, Venus, and other such petty gods, they most wickedly

rob God of his honor, and blaspheme the virtue of his heavenly power." Quoted in Pollard, *Shakespeare's Theater*, p. 132.

39. For a discussion of the problematic relationship between potentially self-damning speech-acts in the play, see Andrew Sofer, "How to Do Things with Demons: Conjuring Performatives in Doctor Faustus," *Theatre Journal*, 2009.

40. Theater-studies includes some work that attempts to conceive of the theatrical interaction in ethical terms. Writings on ancient Greek theater do this as a matter of course. For contemporary versions that focus on the ethics of spectatorship, see Jon Erickson, "The Face and the Possibility of an Ethics of Performance," *Journal of Dramatic Theory and Criticism*, 1999; Helena Grehan, *Performance, Ethics and Spectatorship in a Global Age*, 2009, and Rayner, "The Audience: Subjectivity, Community and the Ethics of Listening." More thematic work on the interface between theater and ethics exists too, e.g. D.N. Ridout, *Theatre and Ethics*, 2009. Nevertheless, these writings do not address the ethics of acting as such.

41. See Burgoyne, Poulin, and Rearden, "The Impact of Acting on Student Actors: Boundary Blurring, Growth, and Emotional Distress." Their paper also refers to an unpublished Ph.D. dissertation by Lisa Tust-Gunn, entitled *A Mirror to Nature: The Theatre Actor's Relationship to Character and Use of Roles for Self-Exploration* (California School of Professional Psychology, 1995) which I have been unable to consult, but that, according to Burgoyne et. al., seems to likewise focus on the emotionally taxing aspects of some self-based acting techniques. Burgoyne's earlier article called attention to the lack of an ethical dimension in theater practice, a lack brought home to her in her own experience as director, see Suzanne Dieckman Burgoyne, "A Crucible for Actors: Questions of Directorial Ethics," 1991.

42. Susan Verducci, "A Moral Method? Thoughts on Cultivating Empathy through Method Acting," *Journal of Moral Education*, 2000. Verducci situates her work in relation to others (Joe Winston and Jonathan Levy) who advance similar claims on behalf of moral amelioration through acting. The idea that becoming through performing can be harnessed to positive and not just negative ends has been raised in older defences of acting as well. Even Prynne includes two examples of actors who were so cynical that they were willing to jokingly undergo baptism on stage, and, as a result, became devout Christians (*Prynne, Histrio-Mastix.*, part I, act 5 scene 5, pp. 118–19 in EEBO).

Part III—Pornography and Acting

1. Nancy Bauer discusses pornography along these lines, characterizing pornographic practice as creating a magical world, a pornutopia, in which every desire is reciprocated and in which the fulfilling of one's sexual wish automatically becomes someone else's vehicle for gratification. See Nancy Bauer, "Pornutopia," *N+1*, 2007.

2. There are similar definitions by Jan Narveson and Alan Soble, both focusing on the intent or likelihood of stimulating the projected audience. For these

definitions as well as a typology and criticism of other possible ones, see Michael C. Rea, "What Is Pornography?," *Noûs*, 2001. Rea's own reservations regarding an intention-based definition strike me as unconvincing.

3. Morse Peckham presents an example of a snuffbox that includes a sexual image amidst highly detailed depictions of flowers, trees and bushes (Morse Peckham, *Art and Pornography: An Experiment in Explanation,* 1969, pp. 51–52). The example is meant to destabilize a sharp disjunction between pornography and art. Yet evident in Peckham's description is how the sexual aspect of the representation is embedded in a context that includes genuinely pursued nonsexusl values. Another potential counterargument to mine is that porn's actual range of interests tends to be systematically underestimated by theorists. At least four contributors to Peter Lehman's anthology allude, for example, to the humor found in porn (Peter Lehman, ed., *Pornography: Film and Culture* 2006). Yet, here too I am unconvinced. Comic appeal is parasitic upon porn's attempt to sexually stimulate the viewer. No one would pick up a porn film if merely looking for a laugh. I will later suggest that pornographic scenarios are sometimes politically subversive, and that such a function may be built into the stimulation they elicit. The intent to arouse is, nevertheless, primary in their production and projected consumption.

4. There are alternative ways of distinguishing pornography from art. Christy Mag Uidhir argues that the essential difference between art and pornography is that art is what she calls "manner specific" whereas pornography is "manner inspecific." Manner specificity is the idea that the artwork aims to achieve not just a purpose, but to achieve it in a specific manner. Pornography, however, aims to achieve the goal of sexual stimulation regardless of a specific manner (Christy Mag Uidhir, "Why Pornography Can't Be Art," *Philosophy and Literature*, 2009). Such approach is similar to Jerrold Levinson's regarding the transparency of pornography as opposed to the opacity of art—the latter typically draws attention to its form (Jerrold Levinson, "Erotic Art and Pornographic Pictures," 2005). For Mag Uidhir, the problem with Levinson's characterization is that it is too restrictive: porn *can* call attention to its form, yet if an interest in form arises, such constitutes a superfluous addition as far as pornographic success is concerned. I do not think that porn is manner inspecific: choice of positions, costumes, tone of voice, and other selections can make the difference between a more or less successful porn (if porn were manner inspecific, porn viewers would be indifferent as to the product they choose, which is not the case). My own characterization is "Aristotelian" in orientation, appealing to an overarching objective rather than to structural features (like those emphasized in Uidhir's or Levinson's). Such a characterization allows for idealized versions of porn, in which form *can* matter to the producer or to the connoisseur viewing it. According to my characterization, if the created work is judged as intending to sexually stimulate, having no other significantly pursued objective, it is porn. If it involves other objectives that are genuinely attempted, it is erotica.

5. Advertising is similar. There too, the overarching objective is not aesthetic, and it is far from obvious that better acting promotes the commercial objective. A producer would accordingly select whatever is calculated to meet the objective of selling the advertised product, even if this means sacrificing aesthetic values. For the similarity between pornography and advertising, see Christy Mag Uidhir, "Why Pornography Can't Be Art," 2009.

6. Linda Das, "I Felt Raped by Brando," 2007.

7. Marianne Macdonald, "Downhill Ride for Maria after Her Tango with Brando," 2006.

8. See, for example, C. Taylor, *Naked: The Life and Pornography of Michael Lucas,* 2007, p. 121.

9. Drawing on testimonials by porn performers, as I plan to do, will strike some readers as unproblematic. Others would (rightly in my view) demand a methodological clarification. The first problem is that not many of these autobiographical reports exist. The ones that do are mostly written by *successful* performers in the American system. Extrapolating from these to the experiences of thousands of other performers (many of whom work in non-Western cultural contexts) is accordingly precarious. As for the few sources we have, these, too, should be treated with caution: pseudonyms and co-authors abound in this literature; lapses of turning the autobiographical narrative into a form of porn are also frequent. Yet for anyone inquiring into experiential aspects of pornographic performance, such texts are the best we currently have. Bibliographical details for the books by the performers mentioned above are as follows: J. Jameson and N. Strauss, *How to Make Love Like a Porn Star: A Cautionary Tale,* 2004; C. Milne, *Naked Ambition: Women Who Are Changing Pornography,* 2005; R. Richard, S. Thomas and K. Torke, *Anatomy of an Adult Film,* 2009; and G. Spelvin, *The Devil Made Me Do It,* 2008.

10. "On Crossing the Line to Create Feminist Porn," in Milne, *Naked Ambition,* p. 93.

11. In Milne, *Naked Ambition,* p. 95.

12. In Milne, *Naked Ambition,* p. 138.

13. C. Isherwood, *Wonder Bread and Ecstasy: The Life and Death of Joey Stefano,* 1996, p. 68; W. Poole, *Dirty Poole: A Sensual Memoir,* 2011, p. 171; R. Merritt, *Secrets of a Gay Marine Porn Star,* 2005, p. 219; Taylor, *Naked,* p. 202.

14. Isherwood, *Wonder Bread and Ecstasy,* p. 68.

15. Poole, *Dirty Poole,* pp. 144–45.

16. Merritt, *Secrets of a Gay Marine Porn Star,* p. 220.

17. Bauer, "Pornutopia,", p. 70.

18. For analyses of such genres and their ideological implications, see Laura Kipnis, *Bound and Gagged: Pornography and the Politics of Fantasy in America,* 1999.

19. Isherwood, *Wonder Bread and Ecstasy,* p. 58–61.

20. "It was the first time in my life I'd ever been complimented about my body

and I was quite literally dumbstruck. After four dances, I walked away with 20$ and a whole new confidence in my stride. Prior to that day, I'd felt my body was nothing more than a freak-show curiosity, and now I knew, at least within the dark walls of Sugars [a club], that body could be viewed with admiration. That first encounter changed everything, and it was then that I became a stripper." Danni Ashe, in Milne, *Naked Ambition*, p. 224. Nadine Strossen reproduces a letter she received from a striptease dancer who also was a law student, who found dancing naked to be empowering, Nadine Strossen, *Defending Pornography: Free Speech, Sex, and the Fight for Women's Rights*, 1995, pp. 193–95. While one may encounter such testimonials, the overwhelming majority of reports of the experience of sex work one reads in field work are radically different. As will be cited later in this chapter, such reports stress humiliation, fear, rage, helplessness, dissociation from and scorn for the clients.

21. Richard, Thomas and Torke, *Anatomy of an Adult Film*, p. 10.

22. Frances Ferguson, "Pornography: The Theory," *Critical Inquiry*, 1995.

23. See Bauer, "Pornutopia."

24. Jameson Strauss, *How to Make Love Like a Porn Star*, pp. 382–84. It would be tedious to list the numerous references regarding the difficulty of maintaining an erection during porn scenes in the literature written by porn performers and the various inventive strategies devised to overcome this.

25. The simplification in the above claim concerns my use of "sexual gestures" and its relationship with the status of "having sex," a connection that is actually more evasive than what my argument implies. Gestures such as penetration or various ways of sexually climaxing are obviously sexual, and constitute "having sex." Most kinds of porn are fixated on these. But there are less orthodox forms of porn that do not involve penetration or orgasm by the performers, though they are designed to induce this in a projected viewer. Take, for example, porn that specialize in infantilism (being treated as a baby), or in men being defeated by women in mock wrestling matches. Are performers who are genuinely sexually indifferent to what they perform, and who are filmed in fetishistic sequences, masochistic role-playing and the like "having sex" with each other? It would be interesting to ask *why* indifference seems to be more important in acts of this kind than in gestures like penetration, and whether seeing such a difference can be justified.

26. For Jameson and Thomas, see above citations. For Lords, see L. McNeil, J. Osborne,and P. Pavia, *The Other Hollywood: The Uncensored Oral History of the Porn Film Industry*, 2005, pp. 381–83.

27. L. Lovelace and M. McGrady, *Ordeal*, 2006, pp. 63–64.

28. Jameson, (ibid) p. 320.

29. A further distinction that can be introduced here is between agency *determining* role-playing and agency-*affecting* role-playing. Many forms of role-playing—acting aggressive roles for example—might constitutionally transform the agent.

Indeed, learning from the characters one embodies is one of the more gratifying aspects of acting. Agent-determining role-playing is unrelated to such changes; it may or may not be correlated with their occurrence.

30. It might be argued that these examples are all related to the body and that, accordingly, the embodiment of an intrinsic bodily act of this kind renders impossible the separation of role and act. There are, however, non-bodily related examples of the same kind of inseparability of performed and actual agency. A compelling example appears in the context of legal ethics, in which Daniel Markovits considers (and rejects) the possibility that lawyers could defend the immoral conduct that they themselves are sometimes called upon to perform (e.g. suppressing information that is detrimental to their client) through appealing to the idea of (a morally defensible) playing of a role that may itself include immoral acts (D. Markovits, *A Modern Legal Ethics: Adversary Advocacy in a Democratic Age,* 2008).

31. Note that it is not crucial that the value is shown to be a logically necessary dimension of the act as such. There is, for example, no necessary connection between excretion and disrespect, and it is not impossible to imagine a society in which urinating on a prized national monument would be a sign of veneration. It is sufficient that the connection between the value and the act is endorsed by some broader, established social outlook and that the actor recognizes that this outlook exists (the actor does not even have to himself accept this outlook for him to be determined by performing it; for example, one may show disrespect to another by acting in a way that strikes the performer as inoffensive).

32. On the mechanization of sex in the sense of dissociating sensation from feeling, emotion and passion, see Rollo May, "Paradoxes of Sex and Love in Modern Society," in *The Case against Pornography*, edited by David Holbrook, 1972, pp. 13–36.

33. See Alan Goldman, "Plain Sex," in *The Philosophy of Sex: Contemporary Readings*, edited by. Alan Soble, 1980, pp. 119–38. See also Russell Vannoy, *Sex without Love: A Philosophical Exploration,* 1980, ch. 1.

34. Lovelace and McGrady, *Ordeal*, p. 57.

35. Anat Gur, *Women Abandoned,* 2008, pp. 153–54. For the benefit of non-Hebrew readers, here are some translations from the testimonials by prostitutes that Gur provides: "When I am with a trick I fly away from my body" (p. 155); "It was like being a machine. . . . I would see my body as a programmed machine. . . . I would see my body as a business, and I would be indifferent to them (the tricks), precisely as if I was a machine. In — out — bye bye! . . . No feelings or emotion. There is no real body there, merely an external thing" (p. 156). Such dissociation appears to be a prevalent feature of the experience of prostitution when examined in different locations and contexts. For comparative work including Canada, United States and Turkey, see Colin A. Ross, Melissa Farley, and Harvey L. Schwartz, "Dis-

sociation among Women in Prostitution," *Journal of Trauma Practice*, 2004. Melissa Farley has published other relevant works on prostitution and dissociation.

36. Poole, *Dirty Poole*, p. 168.

37. Milne, ibid., p. 110.

Part IV—The Theatricalization of Love

1. I follow Deleuze in his view of masochism and sadism as non-complementary (though, for some reason, Deleuze leaves unmentioned the manner whereby love forms an important distinguishing characteristic between what Sade and Masoch are presenting).

2. All English citations and page numbers refer to the translation of the text included in Gilles Deleuze, *Masochism*, 1991. All references to the German text are to Leopold Sacher-Masoch, *Venus im Pelz*, 1985. The passages cited here are from p. 240, in the English, and p. 104, in the German text.

3. Regarding such scenes as "frozen," as does Deleuze (ibid., pp. 69–70), risks missing the highly energized quality involved in the participation in such theatricality. Severin's feverish devotedness (that Wanda insists on capturing in the painting), is indeed static; but it is not frozen.

4. The opening scene of the book, in which Severin reaches out to whip a maid, suggests that there is nothing conclusive in the specific gendered arrangement portrayed by Masoch: the masculine element can overmaster the feminine one. The crucial factors in this "philosophy" are, accordingly, those of war between the sexes, and the inability to harmonize opposites.

5. The title is borrowed from a novel by Howard Jacobson, which engages in a rich dialogue with *Venus in Furs*' presentment of theatricality as enabling—rather than hampering—intimacy in masochistic role-playing.

6. I accordingly part company from readings that, from Deleuze's stress on the education of the mistress by the slave to Stewart-Steinberg's idea of masochism as a reinstatement of masculine hegemony, have emphasized the masculine orchestration of scenes of male subjection. Sacher-Masoch stresses Wanda's love for Severin in these moments, thus inviting us to relate to this as a love story involving a unique repertoire of gestures. Reading these scenarios for gendered power-play is possible but ultimately indeterminable, because contradictory political interpretations of their cultural significance are equally persuasive (see the next note for an example). For a discussion of the possible political dimension of the masochistic theater, see Suzanne Stewart-Steinberg, *Sublime Surrender: Male Masochism at the Fin-de-Siècle*, 1998.

7. Nick Mansfield's interpretation exemplifies a version of the political readings that unnecessarily use ideological analysis to deny the loving aspect of the relationship. Mansfield dismisses the possibility that the novel explores an alternative

intimacy. He argues that Severin's desire is far more aggressive than his submissiveness would suggest, seeking to annihilate Wanda's own. According to Mansfield, Wanda does not discover dominance within her, but is coaxed into it by Severin in a manipulation involving prolonged objectification. She thereby mirrors back to Severin the shattering of desire that he seems to crave for himself. Mansfield would thus probably deny the possibility that masochism is a form of intimacy or love: "[T]he masochist fulfills his desire by annihilating the desire of the other. . . . The masochist's desire is fulfilled by being extinguished. The other's desire is extinguished by being represented as fulfilled." The citation is from Nick Mansfield, *Masochism: The Art of Power,* 1997, p. 8. Yet since Wanda repeatedly says that something has been liberated in her, Mansfield must reject her explicit language, dismissing it as an outcropping of Severin's own manipulations. To think that Mansfield is right implies adopting the very conservatism that Masoch's novel challenges in spotlighting unconventional modes of intimacy. Mansfield's reading is, from this perspective, a form of critical paternalism, potentially instancing the annihilation of Wanda's desire, the very act that he ostensibly criticizes.

8. Female masochism (sexual or not) has been extensively discussed, e.g. J. Benjamin, *The Bonds of Love,* 1988. It has even been implicitly identified with masochism as such. But narratives focusing on feminine masochism tend to situate the heroine in relation to male sadists rather than lovers. The latter narratives are more aligned with Sade's protagonists than with the theatrical and loving quality of humiliation expressed in Sacher-Masoch's work. I suspect that for this reason I have been unable to find a discussion of masochism among women in relation to (or as) theatricality. One intriguing exception to this generalization is Anne McClintock's discussion of the relationship between Hannah Cullwick and Arthur Munby (A. McClintock, *Imperial Leather: Race, Gender, and Sexuality in the Colonial Contest,* 1995, ch. 3). McClintock ably reads subversion into Cullwick's theatricalized forms of submission. Even in McClintock's analysis, however, theatricality is not a facilitator of love but, mostly, a means of articulating classed or gendered resistance (perhaps because for some—though I am unsure about McClintock—"love" cannot be dissociated from power dynamics in the first place).

9. The German original stresses the scorn aimed at Severin's manhood even more than the above translation conveys: "jetzt bildest du dir ein, ein freier Mensch, ein Mann, mein Geliebter zu sein" (p. 96).

10. Hornby's association of acting with the oceanic was cited earlier in this book. Cynthia Marshall incorporates accounts of the self by Laplanche and Bersani that situate the self between the need to consolidate identity and the counter-desire to shatter it. She carefully reconstructs developments in the concept of masochism—its movement from a mere perversion into a primary drive and the implication of this for the self within psychoanalytic theory—arguing that the emergence of early

modern subjectivity was linked to a proliferation of representations of shattering bodies on the early modern stage. See Marshall, *The Shattering of the Self: Violence, Subjectivity, and Early Modern Texts*. In terms of historicizing the argument of this chapter, while I welcome the suggestion that some dimensions of acting and masochism could be profitably understood as historically situated in relation to overarching transformations in personal experience, I would not go as far as Carol Siegel and John Noyes in suggesting that masochism is an invention that should be understood in terms of a particular formative moment in European history and literature. For this latter argument, see J. K. Noyes, *The Mastery of Submission: Inventions of Masochism,* 1997, and C. Siegel, *Male Masochism: Modern Revisions of the Story of Love,* 1995.

11. Being shot, wounded or burned as part of a performance, may form part of such art. For discussion, see K. O'Dell, *Contract with the Skin: Masochism, Performance Art, and the 1970s,* 1998. O'Dell draws on Deleuze to posit an implicit "masochistic contract" between performer and audience in such works.

12. Donnellan, *The Actor and the Target*, p. 108.

Part IV—The Theatricalization of Death

1. C. B. O'Neill, *Starving for Attention,* 1983, pp. 86–7.

2. G. Bowman, *Thin,* 2007, p. 73.

3. On the distinction between suicide and gesturing at suicide, as well as on the theatricality of the latter, see G. Fairbairn, *Contemplating Suicide: The Language and Ethics of Self-Harm,* 1995, pp. 92–102.

4. While, to my knowledge, there are no sustained discussions of the anorectic as actor/director, there are important anticipations and overlapping claims that should be read alongside this chapter as part of a comprehensive consideration of anorexia as theatricality. Maud Ellmann writes about the interdependency between the ability to maintain hunger and the state of being perceived, and many of her insights regarding the communicative aspects of refusing food could be cast as claims regarding performance; see M. Ellmann, *The Hunger Artists: Starving, Writing, and Imprisonment,* 1993, esp. p. 17. For the spectacle-based dimension of various forms of performed hunger in the nineteenth century, see Sigal Gooldin, "Fasting Women, Living Skeletons and Hunger Artists: Spectacles of Body and Miracles at the Turn of a Century," *Body & Society*, 2003. In her analysis of contemporary anorexia, Gooldin perceives anorexia as a self-orchestrated heroic drama; see Sigal Gooldin, "Being Anorexic," *Medical Anthropology Quarterly*, 2008.

5. See Burns, "Bodies as (im)material?: Bulimia and body image discourse"; Probyn, "Fat, feelings, bodies: A critical approach to Obesity"; and Malson, "Appearing to disappear: Postmodern Femininities and Self-starved Subjectivities," (all in H. Malson and M. Burns, *Critical Feminist Approaches to Eating Dis/Orders,* 2009,

pp. 113–45). See Burns's essay for others who doubt the tendency of first-wave feminist writings on eating-disorders to "over-emphasize the inscriptive power of cultural images of thinness" (Burns, p. 124).

6. J. Améry, *On Suicide: A Discourse on Voluntary Death,* 1999, ch. 1.

7. Online sites such as the Renfrew Center Foundation for Eating Disorders, or the National Eating Disorders Association provide statistics that undermine ethnic stereotyping of eating disorders. For a relatively recent survey of the studies on the actual ethnic dissemination of eating disorders and the methodological problems of generating reliable data in this field, see Lillian Huang Cummins, Angela M. Simmons, and Nolan W. S. Zane, "Eating Disorders in Asian Populations: A Critique of Current Approaches to the Study of Culture, Ethnicity, and Eating Disorders," *American Journal of Orthopsychiatry*, 2005.

8. Salvador Minuchin, B. L. Rosman, and L. Baker, *Psychosomatic Families: Anorexia Nervosa in Context,* 1978, p. 59. Minuchin does not explicitly mention theatricality; but his claims regarding anorectic families suggest that such families unwittingly create performers.

9. Quoted and translated from "Theatre and Science" in Benedetti, *The Art of the Actor*, p. 225.

10. The blog is called Yummy Secrets—A Proana blog (http://yummy-secrets.blogspot.com). I will say more about the function of such sites later.

11. A physician quoted in Joan Jacobs Brumberg, *Fasting Girls: The Emergence of Anorexia Nervosa as a Modern Disease,* 1988, p. 16.

12. Bowman, *Thin*, p. 49.

13. Emily Halban discloses a similar combination of theoretical clarity regarding her situation coupled with an inability to put this understanding into practice. See E. Halban, *Perfect: Anorexia and Me,* 2008, p. 116.

14. For an extensive reflection on this phenomenon, see O'Dell, *Contract with the Skin: Masochism, Performance Art, and the 1970s*. See also L. J. Lieberman, *Leaving You: The Cultural Meaning of Suicide,* 2003, ch. 5 ("Tragic Artists).

15. Bowman, *Thin*, pp. 72–3.

16. Halban, *Perfect*, p. 131.

17. For the communicative and subversive dimensions of suicide, see Lieberman (ibid.), esp. ch. 1 ("Defiant Death").

18. Bowman, *Thin*, pp. 58–59.

19. I will not attempt to catalogue the various strands of feminist responses to anorexia, and am drawing upon them only when they meaningfully inform my performance-centered analysis. I am aware that many of the gender-related patterns highlighted in feminist writings on anorexia can be recast as claims about performing gender, or (subversively) "dis-performing" it in order to awaken a deautomatization of expectations, or as vain attempts to perform a gender-neutral identity. For

the latter, see M. MacSween, *Anorexic Bodies: A Feminist and Sociological Perspective on Anorexia Nervosa,* 1993, p. 4, p. 252. Relevant too, is Susan Bordo's proposal to relate to eating-disorders as a personal enactment that reproduces (in my terms, dramatizes) social categories and issues relating to the shifts between calculated parsimony and gluttonous self-indulgence in consumer cultures. See S. Bordo, *Unbearable Weight: Feminism, Western Culture, and the Body,* 1993, pp. 198–99. A less familiar suggestion in this context is that feminism is itself somehow importantly linked to the appearance of eating disorders, thereby attempting to account for the disturbing conjunction of first-wave feminism with the emergence of eating disorders precisely in socio-ethnic contexts in which the woman's liberation movement was most effectively felt. The suggestion would be that anorexia presents itself as a distorted possibility for a total form of self-theatricalization: it relies upon the same capacities that would have enabled a woman to become a perfect mother and wife in the past, precisely as a crisis in women's self-theatricalization was set in motion by feminism. For thoughts regarding such crisis (though not in terms of a crisis of shifting paradigms of self-theatricality), see K. Chernin, *The Hungry Self: Women, Eating, and Identity,* 1986, p. 17.

20. G. Minois, *History of Suicide: Voluntary Death in Western Culture,* 2001, p. 302.

21. A structurally similar argument has been made in fat studies: obesity as a use of fat designed to defend the woman from the impossible demands of a sexist society by isolating her from it. The thesis is that putting on weight is a mode of unsexing a body once it is being called upon to enter social regimentation. The thesis was proposed by Orbach in her *Fat is a Feminist Issue*; for relevant discussion and criticism, see Elspeth Probyn, "Fat, Feelings, Bodies: A Critical Approach to Obesity," in *Critical Feminist Approaches to Eating Dis/Orders*, eds. H. Malson M. Burns, 2009, pp. 113–23.

22. For a sustained argument in which this claim is further restricted to the relations between mothers and daughters (rather than my use of the gender-neutral "child"), see Chernin, *The Hungry Self.* I do not see these routes as mutually excluding: being a child and being a daughter can actively shape the same process in different ways.

23. O'Neill, *Starving for Attention*, pp. 84–5.

24. "The options before me were equally abhorrent. I could slow down my exercise, eat more food, and gradually inflate into the monster I was so desperately fleeing, or I could continue my weight control efforts and ultimately end up in the hospital—*Children*'s Hospital at that!" (ibid., pp. 92–3, emphasis in the original). "My dad decided that if I was going to act like an obstinate child I should be treated like one. At five foot seven and 92 pounds, perhaps I even looked like one" (p. 103, cf. p. 145).

25. Halban, *Perfect*, p. 78.. She later describes herself as ". . . torn between the child inside asking only to be taken care of and the growing daughter determined to show her parents that she could do it on her own" (p. 132).

26. Bowman, *Thin*, pp. 60–63.

27. Ellmann, *The Hunger Artists*, p. 112.

28. M. Hornbacher, *Wasted: A Memoir of Anorexia and Bulimia*, 2006, p. 136.

29. I am here adopting Brumberg's two-stage model: the first stage—"recruitment into starvation"—is followed by a second, "career" stage. The first stage can be culturally induced, and is, to some extent, voluntary. In the second stage, the persistent self-starvation is no longer willed and involves its own mechanisms. The theater I describe moves between these "stages." See Brumberg, *Fasting Girls*, ch. 1.

30. Bowman, *Thin*, p. 195. Similar diets are presented in other memoirs.

31. Anorexia's taxing nature may explain pro-anorexia websites that provide support to the exacting performance undertaken by the anorectic. On such sites, see Jenni L. Harshbarger, Carolyn R. Ahlers-Schmidt, Laura Mayans, David Mayans, and Joseph H. Hawkins, "Pro-Anorexia Websites: What a Clinician Should Know," *International Journal of Eating Disorders*, 2009.

32. Maisel et. al, present an elaborate attempt to personify anorexia as a dangerous possessive entity that insinuates itself into the would-be anorectic through various tactics combining feigned friendliness and prescriptive demands. The letter is cited in pp. 66–7 in R. L. Maisel, D. Epston and A. Borden, *Biting the Hand That Starves You: Inspiring Resistance to Anorexia/Bulimia*, 2004.

33. O'Neill: "6:00 A.M. Rise, coffee, read Bible, dress for jogging; 6:30. Jog four miles; 7:15. Stretching exercises; 7:45. Dress for school, join family devotion." And so it goes on, including two hours of calisthenics and weight lifting (between 15:00 and 17:00 followed by forty five minutes of swimming or leg exercises with an occasional consumption of an apple thrown in), see O'Neill, *Starving for Attention*, pp. 80–81.

34. For an extensive discussion of the abjectness of food, see Megan Warin, *Abject Relations: Everyday Worlds of Anorexia*, 2010, ch. 4. Of the memoirs I have studied, the one that most poignantly brings out this dimension is Emily Halban's: "I have effectively become afraid of such foods [fats]; they are the enemy. Taking the step to swallow any from the barred list remains such a frightening task though I know, I know, I should"; "[w]hen we have chicken I take a piece and squeeze it in my napkin when no one is looking my way so as to pump out every last ounce of grease" (Halban, *Perfect*, p. 117; p. 123). One of her strategies to avoid fats in restaurants was, she says, to "douse [her] food in vinegar, allowing it to soak through the food . . . to see whether there were any floating particles." (p. 92).

35. Erving Goffman, *The Presentation of Self in Everyday Life*, 1958, p. 10.

36. Psychodramatist M. Katherine Hudgins provides material from self-psychology regarding the self-fragmentation and discontinuous sense of self in ano-

rectics, describing psychodramatic interventions that aim to empower and solidify the self that is there, (see Katherine Hudgins, M., "Experiencing the Self through Psychodrama and Gestalt Therapy in Anorexia Nervosa," in *Experiential Therapies for Eating Disorders*, eds. Ellen K. Baker Lynne M. Hornyak, 1989, pp. 234–51). In the same collection, dance therapists Julia B. Rice, Marylee Hardenbergh and Lynne M. Hornyak note that in anorectics, "movements tend to be initiated in the peripheral body parts, as opposed to centrally in the trunk. These peripheral movements do not travel in a natural flow. They remain gestures, separate from full involvement with the body [which reflects] detachment from the self." See Julia Rice, Marylee Hardenbergh, and Lynne Hornyak, "Disturbed Body Image in Anoerexia Nervosa: Dance/Movement Therapy Interventions," in Experiential Therapies for Eating Disorders, edited by Ellen K. Baker and Lynne M. Hornyak, 1989, pp. 252–78, p. 260.

37. See Astrid Jacobse, "The Use of Dramatherapy in the Treatment of Eating Disorders," in *Arts Therapies and Clients with Eating Disorders*, edited by Ditty Dokter, 1995, pp. 124–43. Another dramatherapist reports that in her mixed bulimic-anorectic group, "[e]mbodiment, either in movement or enactment, was felt as too threatening. To stand up and be seen was a very prominent fear in the beginning of the group." See Ditty Dokter, "Dramatherapy and Clients with Eating Disorders: Fragile Board," in *Dramatherapy - Clinical Studies*, edited by Steve Mitchell, 1996, pp. 179–93, p. 188.

38. O'Neill, *Starving for Attention*, p. 130–31.

39. Peggy Claude-Pierre, *The Secret Language of Eating Disorders: The Revolutionary Approach to Understanding and Curing Anorexia and Bulimia*, 1999.

40. In *Psychosomatic Families, Salvador Minuchin* advocates a "systems model" rather than a "linear approach" to understanding the dynamics of anorexia. In the latter, the therapist isolates the anorectic, relating to her as the entity that should be explained and treated. In the former, the family is the basic unit, and the anorectic is merely one of its parts. The theatrical claims above, suggest that sometimes it might be useful to perceive the anorectic *and her family* as enmeshed in co-producing and reciprocally directing and acting in a jointly staged play.

41. "Spectacle" is a good term to employ here, since it captures the continuity between contemporary anorexia and past forms of performed hunger (religious or theatrical). Again, see Gooldin's work on hunger as enacted spectacle in the context of nineteenth-century performance.

42. O'Neill, *Starving for Attention*, pp. 143–44.

43. O'Neill, ibid. p. 83.

44. See Warin, *Abject Relations*. Ch 6.

45. The same vagueness as to that which must be externalized surfaces in dramatherapist Maggie Young's description of a drama exercise dealing with the concept of rubbish in a group of bulimic women: "Each member was asked to draw their image of rubbish and how it was contained, prior to expressing this through the

body. Some members found the exercise difficult, saying that rubbish could not be drawn or represented as 'rubbish is inside me and I am the rubbish.'" It is the unrepresentable, unfocused nature of the inner polluting element that should impress us in this context—a non-definable foreign essence that cannot be assimilated into the self and yet, precisely because it is unrepresentable, can never be satisfactorily and finally expunged. See Maggie Young, "Dramatherapy in Short-Term Groupwork with Women with Bulimia," in *Arts Therapies and Clients with Eating Disorders*, edited by. Ditty Dokter, 1995, pp. 105–23, p. 116.

46. Halban, *Perfect*, pp. 61–2.

47. Bowman, *Thin*, p. 131.

Works Cited

Abel, Lionel. *Metatheatre: A New View of Dramatic Form*. New York: Hill and Wang, 1963.

Alan, J. Pakula. *Sophie's Choice*, ITC Entertainment, USA, 1982.

Améry, Jean. *On Suicide: A Discourse on Voluntary Death*. Bloomington: Indiana University Press, 1999.

Andreas, Veiel. *Die Spielwütigen*, Journal-Film Klaus Volkenborn, Germany, 2004.

Andrew, Sofer. "How to Do Things with Demons: Conjuring Performatives in Doctor Faustus." *Theatre Journal* 61.1 (2009): 1–21.

Arnott, Peter D. *Plays without People: Puppetry and Serious Drama*. Bloomington: Indiana University Press, 1964.

Aston, Elaine. *Feminist Theatre Practice: A Handbook*. London: Routledge, 1999.

Auslander, Philip. "'Just Be Your Self': Logocentrism and Difference in Performance Theory." In Zarilli, Phillip B. *Acting (Re)Considered: A Theoretical and Practical Guide*, 53–56. London: Routledge, 2002. 53–60.

Axson-Flynn v. Johnson, United States Court of Appeals for the Tenth Circuit Feb. 3, 2004. 356 F. 3d 1277.

Barish, Jonas A. *The Antitheatrical Prejudice*. Berkeley: University of California Press, 1981.

Bauer, Nancy. "Pornutopia." *N+1* 5 (2007): 63–73.

Beardsley, Monroe C. "What Is Going on in a Dance?" *Dance Research Journal* 15.1 (1982): 31–36.

Bell, John, ed. *Puppets, Masks, and Performing Objects*. Cambridge, MA: MIT Press, 2001.

Benedetti, Jean. *The Art of the Actor: The Essential History of Acting, from Classical Times to the Present Day*. London: Methuen, 2005.

Benjamin, Jessica. *The Bonds of Love: Psychoanalysis, Feminism, and the Problem of Domination*. New York: Pantheon Books, 1988.

Bentley, Eric. *Theatre of War: Comments on 32 Occasions*. London: Eyre Methuen, 1972.

Berliner, Paul F. *Thinking in Jazz: The Infinite Art of Improvisation*. Chicago: University of Chicago Press, 1994.

Berry, Cicely. *Voice and the Actor*. New York: Collier Books, 1973.
Blau, Herbert. *The Audience*. Baltimore: Johns Hopkins University Press, 1990.
Boal, Augusto. *The Rainbow of Desire: The Boal Method of Theatre and Therapy*. Translated by Adrian Jackson. London: Routledge, 1995.
Boehn, Max von. *Puppets and Automata*. Translated by Josephine Nicoll. New York: Dover Publications, 1972.
Bordo, Susan. *Unbearable Weight: Feminism, Western Culture, and the Body*. Berkeley: University of California Press, 1993.
Bowman, Grace. *Thin*. New York: Penguin Group, 2007.
Branagh, Kenneth. *Beginning*. London: Chatto & Windus, 1989.
Brando, Marlon, and Robert Lindsey. *Brando: Songs My Mother Taught Me*. New York: Random House, 1994.
Briginshaw, Valerie A. "Difference and Repetition in 'Both Sitting Duet.'" *Topoi: An International Review of Philosophy* 24.1 (2005): 15–28.
Brook, Peter. *King Lear*. Ringwood: Athena Films, 1971.
Brown, Lee B. "Phonography, Repetition and Spontaneity." *Philosophy and Literature* 24.1 (2000): 111–25.
Brumberg, Joan Jacobs. *Fasting Girls: The Emergence of Anorexia Nervosa as a Modern Disease*. Cambridge, MA: Harvard University Press, 1988.
Burch, Steven Dedalus. "Imitation of Life: A Meditation on 'Victim Art.'" *Journal of Dramatic Theory and Criticism* XII.1 (1997): 121–32.
Burgoyne, Suzanne Dieckman. "A Crucible for Actors: Questions of Directorial Ethics." *Theatre Topics* 1.1 (1991): 1–12.
Burgoyne, Suzanne, Poulin, Karen, and Ashley Rearden. "The Impact of Acting on Student Actors: Boundary Blurring, Growth, and Emotional Distress." *Theatre Topics* 9.2 (1999): 157–79.
Burns, Elizabeth. *Theatricality: A Study of Convention in the Theatre and in Social Life*. London: Longmans, 1972.
Caine, Michael. *Acting in Film*. New York: Applause Theatre Book Publishers, 1990.
Calderwood, James L. *Shakespearean Metadrama: The Argument of the Play in Titus Andronicus, Love's Labour's Lost, Romeo and Juliet, A Midsummer Night's Dream, and Richard II*. Minneapolis: University of Minnesota Press, 1971.
Callow, Simon. *Being an Actor*. London: Vintage, 2004.
Callow, Simon. *Charles Laughton: A Difficult Actor*. New York: Grove, 1987.
Cameron, John Mitchell. *Shortbus*. New York: Safeword Productions LLC., 2006.
Camus, Albert. *The Myth of Sisyphus, and Other Essays*. New York: Knopf, 1955.
Canby, Vincent. Review of *The Elephant Man*, *The New York Times*, October 3, 1980. http:www. movies.nytimes.com/movie/review.
Carroll, Noël. "Philosophy and Drama: Performance, Interpretation and Intentionality." In *Staging Philosophy: Intersections of Theatre, Performance, and Philosophy*, 104–21. Ann Arbor: The University of Michigan Press, 2006.

Case, Sue-Ellen. *Feminism and Theatre*. New York: Methuen, 1988.
Chaplin, Charlie. *My Autobiography*. London: Bodley Head, 1964.
Chekhov, Michael, and Mel Gordon. *On the Technique of Acting*. New York: Harper Perennial, 1991.
Chérau, Patrice. *Intimité*. Paris: Téléma; Issy-les-Moulineaux: Canal +, 2000.
Chernin, Kim. *The Hungry Self: Women, Eating, and Identity*. New York: Virago, 1986.
Claude-Pierre, Peggy. *The Secret Language of Eating Disorders: The Revolutionary Approach to Understanding and Curing Anorexia and Bulimia*. New York: Vintage Books, 1999.
Coetzee, J. M. *Elizabeth Costello*. New York: Viking, c. 2003. First published 2003 by Secker & Warburg.
Cohen, Matthew I. "Puppetry and the Destruction of the Object." *Performance Research* 12.4 (2007): 123–31.
Cole, David. *Acting as Reading: The Place of the Reading Process in the Actor's Work*. Ann Arbor: University of Michigan Press, 1992.
Cole, Toby, ed. *Actors on Acting: The Theories, Techniques, and Practices of the Great Actors of All Times as Told in Their Own Words*. New York: Crown, 1970.
Collodi, Carlo [Carlo Lorenzini]. *The Adventures of Pinnocchio*. Translated by Carol Della Chiesa, Project Gutenberg.http://www. Gutenberg.org.
Cook, Amy. "Interplay: The Method and Potential of a Cognitive Scientific Approach to Theatre." *Theatre Journal* 59.4 (2007): 579–94.
Crews, Frderick Campbell. *The Pooh Perplex: A Freshman Casebook*. New York: E.P. Dutton, 1963.
Cummins, Lillian Huang, Simmons, Angela M., and Nolan W. S. Zane. "Eating Disorders in Asian Populations: A Critique of Current Approaches to the Study of Culture, Ethnicity, and Eating Disorders." *American Journal of Orthopsychiatry* 75.4 (2005): 553–74.
Das, Linda. "I Felt Raped by Brando."*Daily Mail*, July 19, 2007. // http://www.dailymail.co.uk/tvshowbiz/article-469646/I-felt-raped-Brando.html.
Davies, David. *Philosophy of the Performing Arts*. Chichester: Wiley-Blackwell, 2011.
Deleuze, Gilles. *Masochism*. Translated by Jean McNeil. New York: Zone Books, 1991.
Dench, Judi. *And Furthermore*. New York: St. Martin's Press, 2011.
Derrida, Jacques. "The Theater of Cruelty and the Closure of Representation." , In *Mimesis, Masochism, and Mime: The Politics of Theatricality in Contemporary French Thought*, edited by Timothy Murray, 40–61.
Diamond, Elin. *Unmaking Mimesis: Essays on Feminism and Theatre*. London: Routledge, 1997.
DiBattista, Maria. *Fast-Talking Dames*. New Haven, CT: Yale University Press, 2003.
Diderot, Denis. *The Paradox of Acting*. Miami, FL: HardPress Publishing, 2013.

Dijksterhuis, E. J. *The Mechanization of the World Picture*. Oxford: Clarendon Press, 1961.

Dillon, Cynthia Bishop. "Active Interpretation/Deconstruction Play: Postmodern Considerations of Acting." *Journal of Dramatic Theory and Criticism* 8.1 (1993): 27–44.

Dokter, Ditty. *Arts Therapy and Clients with Eating Disorders: Fragile Board*. London: Jessica Kingsley Publishers, 1994.

Dokter, Ditty. "Dramatherapy and Clients with Eating Disorders: Fragile Board." In *Dramatherapy: Clinical Studies, edited by Steve Mitchell, 179–93*. London: Jessica Kingsley, 1996. 179–93.

Dolan, Jill. *Presence and Desire: Essays on Gender, Sexuality, Performance*. Ann Arbor: The University of Michigan Press, 1993.

Donnellan, Declan. *The Actor and the Target*. London: Nick Hern, 2002.

Dostoyevsky, Fyodor. *Notes from Underground, White Nights, The Dream of a Ridiculous Man, and Selections from The House of the Dead*. Translated by Andrew Robert MacAndrew. New York: the New American Library, 1961.

Dummett, Michael. *Truth and Other Enigmas*. Cambridge, MA: Harvard University Press, 1978.

Ellmann, Maud. *The Hunger Artists: Starving, Writing, and Imprisonment*. Cambridge, MA: Harvard University Press, 1993.

Erickson, Jon. "The Face and the Possibility of an Ethics of Performance." *Journal of Dramatic Theory and Criticism* 13.2 (1999): 5–22.

Fairbairn, Gavin J. *Contemplating Suicide: The Language and Ethics of Self-Harm*. London: Routledge, 1995.

Feldman, Bilha. *Three Approaches to the Art of Acting: Stanislavski, Chekhov, Grotowski: Theories & Exercises*. Tel Aviv: Safra Publishing House, 2011.

Féral, Josette. "Foreword." *SubStance* 31.2 (2002): 3–13.

Ferguson, Frances. "Pornography: The Theory." *Critical Inquiry* 21.3 (1995): 670–95.

Fernandes, Ciane. *Pina Bausch and the Wuppertal Dance Theater: The Aesthetics of Repetition and Transformation*. New York: Peter Lang, 2001.

Fitzgerald, R. Joseph. *My Strange Addiction*. Chicago: 20 West Productions, 2010.

Fuchs, Elinor. *The Death of Character: Perspectives on Theater after Modernism*. Bloomington: Indiana University Press, 1996.

Gainor, J. Ellen. "Rethinking Feminism, Stanislavsky and Performance." *Theatre Topics* 12.2 (2002): 163–76.

Gallagher, Shaun. *How the Body Shapes the Mind*. Oxford: Clarendon Press, 2005.

Garfein, Jack. *Life and Acting: Techniques for the Actor*. Chicago: Northwestern University Press, 2010.

Garner, Stanton B. *Bodied Spaces: Phenomenology and Performance in Contemporary Drama*. Ithaca, NY: Cornell University Press, 1994.

Gaut, Berys N. *Art, Emotion and Ethics*. Oxford: Oxford University Press, 2007.

Gibson, John. *Fiction and the Weave of Life*. Oxford: Oxford University Press, 2007.

Gielgud, John. *John Gielgud: An Actor and His Time*. New York: Applause Theatre & Cinema Books, 1997.

Glasgow, Rupert D. V. *Madness, Masks, and Laughter: An Essay on Comedy*. Cranbury, NJ: Associated University Presses, 1995.

Goffman, Erving. *The Presentation of Self in Everyday Life*. Monograph No. 2. Edinburgh: University of Edinburgh, Social Sciences Research Centre, 1956.

Gold, Jack. *The Merchant of Venice*. London: BBC Television, 1980.

Goldman, Alan. "Plain Sex." In *The Philosophy of Sex: Contemporary Readings*, edited by Alan Soble, 119–38 Totowa: Littlefield Adams, 1980.

Goldman, Michael. *The Actor's Freedom: Toward a Theory of Drama*. New York: Viking Press, 1975.

Goldman, Michael. *On Drama: Boundaries of Genre, Borders of Self*. Ann Arbor: University of Michigan Press, 2000.

Goodall, Jane. *Stage Presence*. New York: Routledge, 2008.

Gooldin, Sigal. "Being Anorexic." *Medical Anthropology Quarterly* 22.3 (2008): 274–96.

Gooldin, Sigal. "Fasting Women, Living Skeletons and Hunger Artists: Spectacles of Body and Miracles at the Turn of a Century." *Body & Society* 9.2 (2003): 27–53.

Gordon, Robert. *The Purpose of Playing: Modern Acting Theories in Perspective*. Ann Arbor: The University of Michigan Press, 1996.

Graeber, David. "On the Phenomenology of Giant Puppets: Broken Windows, Imaginary Jars of Urine, and the Cosmological Role of the Police in American Culture." In *Possibilities: Essays on Hierarchy, Rebellion, and Desire, 375–418*. Oakland, CA: AK Press, 2007.

Greene, John. *A Refutation of the Apology for Actors. London, c. 1615*. Imprinted at London: By W. White, Early English Books Online. http://www.eebo.chadwyck.com.

Grehan, Helena. *Performance, Ethics and Spectatorship in a Global Age*. Basingstoke, England: Palgrave Macmillan, 2009.

Gross, Kenneth. *The Dream of the Moving Statue*. Ithaca, NY: Cornell University Press, 1992.

Gross, Kenneth. *Puppet: An Essay on Uncanny Life*. Chicago: University of Chicago Press, 2011.

Grotowski, Jerzy. *Towards a Poor Theatre*. New York: Simon and Schuster, 1968.

Guignabodet, Valérie. *Monique*. Paris: Pan-Européenne, 2002.

Gur, Anat. *Women Abandoned [in Hebrew] Tel Aviv:* Hakibutz Hameuchad, 2008.

Gussow, Mel. *Michael Gambon: A Life in Acting*. New York: Applause Theatre & Cinema Books, 2004.

Hagen, Uta, and Haskel Frankel. *Respect for Acting*. New York: Macmillan, 1973.

Halban, Emily. *Perfect: Anorexia and Me*. London: Vermilion, 2008.

Hamilton, James R. *The Art of Theater*. Malden, MA: Blackwell Publishing, 2007.

Harrop, John. *Acting*. London: Routledge, 1992.

Harshbarger, Jenni L., et al. "Pro-Anorexia Websites: What a Clinician Should Know." *International Journal of Eating Disorders* 42.4 (2009): 367–70.

Held, Virginia. *The Ethics of Care: Personal, Political, and Global*. Oxford: Oxford University Press, 2006.

Hinz, Melanie, ed. *Chaos und Konzept: Proben und Probieren im Theater.* Berlin: Alexander Verlag, 2011.

Holbrook, David, ed. *The Case against Pornography*. La Salle, IL: Open Court, 1973.

Hornbacher, Marya. *Wasted: A Memoir of Anorexia and Bulimia*. New York: HarperCollins, 2006.

Hornby, Richard. "The Camera, the Actor and the Audience." *Journal of Dramatic Theory and Criticism* 17.2 (2003): 141–47.

Hornby, Richard. *The End of Acting: A Radical View*. New York: Applause Theatre & Cinema Books, 1992.

Horniak, Lynn M., and Ellen K. Baker, eds. *Experiential Therapies for Eating Disorders*. New York: Guilford Press, 1989.

Hudgins, Katherine, M. "Experiencing the Self through Psychodrama and Gestalt Therapy in Anorexia Nervosa." In *Experiential Therapies for Eating Disorders, edited by Lynne Hornyak and Ellen K. Baker, 234–51*. New York: Guilford Press, 1989.

Isherwood, Charles. *Wonder Bread and Ecstasy: The Life and Death of Joey Stefano*. New York: Alyson Publications, 1996.

Jacobse, Astrid. "The Use of Dramatherapy in the Treatment of Eating Disorders." In *Arts Therapies and Clients with Eating Disorders: Fragile Board, edited by Ditty Dokter, 124–43*. London: Jessica Kingsley, 1995. 124–43.

Jameson, Jenna, and Neil Strauss. *How to Make Love Like a Porn Star: A Cautionary Tale*. New York: Regan Books, 2004.

Johnson, Mark. *The Meaning of the Body: Aesthetics of Human Understanding*. Chicago: University of Chicago Press, 2007.

Kipnis, Laura. *Bound and Gagged: Pornography and the Politics of Fantasy in America*. Durham N.C.: Duke University Press, 1999.

Kivy, Peter. *The Possessor and the Possessed: Handel, Mozart, Beethoven, and the Idea of Musical Genius*. New Haven, CT: Yale University Press, 2001.

Komintz, Richard Laurence, and Mark Levenson, eds. *The Language of the Puppet.* Vancouver, WA: Pacific Puppetry Center Press, 1990.

Kozintsev, Grigorii Mikhailovich. *Korol Lir po tragedii Shekspira.* [in Russian] Leningrad [now Saint Petersburg]: Soviet Union, Lenfilm, 1971.

Krasner, David, David Z. Saltz, eds. *Staging Philosophy: Intersections of Theater, Performance, and Philosophy*. Ann Arbor: University of Michigan Press, 2006.

Krasner, David. "I Hate Strasberg: Method Bashing in the Academy." In *Method Acting Reconsidered: Theory, Practice, Future*, 3–33. New York: St. Martin's Press, 2000.

Krell, David Farrell. "The Moment of Nothing: A Philosophical Note on the Work of Kristin Linklater." *Mosaic* 44.1 (2011): 109–19.

Krüger, Sabina. "Die Evokation der Monster: Grenz und Schwellenerfahrung als Probenverfahren bei La Fura Dels Baus." In Melanie Hinz, ed., *Chaos und Konzept: Proben und Probieren im Theater,2011, 262–85.*

Langer, Susanne K. *Feeling and Form: A Theory of Art*. New York: Routledge & Kegan Paul, 1953.

Lehman, Peter, ed. *Pornography: Film and Culture*. New Brunswick, NJ: Rutgers University Press, 2006.

Lehmann, Hans-Thies. *Postdramatic Theatre*. London: Routledge, 2006.

Lenz, Joseph. "Base Trade: Theater as Prostitution." *Elh* 60.4 (1993): 833–55.

Levinson, Jerrold. "Erotic Art and Pornographic Pictures." *Philosophy and Literature* 29.1 (2005): 228–40.

Lieberman, Lisa. J. *Leaving You: The Cultural Meaning of Suicide*. Chicago: Ivan R. Dee, 2003.

Linklater, Kristin. *Freeing Shakespeare's Voice: The Actor's Guide to Talking the Text*. New York: Theatre Communications Group, 1992.

Linklater, Kristin. *Freeing the Natural Voice*. New York: Drama Publishers, 1976.

Loux, Michael J, ed. *The Possible and the Actual: Readings in the Metaphysics of Modality.* Ithaca, NY: Cornell University Press, 1979.

Lovelace, Linda, Mike McGrady. *Ordeal*. New York: Citadel, 2006.

Macdonald, Marianne. "Downhill Ride for Maria after Her Tango with Brando." *The Sydney Morning Herald*, June 22, 2006. http://www.smh.com.au/news/film/downhill-ride-for-maria-after-her-tango-with-brando/2006/06/21/1150845244689.html.

MacSween, Morag. *Anorexic Bodies: A Feminist and Sociological Perspective on Anorexia Nervosa*. London: Routledge, 1993.

Mag Uidhir, Christy. "Why Pornography Can't Be Art." *Philosophy and Literature* 33.1 (2009): 193–203.

Maisel, Richard, Epston, David, and Ali Borden. *Biting the Hand That Starves You: Inspiring Resistance to Anorexia/Bulimia*. New York: Norton & Company, 2004.

Malson, Helen, and Marie Burns, eds. *Critical Feminist Approaches to Eating Dis/Orders*. New York: Routledge, 2009.

Mansfield, Nick. *Masochism: The Art of Power*. Westport, CT: Praeger, 1997.

Margalit, Avishai. *The Ethics of Memory*. Cambridge, MA: Harvard University Press, 2002.

Markovits, D. *A Modern Legal Ethics: Adversary Advocacy in a Democratic Age*. Princeton, NJ: Princeton University Press, 2008.

Marowitz, Charles. *The Act of Being: Towards a Theory of Acting*. New York: Taplinger Publishing Company, 1978.

Marshall, Cynthia. *The Shattering of the Self: Violence, Subjectivity, and Early Modern Texts*. Baltimore, MD: Johns Hopkins University Press, 2002.

Mason, Helen, and Marie Burns, eds. *Critical Approaches to Eating Dis/Orders*. New York: Routledge, 2009.

May, Rollo. "Paradoxes of Sex and Love in Modern Society." In *The Case against Pornography*, edited by David Holbrook, 13–36. La Salle, Ill.: Open Court, 1972. 13–36. 1973.

McClintock, Anne. *Imperial Leather: Race, Gender, and Sexuality in the Colonial Contest*. New York: Routledge, 1995.

McConachie, Bruce, and F. Elizabeth Hart, eds. *Performance and Cognition: Theatre Studies and the Cognitive Turn*. New York: Routledge, 2006.

McNeil, Legs., Osborne, Jennifer, and avia, Peter. *The Other Hollywood: The Uncensored Oral History of the Porn Film Industry*. New York: HarperCollins, 2005.

Meisner, Sanford, and Dennis Longwell. *Sanford Meisner on Acting*. New York: Vintage Books, 1987.

Merlin, Bella. *Beyond Stanislavsky: The Psycho-Physical Approach to Actor Training*. New York: Routledge, 2001.

Merritt, Rich. *Secrets of a Gay Marine Porn Star*. New York: Kensington Books, 2005.

Meschke, Michael. *In Search of Aesthetics for the Puppet Theatre*. New Delhi: Indira Gandhi National Centre for the Arts; Sterling Publishers, 1992.

Milne, A. A. *The House at Pooh Corner*. New York: Puffin Books, 1992.

Milne, Carly. *Naked Ambition: Women Who Are Changing Pornography*. New York: Carroll & Graf, 2005.

Minois, Georges. *History of Suicide: Voluntary Death in Western Culture*. London: Johns Hopkins University Press, 2001.

Minuchin, Salvador. Rosman, Bernice L., and Lester Baker. *Psychosomatic Families: Anorexia Nervosa in Context*. Cambridge, Mass.: Harvard University Press, 1978.

Mitchell, Steve, ed. *Dramatherapy: Clinical Studies*. London: Jessica Kingsley Publishers, 1996.

Moreh, Shmuel. "The Shadow Play (Khayāl Al-Zill) in the Light of Arabic Literature." *Journal of Arabic Literature* 18 (1987): 46–61.

Morrison, Michael A. *John Barrymore, Shakespearean Actor*. Cambridge: Cambridge University Press, 1997.

Murray, Timothy, ed. *Mimesis, Masochism, and Mime: The Politics of Theatricality in Contemporary French Thought*. Ann Arbor: University of Michigan Press, 1997.

Nagel, Thomas. "Sexual Perversion." *The Journal of Philosophy* 66.1 (1969): 5–17.

Nanay, Bence. "Do We Sense Modalities with Our Sense Modalities?" *Ratio* 24.3 (2011): 299–310.

Nehamas, Alexander. *Nietzsche, Life as Literature*. Cambridge, MA: Harvard University Press, 1985.

Nelson, Victoria. *The Secret Life of Puppets*. Cambridge, MA: Harvard University Press, 2001.

Neuringer, Charles, and Ronald A. Willis. "The Psychodynamics of Theatrical Spectatorship." *Journal of Dramatic Theory and Criticism* 2.1 (1987): 95–110.

Nicholas, Rescher. "The Ontology of the Possible." In *The Possible and the Actual: Readings in the Metaphysics of Modality*. Ithaca, NY: Cornell University Press, 1979. 166–81.

Noyes, John. K. *The Mastery of Submission: Inventions of Masochism*. Ithaca, NY: Cornell University Press, 1997.

Nussbaum, Martha C. *Sex & Social Justice*. New York: Oxford University Press, 1999.

O'Dell, Kathy. *Contract with the Skin: Masochism, Performance Art, and the 1970s*. Minneapolis: University Of Minnesota Press, 1998.

O'Neill, Cherry Boone. *Starving for Attention*. New York: Dell, 1983.

Olivier, Laurence. *Confessions of an Actor: An Autobiography*. New York: Penguin Books, 1984.

Onians, Richard B. *The Origins of European Thought About the Body, the Mind, the Soul, the World, Time and Fate: New Interpretations of Greek, Roman and Kindred Evidence Also of Some Basic Jewish and Christian Beliefs*. 2nd. ed. Cambridge: Cambridge University Press, 1988.

Ophrat, Hadas. *Conversations with a Puppet: On Contemporary Puppetry [in Hebrew]* Tel Aviv: Sal Tarbut Artzi, 2008.

Osipovich, David. "What Is a Theatrical Performance?" *Journal of Aesthetics and Art Criticism* 64.4 (2006): 461–70.

Ovid. *Metamorphoses. Books Ix-Xv*. Translated by Frank Justus Miller. Loeb Classical Library 42–43. Cambridge, MA: Harvard University Press, 1977.

Pakula, Alan J. *Sophie's Choice. ITC Entertainment, 1982.*

Patrice, Chéreau. *Intimité*, Téléma, Le Studio Canal+, France, 2000.

Peckham, Morse. *Art and Pornography: An Experiment in Explanation*. New York: Basic Books, 1969.

Poggi, Gianfranco. *Money and the Modern Mind: Georg Simmel's Philosophy of Money*. Berkeley: University of California Press, 1993.

Pollard, Tanya. *Shakespeare's Theater: A Sourcebook*. Malden, MA: Blackwell Publishing, 2004.

Poole, Wakefield. *Dirty Poole: A Sensual Memoir*. Maple Shade, NJ: Lethe Press, 2011.

Probyn, Elspeth. "Fat, Feelings, Bodies: A Critical Approach to Obesity." In *Critical*

Feminist Approaches to Eating Dis/Orders, edited by Helen Mason and Marie Burns, 113–23. New York: Routledge, 2009.

Prynne, William. *Histrio-Mastix*. 1633 ed. London: Printed by Allde, Mathewes, Cotes and Jones for Sparke, 1633.

Pullen, Kirsten. *Actresses and Whores: On Stage and in Society*. New York: Cambridge University Press, 2004.

Quinn, Michael L. "Self-Reliance and Ritual Renewal: Anti-Theatrical Ideology in American Method Acting." *Journal of Dramatic Theory and Criticism* 10.1 (1995): 5–20.

Rayner, Alice. "The Audience: Subjectivity, Community and the Ethics of Listening." *Journal of Dramatic Theory and Criticism* 7.2 (1993): 3–24.

Rea, Michael C. "What Is Pornography?" *Noûs* 35.1 (2001): 118–45.

Rice, Julia, B., Hardenbergh, Marylee, Lynne M. Hornyak, "Disturbed Body Image in Anoerexia Nervosa: Dance/Movement Therapy Interventions." In *Experiential Therapies for Eating Disorders, edited by Lynn M. Horniak and Ellen K. Baker*. New York: Guilford Press, 1989. 252–78.

Richard, R., Thomas, Sunset, and Kyle Torke. *Anatomy of an Adult Film*. New York: World Audience, Incorporated, 2009.

Richardson, Don. *Acting without Agony: An Alternative to the Method*. Boston: Allyn and Bacon, 1988.

Ridout, Nicholas. *Theatre and Ethics*. New York: Palgrave Macmillan, 2009.

Roach, Joseph R. *It*. Ann Arbor: University of Michigan Press, 2007.

Roach, Joseph R. *The Player's Passion: Studies in the Science of Acting*. Ann Arbor: University of Michigan Press, 1993.

Rosenberg, Marvin. *The Masks of King Lear*. Berkeley: University of California Press, 1972.

Rosenfield, L. Davidson. *From Beast-Machine to Man-Machine: The Theme of Animal Soul in French Letters from Descartes to La Mettrie*. New York: Oxford University Press, 1940.

Ross, Colin A., Farley, Melissa, and Harvey L. Schwartz. "Dissociation among Women in Prostitution." *Journal of Trauma Practice* 2.3–4 (2004): 199–212.

Ruhl, Sarah. "Re-Runs and Repetition." *Contemporary Theatre Review: An International Journal* 16.3 (2006): 283–90.

Sacher-Masoch, Leopold von. *Venus im Pelz*. Vienna: Christian Brandstaetter, 1985.

Saltz, David Z. "How to Do Things on Stage." *The Journal of Aesthetics and Art Criticism* 49.1 (1991): 31–45.

Saltz, David Z. "Infiction and Outfiction: The Role of Fiction in Theatrical Performance." *Staging Philosophy: Intersections of Theater, Performance, and Philosophy*. Ann Arbor: The University of Michigan Press, 2006. 203–20.

Saltz, David Z. "What Theatrical Performance Is (Not): The Interpretation Fallacy." *Journal of Aesthetics and Art Criticism* 59.3 (2001): 299–306.

Saltz, David Z. "Why Performance Theory Needs Philosophy." *Journal of Dramatic Theory and Criticism* 16.1 (2001): 149–54.

Schechner, Richard. *Environmental Theatre*. New York: Hawthorn Books, 1973.

Schumann, Peter. "What, at the End of This Century, Is the Situation of Puppets and Performing Objects?" In *Puppets, Masks, and Performing Objects, edited by John Bell*, Cambridge, Mass.: MIT Press, 2001. 46–51.

Scolnicov, Hanna. "Stripping as Gesture." *Assaph* 24 (2010): 139–51.

Segel, Harold B. *Pinocchio's Progeny: Puppets, Marionettes, Automatons and Robots in Modernist and Avant-Garde Drama*. Baltimore, MD: Johns Hopkins University Press, 1995.

Shaw, Fiona. *As You Like It. London*: BBC, 1996.

Shell, Marc. *Stutter*. Cambridge, MA: Harvard University Press, 2005.

Sher, Antony. *Year of the King: An Actor's Diary and Sketchbook*. London: Methuen, 1997.

Shershow, Scott Cutler. *Puppets and "Popular" Culture*. Ithaca, NY: Cornell University Press, 1995.

Shusterman, Richard. *Body Consciousness: A Philosophy of Mindfulness and Somaesthetics*. Cambridge: Cambridge University Press, 2008.

Shusterman, Richard. *Surface and Depth: Dialectics of Criticism and Culture*. Ithaca, NY: Cornell University Press, 2002.

Sichel, John. *William Shakespeare's The Merchant of Venice. London: ATV*, 1973.

Siegel, Carol. *Male Masochism: Modern Revisions of the Story of Love*. Bloomington: Indiana University Press, 1995.

Sivory-Asp, Sirpa. "The Presence of the Gods." In Kominz, Richard Laurence, and Mark Levenson. *The Language of the Puppet, 1990*. Vancouver, Wash.: The Pacific Puppetry Center Press 1990.

Soble, Alan, ed. *The Philosophy of Sex: Contemporary Readings*. Totowa, NJ: Littlefield Adams, 1980.

Sofer, Andrew. "How to Do Things with Demons: Conjuring Performatives in Doctor Faustus." Theatre Journal 61 (2009): 1–22.

Spelvin, Georgina. *The Devil Made Me Do It*. Los Angeles: Georginas World Incorporated, 2008.

Stanislavsky, Konstantin. *An Actor Prepares*. Translated by Elizabeth Reynolds Hapgood. New York: Routledge, 2003.

Stanislavsky, Konstantin. *Building a Character*. Translated by Elizabeth Reynolds Hapgood. New York: Routledge, 2003.

States, Bert O. *Great Reckonings in Little Rooms: On the Phenomenology of Theater*. Berkeley: University of California Press, 1985.

Stewart-Steinberg, Suzanne. *The Pinocchio Effect: On Making Italians 1860–1920*. Chicago: University of Chicago Press, 2007.

Stewart-Steinberg, Suzanne. *Sublime Surrender: Male Masochism at the Fin-de-Siècle*. Ithaca, NY: Cornell University Press, 1998.

Strasberg, Lee. *A Dream of Passion: The Development of the Method*. New York: Plume, 1988.
Streisand, Barbra. *The Prince of Tides*. Culver City, CA: Columbia Pictures, Corporation, Barwood/Longfellow, USA, 1991.
Strossen, Nadine. *Defending Pornography: Free Speech, Sex, and the Fight for Women's Rights*. New York: Scribner, 1995.
Taylor, Corey. *Naked: The Life and Pornography of Michael Lucas*. New York: Kensington Books, 2007.
Thom, Paul. *For an Audience: A Philosophy of the Performing Arts*. Philadelphia: Temple University Press, 1993.
Tom, Hooper. *The King's Speech*. London and Sydney: See-Saw Films; London: Bedlam Productions, 2010.
Valérie, Guignabodet. *Monique*, Pan-Européenne Production, France, 2002.
Vannoy, Russell. *Sex without Love: A Philosophical Exploration*. Buffalo N.Y.: Prometheus Books, 1980.
Veiel, Andreas. *Die Spielwütigen*. Berlin: Klaus Volkenborn KG, 2004.
Verducci, Susan. "A Moral Method? Thoughts on Cultivating Empathy through Method Acting." *Journal of Moral Education* 29.1 (2000): 87–99.
Villiers, André. *La Prostitution de l'acteur*. Paris: Editions du Pavois, 1946.
Walton, Kendall L. *Mimesis as Make-Believe: On the Foundations of the Representational Arts*. Cambridge, MA: Harvard University Press, 1990.
Warin, Megan. *Abject Relations: Everyday Worlds of Anorexia*. New Brunswick, NJ: Rutgers University Press, 2010.
Welton, Donn, ed. *The Body: Classic and Contemporary Readings*. Malden, MA: Blackwell, 1999.
Wiles, David. "Burdens of Representation: The Method and the Audience." In Krasner, David. *Method Acting Reconsidered: Theory, Practice, Future*, New York: St. Martin's Press, 2000. 169–78.
Wilshire, Bruce. *Role Playing and Identity: The Limits of Theatre as Metaphor*. Bloomington: Indiana University Press, 1982.
Wimsatt, W. K. *The Verbal Icon: Studies in the Meaning of Poetry*. London: Methuen, 1967.
Woodruff, Paul. *The Necessity of Theater: The Art of Watching and Being Watched*. Oxford: Oxford University Press, 2008.
Worthen, William B. *Drama: Between Poetry and Performance*. Malden, MA: Wiley-Blackwell, 2010.
Worthen, William B. *Modern Drama and the Rhetoric of Theater*. Berkeley: University of California Press, 1991.
Worthen, William B. "Of Actors and Automata: Hieroglyphics of Modernism." *Journal of Dramatic Theory and Criticism* 9.1 (1994): 3–20.

Young, Maggie. "Dramatherapy in Short-Term Groupwork with Women with Bulimia." In Dokter, Ditty. *Arts Therapies and Clients with Eating Disorders*, 105–23.

Zamir, Tzachi. *Double Vision: Moral Philosophy and Shakespearean Drama*. New Jersey: Princeton University Press, 2007.

Zamir, Tzachi. "Philosophy." In *The Oxford Handbook of Shakespeare*, edited by Arthur F. Kinney. New York: Oxford University Press, 2012.

Zarilli, Phillip B. *Acting (Re)Considered: A Theoretical and Practical Guide*. London: Routledge, 2002.

Zarrilli, Phillip. B., and P. Hulton. *Psychophysical Acting: An Intercultural Approach after Stanislavski*. London: Routledge, 2009.

Index